Simone Alz   Sabine zur Nedden

The Golden View

As you have never looked at your life before

The key to self-realization and becoming conscious

Translated & edited
by
Vidya Bolz & Josephine Beney

wissenstor-verlag.com

Copyright © 2017
Wissenstor-Verlag
Birkenweg 4
74576 Fichtenau
Germany
Fax: +49 7962 710263
www.wissenstor-verlag.com
Email: info@wissenstor-verlag.com

Printed by:
CPI – Ebner & Spiegel, Ulm, Germany

Cover design by:
Atelier Toepfer, 85560 Ebersberg, Germany
Email: info@ateliertoepfer.de

ISBN 978-3-938656-95-2

Table of contents

👁 The 23 perspectives of the Golden View 👁

PART I
SELF-REFLECTION &
INITIAL INSIGHTS

PART II
BECOMING CONSCIOUS

PART III
HEART-OPENING & SELF-REALIZATION

Introduction

I looked down at my shaking hands and realized that I was incredibly nervous. I had no idea who this Dr Seer was. Such an odd name! I'd only noticed the small sign on the gate yesterday – a neat plaque bearing the words 'THE GOLDEN VIEW'. I must have passed it a hundred times before without seeing it.

And now, all of a sudden, it was as though I had been irresistibly pulled into its vortex, and felt myself immediately compelled to make an appointment. It seemed remarkably straightforward, as if my telephone call had been anticipated. *Yes, you could come tomorrow,* said a pleasant male voice on the other end of the line. *At 8 pm. I think the time would suit you, would it not?* "Oh yes – yes, that would be great." But how could he possibly have known that…?

The next day I found myself once again standing in front of the big metal gate. It was much easier to open than I expected. I walked hesitantly towards the house along the paved pathway, a thousand thoughts crowding my mind. I hadn't slept all night, and I could feel my heart beating in my throat, pounding away. Why was I so nervous? 'I'm going to have some *life coaching* – what's the big deal? It's nothing unusual,' I told myself, trying to calm down. 'Nothing to be afraid of. It's not like it's a test or anything.'

I was annoyed at myself. Why on earth did I have to go and make this appointment? Why had I put myself in this awkward position? Couldn't I have just continued living my life along the same old lines? What had brought me here? Some sort of premonition? Or maybe intuition? Destiny, perhaps? Gut feeling? A desire? My desire to finally change my life? Was it my never-ending search for answers – answers to the questions that haunted me, and made me so tired? Or perhaps a longing to feel alive again, at long last: a longing to rise in the morning and not feel depressed and exhausted, but full of energy? Was it the search for the truth? Or some inexplicable yearning, driving me on? Was it a subconscious intention to once and for all understand the sadness that occasionally overwhelmed me out of nowhere? Or was it my memories, ceaselessly flooding my mind, draining me of my strength and energy? Was it the desire to finally understand why we humans do so many things that seem so meaningless?

Is there even such a thing as meaning? What a question... one that has been asked countless times throughout history, by people of every possible origin scattered across all the world's continents.

I've read a lot of books, including so-called self-help books. I've never had a problem understanding them; could always follow their meaning with the rational part of my brain. Perhaps I was simply an ineffectual reader, because so far I hadn't managed to drastically change my life or apply the advice I'd received in any particularly helpful way. Such advice often sounds so simple in theory – the challenge is working out how to properly understand, discern, feel and, most importantly, implement it.
Yes – thinking about it, I was actually really tired. My own life wore me out. And now here I was, standing in front of a big door with a grey sign on which was written in shiny lettering:

THE GOLDEN VIEW

What was hidden behind this door bore no resemblance to anything I've experienced in my life so far.

My name is Allman, and in the pages that follow I will tell you my story.

* * * * * * * * * *

7

First encounter with Dr Seer

The door opened instantly. Had I already rung the bell? I couldn't remember. Was I so nervous that I was getting things muddled in my mind?

Please come in, I've been expecting you.

'Oh no, am I late?' I wondered, my mind racing. Before the next thought had a chance to form I heard his melodic voice speak again.

Don't worry so much. Please come in. You've come to the right place.

I found myself in a wide corridor. It was extremely bright, and I struggled not to squint. Was it the lighting? Or maybe it was sunlight… at 8pm in the evening, though? The walls were covered with all kinds of different mirrors; big ones, small ones, round ones and square ones, and the effect was such that I didn't really know where to look.

Seeing can be difficult, at first. But don't worry. You'll learn.

Dr Seer smiled and shook hands with me.

Good evening!

He was a tall, slim man in his late fifties, perhaps, with a well-proportioned face that carried a friendly expression. His smile was very pleasant, and in spite of the strange environment I already felt at ease. He looked at me with eyes that were remarkably green. I felt myself calming down, and managed to compose myself, a little.

"My name is Allman, good evening. Thank you for finding the time to see me so soon." I nearly added: 'although, to tell you the truth, there wasn't really any particular need.' Or was it simply that I had not been aware of the need?

Trust me, you've come to me at the right moment.

"Oh… right, yes. By the way, I completely forgot to ask on the phone how much your consultations cost…?"

It will cost you a lot of willingness, and courage. You will be able to pay back the value of what you receive here when the time comes. How do you feel?

"Oh, I... I don't really know. I think, right now, I actually feel quite good."

You don't know? What exactly don't you know?

"In all honesty, I don't know where to start..."

Alright. Just take your time. We have all the time in the world.

Dr Seer breathed in and out, loudly enough for me to hear.

Have a look at this. What is it?

He pointed at one of the many mirrors on the wall, one with a simple silver frame. Slightly unsure of myself, I tried to find an appropriate answer. "That... that would be a mirror..."

Correct. And what do you see IN the mirror?

"Hm. Well, there's a flower reflected in the mirror." There was a dark wooden table set back a few metres from the wall, and on it stood a porcelain vase containing a single white flower.

And what does this flower look like?

I suddenly had the feeling that this was really about something else, something bigger and more significant – so I answered as accurately as I could.

"The flower has a dark green stem, about 15 cm long, with four leaves attached to it. The blossom is white and consists of many small, hard petals."

How can you tell that the petals are 'hard'?

For some reason I was finding Dr Seer's questions really challenging. And yet, at the same time, this curious game intrigued me.

"Well, I... I think that the blossom would feel hard. Those kinds of blossoms tend to be pretty firm to the touch. And they're usually not scented."

Ah, I see: So you look at the reflection of the flower and imagine that the blossom feels a certain way because that's usually how it is. I understand.

I felt caught out. Had I said something wrong? He looked at me intently.

Now please approach the flower and get as close to it as possible. Disengage your mind from its reflection. Position your face above the blossom and look at it. What do you see now?

"I see a white blossom, and deep inside it, an orange spot."

My head was so close to the blossom that I was nearly touching it with my nose. To my surprise, I could smell a sweet scent.

"And – wow! The scent is so intense that it's almost making me dizzy."

Dr Seer smiled.

Aha, so that's the absence of perfume then, is it? Have you ever seen a blossom such as this before?

"No, I haven't actually. When I examine it from this close up, I have to say that no, I've never seen anything like it."

He seemed satisfied.

Look at it again, even more closely. Look deep into the blossom. Do you see anything else?

I rubbed my eyes briefly and looked again. The blossom now seemed to resemble some sort of living kaleidoscope. My heart started beating faster. What was happening to me?

"Yes, I see sparkling drops of water inside the petals. They look like dew drops on a meadow in the morning."

So these drops remind you of something? And you like them?

"They remind me of how, as a child, I used to try and collect dew drops with a leaf in the mornings on my way to school..."

He seemed to understand me. What's more, he gave me the feeling that he was there for me, that he was interested in me and that he was happy to guide me through this process.

How do the petals feel? Please get very close to the flower.

Now I was so close to the white blossom that I was touching it with my face. I felt as if I was being drawn into a cloud of white.

"Oh, they're wonderfully soft!"

Now you see! How easy it is to be mistaken! If you hadn't moved in that closely, and if you hadn't looked at it from above and from such close proximity, the true characteristics and the incredible beauty of this rare blossom would have remained hidden from you. And the same goes for the memories that the blossom reawakened in you!

Suddenly I began to sense what Dr Seer had in store for me. He stepped closer and put his hand gently on my shoulder.

As you have just experienced, the way you think and feel about something is very much dependent on how you perceive it. The perspective that you choose determines what it is that you observe. And these observations lead you to particular feelings, experiences and insights.

He smiled again.

The flower was just the beginning, by the way. It goes without saying that this is about how you see yourself, other people and your life every day, every hour and every minute – it's about how you see every incident and how you view every situation.
You can change everything in your life if you look at it in a new way.

Let me show you THE GOLDEN VIEW!

I took a step back and involuntarily glanced in one of the mirrors. All of a sudden and quite unexpectedly I felt a few slight reservations. Was I doing the right thing here?

"What exactly is THE GOLDEN VIEW, Doctor? A new therapeutic method, something like that? Some kind of life philosophy?

All this and much more, my dear Mr Allman.

"Hm. It would make a good book title, you know."

Indeed, that too. Allow yourself to be surprised.

"And why is it called THE GOLDEN VIEW? Why golden?"

Dr Seer looked at me.

What do you think? What do you associate with the word?

"Hm. Gold is very valuable. People refer to 'golden rules' and the 'golden mean'... you can 'strike gold' and so on... 'Golden', I suppose, always refers to something being ideal, or the very best..."

He nodded at me appreciatively, and paused.

Have you ever heard of the 'golden ratio'?

"I think so. Doesn't it have something to do with art?"

Yes, among other things. The golden ratio is based on sacred geometry, an ancient mathematical formula that manifests itself in art, architecture, nature and – yes, even in the human body. It describes a ratio that is perceived as absolutely harmonious by the human eye. For example, a portrait painted according to the golden ratio produces a face with features that the viewer perceives as beautiful and perfect.

"That's fascinating. And sounds like something with a lot of history behind it. How long has the golden ratio been around?"

The application of this principle goes back thousands of years. Whole cities and temples were built according to the golden ratio. Even the Greek philosophers and scholars of antiquity used this formula, and regarded it as a gift from the gods.

"Oh wow! But, to be honest, these aren't really things I know very much about."

There's no need to, really. Detach yourself from what you know or don't know and give your imagination free reign. So, what could 'THE GOLDEN VIEW' possibly stand for?

He was challenging me again. I'd never heard of any of these things before in my life. A few minutes ago I'd been hovering with my face above a simple white blossom as part of some self-awareness process or something, and now here he was, talking about sacred geometry and Greek philosophers. I tried to concentrate.

"OK. Let's see… According to what you explained a moment ago, THE GOLDEN VIEW is all about looking at things in a certain way. By looking at the flower in different ways I was able to discover new things about it."

Well done! You've been paying attention! So what, then, could be the connection to the golden ratio?

"I'm not really any good at problem-solving tasks like this."

Clear your mind of doubts! Just give it a go. You're very close.

Dr Seer was beaming at me encouragingly. And suddenly it came to me.

"I've got it! What you're saying is that the golden ratio is within the observed object itself, so to speak! If I've understood correctly, then a painting is beautiful when it features the golden ratio. And THE GOLDEN VIEW is something that I can actively apply myself! I can *make* something beautiful by looking at it in a certain way… is that it?"

Very well observed!

13

"Consequently, even though the object I'm looking at may not be perfect, I myself can introduce the element of perfection, to a certain extent. A bit like that saying, 'Beauty is in the eye of the beholder', or something."

Dr Seer clapped his hands.

And not just beauty! It can also be the answer, relief, insight, truth, fulfilment, happiness, self-realization! Just as, for the human eye, there exists the perfect perception of things, there also exists a perfect perspective for each human situation – a magical way of seeing that changes everything.

He leaned in closer to me, dropping his voice to a whisper.

With THE GOLDEN VIEW you are not looking at a painting in a museum, but at your own life. All you have to do is to understand and apply the secret.

This particular message seemed to be immensely important to him.

You will find solutions to your problems, answers to your questions, and make new discoveries about your life that have remained hidden until now. You can create a conscious and fulfilled life for yourself, if you so wish.

What do you say?

I couldn't speak. I don't know how else to describe it... I felt deeply moved, overwhelmed with emotion. Perhaps it was also a kind of budding hope. I had absolutely no idea what lay ahead, but something told me that it was a good thing that I had found my way to Dr Seer.

Over the next weeks and months I visited him many times. We often spent several hours together, with many sessions lasting deep into the night.

Thus he introduced me, step by step, to the secrets of

THE GOLDEN VIEW.

Part I

SELF-REFLECTION
&
INITIAL INSIGHTS

1 Look in the mirror!

How do I actually feel?

Three days had passed since my first meeting with Dr Seer. I had lain awake the last few nights with countless thoughts churning over and over in my mind in no particular order. It was as though he had set something in motion inside me that now wanted to be discovered. I felt very nervous again.

Dr Seer greeted me warmly. He seemed genuinely pleased to see me.

How are you doing today?

"Good question. I'm not really sure. I've hardly slept at all."

Weren't you tired?

"Oh yes, I was tired! I AM tired, massively tired!"

He waited, watching me with his eyes half closed. After what felt like an eternity he spoke in a gentle voice.

I quite understand. Tell me – what was going through your mind last night?

"Oh, you know, there's so much. My job, day-to-day stuff, my life... I don't know, exactly. I simply don't know how to deal with certain things. I feel overwhelmed by it all, and then I often find myself wondering: where's the joy in all this? And why can't I ever seem to finally make more money? Why does life always have to be such a struggle? I feel like all I do is function, all the time."

You are very confused.

"Yes. That feels about right."

You are preoccupied with so much that you don't know where to begin.

"Yes..."

Take a deep breath in, and then breathe out.

"Why? I'm doing that anyway."

Please, I'd like for you to now breathe more deeply and consciously than usual.

I breathed in and out, deeply. And, strangely, I immediately felt different – a little lighter, somehow.

When you're thinking of something that makes you worried, breathe deeply in and out! Just do it, even if only once. It will help you! Simple methods are often the best.

Dr Seer winked at me.

Follow me!

"Am I going to look at some flowers again?"

You'll see. Come with me!

He led me to the big wall with the mirrors.

Which one do you like best?

Inexplicably, my heart now started to beat faster. I pointed to one of the mirrors, one with a white painted wooden frame. Dr Seer nodded at me.

Please come and stand here.

He carefully positioned me in front of my reflection.

Look into the mirror!

So there I stood. And strange as it may seem, I had a hard time looking at myself. Dr Seer noticed my uncertainty.

Take your time!

"What's the point of this exercise?"

If you open yourself to it, you will experience the significance of it. Once you experience it, you will understand. Please look at your reflection. What do you see?

"Hm, well: I see that there's a button missing on my jacket. And that I could do with a haircut."

He wasn't going to be led off topic, and continued very earnestly.

What else do you see?

Since I knew I wasn't going to get out of this one so easily, I tried to go along with him.

"I see a man who looks pretty exhausted. Who's in desperate need of a holiday. And who could do with losing a few pounds... But how can I possibly stick to some ridiculous diet on top of everything else? I already have to abide by so many rules and uphold so many obligations all the time as it is. Am I not allowed to just enjoy my life?"

I surprised myself by quite how vehemently all this anger burst out of me. My heart was thumping and I felt the blood rush to my head.

"I think we'd better leave this be!"

I found the situation very uncomfortable. But Dr Seer remained unchanged. He glanced sideways at me, benignly.

What else do you see?

Purely out of politeness, I forced myself to give an answer: "I... I don't see anything. I just feel angry, to tell you the truth. I've no idea what's going on with me right now."

Please remain standing in front of the mirror. What is making you angry?

18

"I'm angry at my life! Or at myself! Or both – oh, I don't know!"

He nodded that he understood. That calmed me, a little.

Now look yourself in the eyes!

And as he noticed my resistance, he added, encouragingly:

It's entirely up to you. If you open yourself and embrace this, you'll go home later having gained an entirely new perspective. Please breathe more deeply. And look deeper into your reflection. Gaze deeply into it.

I shook myself a little, and tried to pull myself together. I looked into my own eyes. It was an odd experience. Quite different to those hurried moments when you glance at yourself in the mirror on a daily basis. I concentrated on not averting my eyes despite constantly feeling the need to do so. My initial anger diminished. And I noticed something emerging within me that was somehow softer.

Dr Seer whispered:

What do you see?

I found it difficult to answer him. What's more, I had the impression that he wasn't waiting for an answer at all, but that his primary aim was to support me in not giving up. Slowly my thoughts calmed.

"I… see… me."

I looked myself in the eyes. And it was as though my facial expression kept changing every few seconds. Was I standing in front of some kind of magic mirror?

This is a completely normal mirror. It shows you whatever you are ready to see. What do you feel when you look at yourself?

"I feel… I feel sad. Yes, I'm sad. I feel alone. I… often feel very lonely…"

Tears welled up in my eyes. But this time, unlike before, when I felt anger, I didn't try to suppress my feelings. I let it happen.

It's good if you feel the need to cry. Go ahead and cry. I understand you.

"I don't usually cry in front of other people. Whatever must you think of me?"

Dr Seer had a certain quality about him that made me feel that he liked me, no matter how I behaved. He radiated warmth and trust.

I think it's a very good thing that you're here.

Tears were flowing down my cheeks and I didn't try to hold them back. Several minutes passed during which we just stood as we were – me in front of my reflection, with Dr Seer beside me, calm and patient. I cried. I cried in a way I haven't done in a very long time. I felt the memories of the last few years rise up in me, all that pain; my lost love; all the hurt; the fear of not ever being able to change my life; my worries about the future. It was this sudden, ruthless confrontation with an honest, direct appraisal of myself that brought out all my sadness. Had I ever really been happy?

Dr Seer handed me a tissue. I tried to collect myself.

"Why are we doing this?"

What do you think?

"I'm learning to be aware of myself."

That's one way to look at it, yes. And it goes even further.

"Really?"

You have just made contact with your innermost self.

Smiling, he stepped behind me and put his hands on my shoulders. He looked at me in our shared reflection.

By truly looking in the mirror, you open the door to what you feel.

He held my gaze for a while, as if he wanted to make sure that I understood what he meant.

And when the doorway to those feelings is open, hurtful experiences can heal. It allows you to draw new strength, and to realize more truthfully what it is that you want to change. In this way, new paths can open up in your life. You can move closer to your dreams and desires, while firmly holding your own hand. You stay connected to your innermost self. You protect yourself, your feelings and your dreams, and this allows you start on a new path.

He took a deep breath.

When you look in the mirror with absolute intention, it allows you to see into your own heart.

I was still numb from having cried so many tears. But I felt in good hands here, in this special place – standing in front of all the mirrors, enveloped by Dr Seer's benevolence and acceptance.

We shall work through everything that preoccupies and burdens you, step by step. We shall look at your inner sadness. Trust me, it will get easier for you. We shall take a look at what happened to your love. Why you lost it. What you wish for. How you can make your work more satisfying. And what you might want to change, and realize. You will be happier and you will rediscover the meaning of your life!

I let myself tumble into his words. I felt the need to cry again, a little. How did he know all these things about me?

"Are you... psychic?"

I merely look very closely.

Dr Seer smiled.

Go home now. I thank you.

"Thank me? For what? It's I who should be grateful to you."

I appreciate you wanting to go down this road – the road to yourself. Very courageous!

I didn't know what exactly he meant by that. At the time I had no way of knowing how intense the process of change that I had already begun would become. But it felt right to have ended up here at this point in time.

"Can I come back tomorrow?"

Yes. Come back tomorrow evening at the same time.

"I'm very grateful to you."

I know. I see it.

2 See yourself from the outside!

*Gaining awareness of the impression
you make on your surroundings*

I was glad that I was able to go straight back to see Dr Seer the next day.
I felt at ease in his presence, and it was obvious quite how much he wanted
to help me. I rang the bell, filled with curiosity and, I freely admit, another
little bout of nervousness.

How are you doing today?

Dr Seer extended his hand to me, inviting me in.

"Oh, pretty good, thank you. Good evening."

Good evening! Please, come in!

He led me through the corridor of mirrors to a room containing nothing
but a small glass table and two armchairs, one green, one white. The floor
and ceiling were also white. Dr Seer indicated I should take a seat.

How was your day today?

I took off my jacket and fell into the green chair.

"Well, I'd booked the day off quite a while ago, but it's not always a given
that I can then actually take the leave. I went for a walk, spent a long time
in a café reading the newspaper – nothing special."

Nothing special, I understand. How did you feel doing it?

"Doing what?"

Sitting in the café, for example.

Suddenly I was thrown, without having the slightest idea why. I didn't
really understand what his question meant. Dr Seer noticed my puzzled
expression, and smiled.

23

I meant exactly what I asked. I'd really like to know.

"Oh. OK."

What are you unsure about?

"I don't know, I thought maybe you were getting at something else."

He studied me carefully and said, in a firm voice:

When who you are on the inside matches who you are on the outside, clarity is the result. When you present to the outside world who you really are and what you really mean, then you are able to communicate with other people on a whole new level. You can express your desires much more clearly. And you are able to get much closer to others. This creates authenticity. Do you understand?

"No, I don't think so, not quite…"

I felt somewhat overwhelmed by his delivery of so much wisdom, so soon after arriving. Dr Seer, however, did not seem the slightest bit phased by my confusion.

I asked you how you felt. And you assumed there was more to my question than the question itself. It unsettled you. Why? Because you didn't trust in the authenticity of our conversation.

"Goodness, no, I didn't mean to imply that at all. Apologies. I… I do trust you."

Don't worry, I'm not offended. On the contrary, I'd like to thank you for creating this situation. Because it's something you can learn a lot from.

He smiled, and seemed genuinely to be enjoying our little misunderstanding.

Have you ever asked yourself how other people perceive you?

"Hm. Sure I have, it's something everyone thinks about, all the time, isn't it? I for one always try to be friendly. I think I behave pretty decently, on the whole."

My answer evidently didn't seem to satisfy him.

Do you recall how, yesterday, when you were looking in the mirror, it made you very sad? You said that you often feel lonely. Do you remember?

"Yes, I remember."

Do you show that to the world around you?

"That I'm lonely? No, of course not. Who would do such a thing? Besides, how would I go about *showing* it? Should I hang a sign around my neck bearing the message: 'Hello, I'm lonely!', or something? Why would I want people to see it, anyway?"

Dr Seer refused to be swayed off course.

Each feeling that burdens us is connected to a desire, a desire that is hidden in our heart and that is not allowed to be revealed because we block it off, emotionally. What could this desire be, in your case?

He certainly had a way of surprising you. Once again he was saying things that seemed to echo the deepest truths with such natural ease that he might as well have been reading out the weather report. How did he know all this?

Do you understand?

I nodded and tried to focus.

So, what desire is connected with the feeling of loneliness?

"Well, the desire to meet and befriend people who like me... who accept me as I am, without me having to pretend to be anything else."

You see! And how much of that do you show those around you?

"Well now, when you put it like that… I don't think I show any of it to anyone."

How did you feel today in the café? Please, take a deep breath in, and then out again – and now revisit the situation in your mind.

I took a deep breath, and as I breathed out again I let myself sink deeper into my chair.

Please, close your eyes. Describe what you experienced as you sat in the café.

I closed my eyes and started to speak:

"I had ordered a cappuccino. I sat at a table in the back, in the left-hand corner. It was very crowded, and almost all the tables were occupied. There was a nice mix of friendly-looking people: a pretty woman with blond hair three tables away from mine who'd caught my eye a few times already; a kindly elderly couple with a big dog. It was very loud, what with all the voices and the clatter of dishes; a woman laughed heartily… Sunlight was streaming into the room, and I would have liked to strike up a conversation with someone. Yes, I suppose I felt isolated. Luckily I had my newspaper and my coffee…"

How do you think the other people perceived you?

"I don't know if they even noticed me. Most of the time I hid behind my newspaper."

Now, please open your eyes and look at me.

Dr Seer fixed his gaze on me. I knew something important was coming.

The best perspective for ascertaining whether what is inside us corresponds with what we reflect on the outside – that is to say, whether we show the outside world our true innermost desires – is the 'outside perspective'. See yourself from the outside!
In your mind, return to the situation in which you felt uncomfortable, and be the invisible eye observing yourself. What do you see?

26

"Ok... let me think. Well – the eye sees a guy who is totally fixated on his newspaper, who doesn't speak or so much as smile at anybody – someone who is only interested in reading the paper and who doesn't seem to care about the people around him at all. What's more, he's clutching his cup of coffee as though afraid someone might take it away from him."

Dr Seer couldn't help but smile, and even I couldn't refrain from chuckling. It felt very liberating to take a distanced look at myself. I suddenly began to laugh out loud. It felt good and made me feel connected to laugh at myself like this with Dr Seer. I knew that he understood me. We laughed and laughed.

Do you know that not taking yourself too seriously can be very uplifting?

I wiped a tear from the corner of my eye.

"Yes, absolutely. You're so right!"

What do you realize when you take a step back and look at yourself from the outside like this?

"Hm... that the impression I give others is nothing like the impression I wish to make."

My insight seemed enormously important to him.

Just to reiterate and be clear: what we're talking about here is not trying to see if you can appear as you would like to appear, but rather if you reveal to the outside world that which you desire within. What was your inner-most desire in this situation?

"To have a conversation with a nice person, to exchange ideas with somebody, maybe to make friends with someone."

And now, seeing yourself from the outside, what impression did you give, would you say?

I answered as objectively as possible.

"Not interested, not friendly – you might even say unapproachable. Like somebody who wants to be left alone, and for whom reading the newspaper is more important than communicating with others."

Dr Seer seemed satisfied.

You see! Who you were on the inside did not match what you were presenting to the outside world. It really is as simple and clear as it appears. How would things have panned out if these two aspects had corresponded with one another?

"Hm. I suppose I would have smiled at people, might even have asked if I could join somebody at their table; I wouldn't have hidden behind the paper and instead would have shown myself to be more open and more interested..."

As if out of nowhere, a feeling of annoyance arose in me.

"But you know, if it was as simple as all that, then I wouldn't be so lonely..."

I didn't say that it was simple.

"Very funny."

Dr Seer definitely had a knack for challenging you.

Trust me! I can see what it is you wish to communicate to me. You have gone through life and had your own particular experiences, naturally. These experiences are connected to certain emotions. These connections have led you to develop unconscious behaviour patterns, which you allow yourself to be steered by. We shall be taking a closer look at these experiences, emotions and behaviour. You will come to know yourself much better.

I listened to his words. He paused for a moment.

THE GOLDEN VIEW will guide you to new levels of insight. You will realize that you can change your experiences whenever you open up and look at yourself in a new way. When you choose the right perspective you will become conscious of what you feel and why you behave in a certain way. You will be able to heal your heart. You will have new experiences, and discover new feelings.

He winked at me, encouragingly.

That's something you have already begun to do.

I sensed very clearly that he was right.

'Seeing yourself from the outside' is a wonderful method with which to become conscious of your own behaviour, and a way to discover that very often it is because of us and no-one else that situations don't turn out the way we want them to. More often than not it is because we don't present ourselves authentically, or we show something else entirely – perhaps even the very opposite of our actual concerns, needs and desires.

"I understand."

Use this perspective to recognize what impact you and your behaviour patterns have on the outside world. Then change your behaviour when it doesn't correspond with your inner truth! Very often it is just a nuance. Imagine, for instance, a man who never manages to get people to agree with him in meetings. To all intents and purposes, it seems like everybody is against him. Why? 'The outside perspective' would reveal that his facial expression is always grim. He frowns constantly. In reality, the man only does it because he's trying to concentrate. And yet, for the longest time, he's been wondering why his ideas get rejected so much. So if he simply pays more attention to looking friendly, especially when he's concentrating, then he will make a totally different impression on those around him. His colleagues would be sure to listen to him more attentively, and take more of an interest.

"I think I understand."

Yes, you do – I can see it.

He put a friendly hand on my shoulder.

29

Please try to pay attention to this over the next few days! Observe closely those situations that go awry, that turn out differently to how you want them to; in which people have a different understanding of you from what you actually meant; in which you feel misjudged. And then assume the outside perspective. You'll be surprised at what you discover.

"Ok, great. I'll do that. Thank you!"

Fascinated by this new insight, I took my leave from Dr Seer.

"Goodbye!"

He gazed at me, smiling, as I left.

3 Look at the situation from above!

Being the neutral observer

Roughly a week had passed since I had last seen Dr Seer. I had to hurry to make our appointment on time. Over the last few days I had often remembered to use the 'See yourself from the outside!' perspective, adopting it time and time again as a way to see myself and the situations I found myself in. And I had to concede that, if truth be told, I'd never really revealed myself to those around me. How are people supposed to approach me when I'm so closed up? I'm not saying that my life had suddenly changed in just one week, but at least I now had an idea of how I could emerge from my isolation – and that feeling gave me a certain boost.

But that's by the by. Because today, unfortunately, everything was different. To be honest, today had totally stressed me out. Dr Seer was smiling when he opened the door, and for some inexplicable reason it immediately made me feel uneasy. 'Perhaps I shouldn't have come' – was the thought that shot through my mind. I wasn't in the mood to be on the receiving end of any philosophical insights – I had more pressing issues of my own. But now it was too late – I was here.

You're feeling stressed.

"You could say that, yes! But how do you know? I haven't even set foot inside yet!"

Well, come on in, then. Good evening, Mr Allman! Please take a deep breath.

Oh, what a surprise – that again. 'Before you do anything else, breathe.' My tension grew.

Please sit down. Would you like a glass of water?

"Yes, thank you."

While Dr Seer went to get the water, I tried to collect myself and to breathe deeply. Sure enough, my pulse began to slow. And, surprisingly, that was all it took for things to seem less dramatic. How quickly the right method can help you to calm down. Interesting!

Well, today is obviously the day for tackling the 'view from above'.

He handed me a big glass of water.

"Sorry?"

It was unbelievable. I hadn't even spoken a word, and already he seemed to have a solution at the ready. This was all happening too fast for me.

"Doctor, I don't wish to be impolite, but I'm not in the mood for mirror experiments and that kind of thing right now. I've had a miserable day."

I can see that. And that's exactly what we shall address. Tell me about your day!

"Well, the whole day felt cursed. It started in the subway in the morning. Everywhere I looked, someone seemed to be having a bad day – everybody was completely stressed out. Some passenger flared up at me, claiming I had pushed him."

Had you?

"Whether I did or didn't is totally irrelevant! That's simply no way to talk to your fellow human beings! So then I arrive at the office, and attend a team meeting arranged by my boss. We're behind schedule in a strategically important project. And – would you believe it – he then proceeds to try and blame it on me. When it wasn't even my fault!! He knew that, and all the others knew it, too. But they all kept their heads down. Nobody spoke up in my defence. And my boss kept banging on at me. It was a total joke. Shall I go on?"

But of course!

Dr Seer radiated such serenity that my angry outburst began to subside. Had my day really been all that bad?

"Well, as it turned out we did then manage to come up with a solution to our deadline problem, but I'm utterly disappointed in my boss and my colleagues! And the stressful day didn't end there: to round things off, I end up in a horrendously full supermarket. Endless queues at the cash registers. All the customers waiting in line, totally stressed out. And when it finally gets to my turn, the cashier snaps at me in a nasty tone for no reason whatsoever. Is that fair? To cap it all, this all meant I was nearly late for our appointment because everything took so long. Today was just one of those days when everything seems to go wrong."

He studied me carefully. It almost felt as if he was trying to read me.

How do you feel now?

I almost wanted to reply with: "How do you think I feel?! Shitty, of course!" But as I thought for a brief moment and tried to gain some clarity about how I actually felt in this very moment, I sensed, to my surprise, an unexpected calm spreading through me. It was very strange.

"I actually feel kind of OK."

That's something, at least. Thank you for describing your day to me. Now lean back and relax. I'd like to tell you about a perspective called 'Look at the situation from above!'.

Now I felt ready to listen to what Dr Seer had to say. It seemed that his initial plan to teach me a new perspective today was still on the cards. So I let myself sink deeper into the chair and waited with keen anticipation. After what felt like five minutes – in reality it was probably only a few seconds – he began to speak in a soft voice:

Human interactions are always full of challenges. Individuals bring their emotions and experiences, their own stories, into every interaction they share, so all kinds of factors play a role in the communication between two people or within a group. So much more happens during communication than simply talking about a certain topic – and this is what frequently causes conflicts to arise. Viewing things from above helps us to realize this – to see what is actually happening, to be aware of what else may be going on during the conversation besides the spoken word. It's a matter of backing out of the conversation on an emotional level, assuming a bird's eye perspective whilst simultaneously carrying on being in the situation. Do you follow?

"More or less. It sounds good, but backing out of things whilst at the same time carrying on sounds somewhat contradictory, don't you think?"

What it means is that, for a particular situation, you imagine climbing one storey higher and stepping out onto a balcony from which to observe the situation in which you find yourself. You pull yourself out of the drama and assume a more objective position or perspective. You look at the scene from above. Your field of perception expands and you see the other people, their individual stories and their emotional lives independently of your own emotional state. You have become the neutral observer.

Dr Seer paused.

Do you get the gist of what I'm saying?

Suddenly, I had to smile at him. I was somehow touched by how patient he was with me. How was it possible for someone to wish me so well? He winked at me in acknowledgement.

Let's run through it once, based on your experiences today! Let's start with the situation in the subway. Close your eyes, that often makes it easier.

"Umm... OK. So, I'm to imagine that I take myself out of the situation, climb up onto some sort of balcony and look down on the entire situation from above. Is that right?"

Precisely.

"Sounds a bit funny, to tell you the truth. It's hard to imagine a balcony above the subway. But OK, so I zoom out and look at the goings-on from above, and I see... a lot of tired people. The carriage is full and stuffy. I manage to jump aboard the train just in time, and elbow my way to the very back of the carriage. In the process I bump into a man who is just starting to nod off. It startles him. He looks even more tired than the others. He mutters to himself, and looks sad."

This new perspective took me completely by surprise; it allowed me to see totally different aspects of the situation. So I continued:

"Oh, that poor guy!! I think he wasn't feeling at all well. He was so startled, I suspect he was just about to fall into deep sleep. Looking at it now, it seems likely that his outburst wasn't even aimed at me. He was just cursing to himself instead. If I'm completely honest, I feel sorry for him now. Sure, it wasn't pleasant for me either – I was tired, too. And it's not like I shoved him intentionally..."

I opened my eyes. Dr Seer seemed satisfied.

How do you feel now?

"I feel sorry for the man. I feel bad. I could have apologized. And we could have shaken hands. We were all of us having a bad morning. In situations like that, people should stick together, not make matters worse by fighting each other on top of everything else."

Now you see how adopting the right perspective makes the situation appear completely different. And your resentment is gone! Let's move further through your day. Have a look at your team meeting from above.

"That's more difficult. There are more people involved, and I've known them all for quite some time."

Give it a try.

"OK. So I zoom out and look from above again. I stand on the invisible balcony above the situation and look down. I watch myself enter the room. My boss is sitting at the head of the conference table. He looks stressed out, as if he's under a lot of pressure. He's probably got management breathing down his neck because we're falling behind schedule. He's sweating, and his neck is flushed and red. He looks helpless. But all that being said, Dr Seer, there's still no reason for him to lay all the blame at my door!"

Absolutely not. What do you feel?

"His behaviour was inappropriate. However, I confess that I can also understand him. Chances are it wasn't his fault, either, but he still gets all the pressure from higher up the chain. Oh well!"

What else do you see in the team meeting?

"My colleague Carl is sitting across from me and looking around the room feeling insecure. He's avoiding eye contact with the boss. It looks like he feels guilty. And he is! And he's afraid – you can see that. I think he's incredibly afraid to fail, and lose his job. Oh boy, that Carl – what a sorry figure he makes. But he's actually quite a nice guy. Likeable. Only a bit too soft. He looks at me, guiltily. He doesn't want all the criticism to be directed at me, but he just can't bring himself to open his mouth."

I understand. Do you see anything else from above?

"The others seem to be fairly neutral. They don't really play a significant role. In the end, we discuss possible solutions, and then the meeting is brought to a close."

Dr Seer raised his voice.

Please explore your innermost self. How do you feel?

"Well, I think everything feels a bit lighter now, somehow. It is what it is, and it can be explained. I understand the situation. After all, it wasn't actually all that dramatic. At least not if you zoom out and observe from above."

Are you still angry about your day?

I couldn't help but grin. How did this happen? A few minutes ago I thought that I had just survived a truly horrible day. Then I mentally positioned myself on this balcony, looked down on the day from above, so to speak, and the drama disappeared as if it had simply evaporated!

"No, somehow not at all! The anger is gone! You know, we don't have to take a look at the supermarket situation. I can already imagine how that's going to play out. I can imagine that the cashier was simply over-worked. Customers aren't always easy to deal with. Besides, it was full, and loud, and everyone was in a hurry to get home. And so everybody, without noticing it, had contributed to the general tension. In reality, nobody was out to harm anyone else. Hm, I guess that means my day wasn't so full of drama after all. But nonetheless, while it lasted it all felt very stressful – and nothing you can say will make me feel otherwise!"

That is not my intention. What you have now understood is that our own emotions undergo a considerable change when we metaphorically look down upon each situation from above. In so doing, you choose a particular mental perspective, and that has immediate consequences for the emotional processes. You become calmer and are able to step out of a stiflingly negative situation that it seems would have been almost impossible to change through your own behaviour. By adopting this mental meta-plane even your body posture relaxes, and you breathe more calmly. You are no longer dominated by negative emotions and sensations.
Besides, as a neutral observer from above, you can more easily develop an understanding for yourself and others that enables you to handle emerging conflicts much better. Ultimately, this influences the entire situation in a positive manner. Reaching insights and finding solutions becomes much easier.

"Incredible! What a fantastic method! I reckon it can help in so many situations. I didn't realize that creating an inner image or assuming a mental perspective could actually help me become more relaxed and calmer in everyday stressful situations. Does it really work? I'll definitely try it out. There's bound to be another occasion when it'll come in handy."

Definitely! I'm very happy for you. Do you want to come back next week?

"Yes, I'd love to! I'm all for it. THE GOLDEN VIEW, what a great method!

Thank you! Goodbye!"

Goodbye!

I left Dr Seer's practice in a good mood. This time I walked quickly past the mirrors and made a deliberate effort not to look, because my number one priority was now this bird's eye perspective idea. Be a neutral observer. Up on the balcony! I was all fired up and ready to try out 'Look at the situation from above' in the days to come.

4 See with the eyes of a tiger!

Finding the courage to face upcoming changes

My pace quickened as I neared Dr Seer's office. It was early evening, and I urgently needed to ask his advice. This time I wasn't looking for a new way of seeing things – I was in need of specific advice on what to do. This desire for guidance had been gnawing away at me since yesterday, the result of relentlessly mulling over a problem that I had in fact been carrying around with me for years. I'd already planned what I wanted to say to Dr Seer, and rehearsed the sentences over and over as I hurried to meet him.

The door swung open before I reached it. It baffled me that he always seemed to know I was coming before I even rang the bell. It occurred to me that I should take the next opportunity to check whether the entrance could be viewed from inside. 'Viewed' certainly struck me as the appropriate word to use.

My dear Mr Allman, how are we today?

"Hello, Dr Seer. I'm fine, thanks. But I've come with a very specific question today."

Wonderful. But don't you want to come in first?

"Oh, yes. Of course."

We quickly made our way to our room and took our seats. 'Now, whatever you do, don't get side-tracked,' I told myself. I tried to focus on my question, and nothing else. As if wanting to test my patience, Dr Seer began the conversation with a calmness that lay at odds with the urgency I felt inside.

How was your week? Were you able to apply the perspectives you've been learning about?

"Yes, it was great. But I'd like to talk to you about a different topic today."

I can see that. Alright then – let's hear it!

39

"Well, after repeatedly zooming out and looking at my work situation from above, I once again realized that I should definitely be asking for a pay rise. I'm the one who always comes up with the decisive solutions, who drives projects forward and motivates the people around me, who takes responsibility for everything and can be completely relied upon..."

I took a deep breath.

"And... well, I don't know how else to put it – I'm a great asset, and I haven't had a significant salary increase in years."

And you recognized all this by looking at the situation from above? Well done!

Dr Seer seemed visibly pleased by my observations.

"Well, I've known for a long time that I'm getting too little money for what I'm doing. It's just that I was so deeply caught up in my day-to-day work that I kept 'losing sight' of this thought, to put it in your words."

You recognized something very significant by taking a step back from everyday events and looking at the situation from a distance.

"That's true. But my problem is that this doesn't solve anything. Recognizing what's going on and doing something about it are two completely different issues! Since opening my eyes to the reality of the situation and understanding that part of my dissatisfaction arises from the fact that my tireless efforts are not being appropriately remunerated, I'm even more frustrated than before."

I understand. In and of itself, recognition is often not particularly pleasant. It brings us face to face with the truth. However, it is then, and only then, that positive change can take place.

I felt frustration welling up inside me. It was a familiar feeling, one that accompanied me on an almost daily basis. Only this time it manifested itself much more distinctly – and as a result, was much more painful to bear.

"Great. So what do I do now?"

What do you mean, exactly?

"Please, don't pretend not to understand! It's obvious, isn't it? The question is how do I go about getting more money?"

Dr Seer took his time. Maybe he wanted my frustration to intensify, in order to motivate me. This was one of countless moments during our many talks in which I started out with absolutely no idea where he was going with things. But since I trusted him, I could safely assume that he took me seriously, and had my best interests at heart.

He smiled at me in encouragement.

What you want is clear: an increase in salary. And I get the impression that you have been concerned with this issue for quite some time, even though you are only now seeing it so clearly.

"It's been like this for years, actually. I've thought about it time and again. I've had enough – I want things to change."

From one second to the next there was a change in my mood. My frustration gave way to an inner weariness that threatened to completely overwhelm me. I felt incredibly tired. My desire to find a solution, and the urgent question of how to go about tackling this problem, both receded into the background. Dr Seer immediately noticed the change in me.

You suddenly look tired. This issue has taken its toll over time, and cost you a lot of personal energy, am I right?

"Spot on."

Have you ever discussed this matter with your boss?

"No, I haven't."

All these years? Why not?

"I simply assumed that my boss would come forward and offer me a pay rise himself. It's obvious that I earn way too little! It should be self-evident!"

Dr Seer calmly settled his gaze on me. I felt a sense of despair unfold within me.

I understand. But as far as I'm aware, salary increases don't usually just appear out of nowhere without any proactive effort to make them happen.

His comment seemed to touch a nerve. All of a sudden I actually felt offended.

"You can spare me your sarcasm. I'm fully aware how these things work! You don't understand where I'm coming from."

I do understand you – and I'm trying to find out what's really going on inside you. We need the whole picture – even if it makes you uncomfortable, in the beginning. Trust me! You're going to go home feeling much better. And you shall have the answer you're hoping to find. Once we've finished, you will know what to do.

Without warning, a big sigh escaped my lips. In spite of my bad mood I could sense his genuine interest in helping me. And despite everything, I felt supported, even though his constant line of enquiry was not particularly enjoyable. After a few seconds, I shook myself, and continued.

"OK then, it's like this: I didn't dare ask. To be honest, I shied away from doing so."

I see. Do you think your boss could actually be of the opinion that you don't deserve a pay rise?

"No. That's not the problem! I'm certain he sees it the same way I do. It's pretty obvious! And he should have approached me and offered me the increase a long time ago."

But clearly he hasn't yet done so. For reasons that are perhaps not even important right now.

He gave me an intense look.

Why didn't you initiate the discussion yourself? Why did you shy away, as you put it?

I took a deep breath.

"My boss is quite an explosive character. Depending on his mood on any given day, it's entirely possible that he could completely flip out if you approach him to talk about any issues you might be having. Particularly when he thinks it's a non-urgent matter that is therefore irrelevant in his eyes."

Yes, that is unpleasant. Do you believe that, as a result, the conversation would lead to nothing?

"Hm. Well, I suppose that once you get through to him, it's possible to discuss things with him and find solutions. It's more the whole 'flipping out' thing."

I understand. The possibility of encountering this initial, potentially unpleasant situation worries you: the thought that he could immediately 'flip out' if you were to approach him at the 'wrong time'.

"Precisely. I'm a big fan of harmony, you see! I'm not interested in getting into loud confrontations. It costs me a lot of energy, and I tend to withdraw immediately. Or I keep out of these sorts of situations and steer clear of such conflicts from the outset. But that means I never get where I'm trying to go."

Anger and disappointment churned inside me. Why on earth was I so afraid of my boss' moods? Why had I never tried to tackle this before? For years and years I had sat on my concerns and done nothing. I almost felt ashamed in front of Dr Seer. But he was nodding at me encouragingly – and that made me feel a bit more secure. 'If my boss was even just a tiny bit like Dr Seer, everything would be totally straightforward,' I thought to myself.

So, in summary: You have been due a pay rise for a long time. There's no question that you deserve one – the arguments for it are clear. And your boss is bound to see it that way too, were you to have an appropriate conversation with him. You want to initiate this conversation; however you are undecided about it because it could start out on an unpleasant footing. In your opinion, your boss has explosive personality traits. You expect him to react in an angry and indignant manner. And harmony is so important to you that this is the reason you have avoided the conversation about salary altogether.

"You've hit the nail right on the head!"

Dr Seer didn't hesitate for long.

See with the eyes of a tiger!

"Say what now?"

Now I was confused. What had felt like making gradual progress towards finding a solution had ended – how could it not? – with the presentation of yet another new perspective. All of a sudden I started to doubt Dr Seer after all. See with the eyes of a tiger? What a load of nonsense! Was he really taking me seriously?

You're thinking that our conversation was all about clarifying things up until now, and that we were getting closer and closer to finding a solution... and now all this nonsense, right? And to cap it all, I then start talking about animals!

He was smiling. Unbelievable – he knew exactly what I was thinking.

And yes, I do take you seriously.

"Are you able to read people's minds?"

He didn't answer that particular question. At least not during this session.

Allow me to explain the perspective that's going to help you. 'See with the eyes of a tiger' can give the decisive impetus to act in all kinds of situations, and so enable thoughts to be turned into actions. This decisive 'kick' is what you currently require to be able to initiate the conversation with your boss!

"Hm. But why haven't I managed to do it all these years? How can I be certain that I'll go through with it now?"

You were afraid. And that is a natural human response. Please consider the following: Anxieties, limiting belief systems and behaviour patterns can prevent us from engaging with things, persons and above all ourselves. If, consciously or unconsciously, you believe that your boss will react angrily, and this thought unsettles you – or, indeed, if bad experiences you've had in the past cause you to fear the situation you're facing in the present – then you limit yourself and restrict the possibilities available to you.
In order to take action and make a change, we first have to really want it, and second we need to find the power and courage to make it happen.
You want to change your situation. By seeing with the eyes of a tiger you will acquire the power and courage for this first step. This perspective will give you the decisive impulse you need to take action.

"That sounds plausible, but what does a tiger have to do with it all?"

The tiger represents the qualities you require in anxiety-filled situations. Tigers are strong, fast, lithe and confident. They have unwavering self-belief. A tiger will fix their sights on the target, and remain absolutely focused. A tiger exudes dignity. It is a strong and courageous animal. How does that sound to you?

"Wow. Sounds powerful. But how do I do that – how do I see with the eyes of a tiger?"

Dr Seer was clearly pleased that I was starting to come round to his new perspective. His green eyes twinkled – and suddenly it was as though there was something tiger-like in his facial expression. I had never seen eyes quite like it before.

It's very simple: Breathe deeply, and focus on yourself. Imagine adopting these characteristics and embracing them, fully. You ARE the tiger. You feel strength, fearlessness and power. You are focused and determined, and it is from this position that you turn your imaginary gaze on the situation – on the conversation with your boss. You have a clear objective: You want the conversation to be a success, you want to stand your ground and achieve a salary increase. And you focus. You keep this firmly in your sights. You have the power and courage to make it happen. Now you try, in your mind! Please close your eyes.

I did as I was asked. Dr Seer's vivid description allowed me to imagine it vividly. As absurd as it sounded to me at first, I imagined that I was the tiger, and pictured walking into my boss' office, full of confidence, to ask to speak with him.

And I felt new strength rising up in me. It did indeed feel like a 'kick'. I saw with the eyes of a tiger. I went through the situation in my mind, all the while assuming this tiger-like attitude. My objective was to tackle the conversation and to not give in until I had seen it through. I could do it. I would cope, even if things became unpleasant. I would not allow myself to be swayed from my goal, and I was determined to get my salary increase.

I opened my eyes.

It works, am I right?

"Woah, yes... I think it really does!"

The discomfort I'd felt about confronting my boss was gone. Instead, unexpected anticipation rose up in me. And a desire to act, to finally stand up for myself.

"First thing tomorrow morning I'll arrange an appointment to talk to my boss. Fantastic. Thank you."

My pleasure. I am very happy for you! Start seeing with the eyes of a tiger before you even enter the meeting! Walk through the conversation before-

hand, with this perspective in mind. Feel it. And, if you wish, you can call me afterwards to tell me how it went.

"I will. How come I didn't meet you much earlier in my life?"

Perhaps you were only ready for it now.

"Hm, do you think so?"

Dr Seer gave me a knowing look, and shook my hand.

"Can I come back next week?"

I would like that, very much.

"How come you have such faith in me?"

I see who you are. And how much potential rests inside you. Goodbye!

Even though at the time it wasn't clear to me what Dr Seer meant or what exactly he saw in me, it felt really good to hear him say it. There was something about him that gave me strength and made me feel a kind of lightness that I hadn't felt in years. It seemed that, as far as he was concerned, there was not a single problem in the world that couldn't be solved. It filled me with hope, such that I returned home that evening with a spring in my step.

5 Look in their eyes!

Truly connecting with those around you

I did it! Finally, after years of putting it off, I'd found the courage to have the talk with my boss that I'd been dreading for so long – and what's more, I came out of with the pay rise I'd been hoping for! I was pleased with myself for the first time in ages. Strange as it might seem, I'd nearly forgotten what that felt like. While sipping a cappuccino in my favourite café, I gazed out of the window and thought through the events of the last week. I was proud of myself, and yes – perhaps even a little happy.

After about an hour I headed over to Dr Seer's place. I wanted – no, *had* – to thank him and celebrate my success with him. He beamed at me when he opened the door.

You did it! Congratulations!

Again, how did he know? To be honest, I was getting to the point where nothing surprised me anymore. Dr Seer was psychic, pure and simple – if such a thing is possible.

"I won't even bother asking how you know that."

You are most welcome to ask! The answer is: why, it's obvious. You are radiating success and contentment. I'm proud of you! You did a great job! Come on in, let's look happiness straight in the eye!

He had a singular way of expressing himself sometimes, but each time his words resonated with me on some level. Dr Seer once again led the way into the white room with the green and white armchairs. I felt relaxed and at ease, and fell into 'my' chair with a smile on my face.

"Thank you! And above all, thank you for sharing the tiger's perspective! It gave me the decisive kick I needed."

Well done, Mr Allman!

He smiled at me approvingly. It was a completely new experience – for me to witness somebody else sharing my joy from the depths of his heart. I thoroughly enjoyed it. After the longest time I'd finally achieved something and had a taste of success. My spirits were high, and, with a secret desire for yet more praise, I kept talking.

"You know, I was just sat in my favourite café round the corner, thinking to myself how incredible it all is!! All the things I've learned in just a few weeks! I've taken so much on board – and now I've even managed to implement this understanding. It's a great feeling!"

Dr Seer looked at me with a mischievous smile and said nothing. After a while he suddenly asked a question out of the blue that totally threw me off course.

Was the woman in the café, too?

"Sorry? What woman?"

The pretty woman with blond hair who was sat three tables away from you last time.

"How come you're mentioning that now? I'm surprised you even remember!"

Oh, when you look at it that way it's not so very unusual. I listen attentively when you talk, and I remember the scenes that you describe. I retain everything very vividly in my memory, like photos or movies that I can retrieve at will. So, was she there?

I have to admit that I wasn't really in the mood for a change of topic at that particular moment; or rather, I had absolutely no desire to change tack and head in that particular direction. I felt I was due some more well-deserved appreciation, and saw no reason not to bask in it for a little while longer.

"Yes, I think she was there."

You think? Did you see her?

I felt myself growing indignant. He just didn't want to let it go, this insistent line of enquiry.

"Dr Seer, I'm so thrilled about my salary increase, and yet you don't want to dwell on it, not even for a few minutes."

You're more than welcome to tell me more about your success. You did an absolutely fabulous job!

Feeling almost a little offended, I suddenly realized I no longer felt in the mood to talk about my recent achievement. How quickly emotions can change – sometimes just thanks to a couple of questions...

"No, it doesn't matter."

I was actually hoping that Dr Seer would manage to reinstate my good mood – after all, he had been the one to steer us away from our happy exchange. But no, he took me literally.

Good! Then let's return to thinking about the woman. Did you see her?

"Yes," I answered, curtly.

And did you make contact with her?

Realizing I didn't really have any other choice, I gave in. Right, so now we were going to be talking about the woman in the café. In any case, Dr Seer was like a dog with a bone – there was no way I'd be able to dissuade him. And besides, by now I'd come to realize that there was inevitably some significant point to be made whenever he became so intensely insistent on confronting me with my experiences.

"No, I didn't make contact with her. We don't even know each other."

Would you like to get to know her?

"Umm... I don't know. I haven't really thought about it. I suppose... yes, I suppose I would. I've often noticed her, in any case..."

He straightened up, and looked at me as though to challenge me.

Did you look her in the eyes?

"Pardon me? No. Of course not! Why would I? Like I said, I don't even know her! I can't just start staring at her. That would be incredibly embarrassing!"

He smiled, and carried on talking, unperturbed. He seemed to like this particular topic, and undoubtedly had some specific intention in mind.

I didn't ask if you stared at her. Did you look into her eyes?

"I repeat: no! I didn't look her in the eyes. You know, it's just not my style to make direct eye contact with every woman I meet. Chances are it would only be misinterpreted."

I see. So the reason you avoid looking the woman in the café in the eyes is to prevent her from thinking that you might want to flirt with her?

This reasoning bothered me, even though his tone of voice was as soft and pleasant as always. I didn't care to admit the truth of the matter, which was that I didn't dare look directly at the pretty woman in the café – whom I had in fact secretly observed on numerous occasions – let alone look her in the eyes. I didn't want to admit to myself – or Dr Seer – that I had come to think of myself as a bit of a chicken, a hopeless case who had completely forgotten how to flirt over the course of the last few years. For a long time I'd been blocking out the fact that I'd simply given up on women because I was afraid of rejection. But, without meaning to, the words slipped out anyway:

"In all honesty, I just *can't!*"

You can't look into that woman's eyes?

"Yes. I mean, no! I can't. I can't flirt. I'm afraid I'll be met with a rebuff. So I just leave it be. Period!"

Whilst pursuing this line of inquiry, Dr Seer in no way made me feel I was being ridiculed for my supposed incapability – which was extremely helpful, since otherwise I would have balked at such an uncomfortable topic.

You would actually like to get to know this woman, if only you could find the courage and the self-confidence to approach her and strike up a conversation. Am I right?

He was remarkably persistent. It dawned on me that I had no choice but to go through this with him.

So, out of sheer desperation, I exclaimed: "Yes, for goodness' sake!" and fell back into my chair.

This is not just some fun exercise, you know.

"Of course not! It certainly doesn't strike me as particularly amusing!"

Dr Seer waited as if wanting to give me time to pull myself together.

It is helpful to have a clear understanding of one's deepest desires and to recognize why one's actions don't align with achieving these desires.

At that point I had to just let his words flow over me. It all made a lot of sense, of course, but I didn't feel very comfortable about it at all – quite the contrary. Thankfully what followed turned out to be more of a monologue than an interrogation, so I was spared having to answer any more questions for the time being.

By making direct eye contact with another person, you establish a real connection. You connect at a deep level. This allows an emotional bond to be created before a single word has been spoken. It is a silent, inner 'getting to know each other'. Do you understand?

I tried to pull myself together.

"It sounds pretty plausible."

I'll reveal something else to you: Looking into the eyes of another person can also help in situations in which we feel we have lost the connection to that person. When it feels like things are not flowing properly – when it feels like there's an obstruction, and it's as though you can't reach each other. It might feel like the other person is somehow against you, or avoiding you. And that makes you feel insecure. Direct eye contact re-establishes a connection with the person you are talking to on the emotional level. You open up, and so do they, allowing any resistance to be set aside. How does that sound to you?

Actually, I didn't feel like being drawn into the conversation. For the time being it suited me much better to just listen to his words, in truth because I was afraid of once again having to face up to my inability to flirt. So I answered with a very clipped:

"Good."

Can you describe a situation to me in which you noticed that there was a lack of eye contact?

Somewhat reluctantly, I pondered the question.

"Yes. I have a colleague who categorically avoids eye contact when anyone talks to him."

I see. And how is that for the people he engages with?

"It's awkward, somehow. For a while we all thought that maybe he has something to hide, or that he was up to something. That he had a hidden agenda. Then we thought that he might perhaps just be insecure, or simply uninterested in making social contact. And finally, it occurred to us that it was probably a habit he developed in Asia. He spent several years working there, and, as far as I know, direct eye contact is considered impolite in that part of the world. I haven't a clue what's behind it all, but safe to say our relationship is somewhat distanced as a result."

53

It goes without saying that cultural differences influence our behaviour and our interactions. However, let's stay in our own cultural sphere for the moment. You find it unpleasant that your colleague doesn't look you in the eye when you speak with each other. And you have tried to come up with a number of possible explanations for his behaviour, but at the end of the day you don't truly understand why he reacts this way. In the end you have accepted that this is how things are, but the relationship between the two of you is distanced as a result. Correct?

"Yes."

This illustrates how important it is to look your fellow human beings in the eyes, especially when professionally involved with them and having to work together on a daily basis. It might appear banal, but it is a key component of every interaction.

As if wanting to demonstrate what he meant, Dr Seer looked me straight in the eyes and held my gaze for several seconds.

When engaging in direct communication with someone, it is very difficult to make a true connection without looking in their eyes. It doesn't matter what kind of relationship exists between the two parties. You can recognize it straight away through the inner feelings that arise. I would like you to really understand this. There's more to it than meets the eye.

"I thought as much."

Let's go back to the lady in the café.

I knew it: here he was, confronting me with that tiresome topic all over again. Dr Seer clearly didn't lose sight of his original point no matter how far he strayed from the subject.

Now, take a moment to put yourself in her shoes. She sees you sat at an adjoining table, and has perhaps noticed you there on several previous occasions. But you never make eye contact. You always just read your newspaper or look out of the window. What does she make of it all?

54

"No idea. I'm not psychic."

It's not a question of being psychic. Look at the situation from the woman's perspective. You're not a beginner anymore – you've already started learning how to change your view of a situation! Think of the explanations you came up with for your colleague who always avoids eye contact. Would any be a good fit for this particular situation? What might this woman think about you?

"Hm. Well, I suppose she'd probably assume that I'm not interested in her."

Exactly! So if you'd like to get to know this woman, you have no choice but to look her in the eyes. You have to establish a connection first, before anything else can happen! Bridge the gap between you and her.

"I don't know."

What don't you know?

"I don't know if I can bring myself to do that."

Most people find it takes a bit of courage. We tend to want to shy away from the authenticity that is created, at first – the exposure of the truth. Would it help you if I provided detailed instructions for how best to handle the situation?

"Maybe."

I was growing increasingly concerned that Dr Seer was seriously going to require me to look into the woman's eyes.

Alright: So you enter your café, and take a seat from which you have a good view of the whole room. If the woman is already there, choose a seat that allows you to make easy eye contact with her. Then take a deep breath, and smile at yourself.

He winked at me.

You see, moments like these work best when we're relaxed. Say to yourself: 'I feel secure. This is a lovely moment!' Then look at the woman, and keep looking at her until she returns your gaze. If she doesn't respond, simply try again. While you look at her, imagine that your direct gaze is building a bridge between the two of you, and so creating a positive connection between you and her. And then you smile at her.

Dr Seer nodded at me in encouragement as hc spoke these words.

"So, on top of everything else, I have to smile, too."

The subject matter was starting to get to me. I had the growing concern that I would actually have to put these instructions into practise, and so be forced out of my presumed comfort zone. At some point in the past I had withdrawn from the world of women, and had somehow resigned myself to the fact that I was alone. And at this particular moment, I wasn't even completely sure that I wanted things to change.

Of course you smile at her! You'll feel more confident if you smile. Your body will signal this to you – along the lines of: I'm smiling, so I must be feeling good! To put it in simple terms. What's more, a smile radiates friendliness and trustworthiness. And the woman will respond. She will turn towards you, and initial contact will have been established.

"I just hope you're right, Doc. There's a chance she might also react in an unfriendly or irritated manner, because every guy who walks into the café starts flirting with her."

If you don't try, everything will remain the same. You have nothing to lose, and your intentions are good. That is reason enough.

"That's true. And you really think I should give it a go?!"

Yes, of course. That is what this is all about. You said yourself that understanding something is one thing, but implementing it is something else entirely. So do it! Have faith in yourself! And next time we meet, we will take a look at the outcome.

Dr Seer was evidently very pleased about this homework exercise that he'd so nonchalantly sent my way. I bet he could hardly wait to see how it would turn out. 'Well, it's easy enough for him to say, he doesn't have to *do* it,' I thought to myself.

"Alright then. I'll do it. I've got nothing to lose."

Wonderful. I'm proud of you. You're making great progress.

"Oh. Thanks."

Once again, I couldn't help but smile. In no time at all, Dr Seer had managed to put me back in a good mood, and just as I did after every session to date, I left him feeling full of energy and free from the thoughts that were holding me back. It was incredible.

We walked down the hall together. Dr Seer opened the door. The evening sun was shining, and it smelled of summer outside.

"Thanks, Doc! See you next week. Goodbye!"

A feeling of joyful anticipation spread through me. Ideally I'd have loved to head straight to the café to put this latest perspective into practise. But the likelihood of the woman being there right now was fairly small. So I went home instead, and thought through how I'd look at her when I next got the chance. And how, just maybe, I might even smile at her, too.

6 See with the eyes of a role model!

Achieving the seemingly impossible

Lost in thought, I made my way to see Dr Seer. There wasn't really any particular need to see him today. I felt pretty good, and nothing much had really happened since our last session. I didn't have any pressing concerns, or any specific questions I hoped he could answer. But chances are he'd have yet another perspective up his sleeve that he would want to introduce me to. In fact, I was fairly certain of it. I chuckled to myself, thinking about how passionate the Doc got each time he explained how to solve a particular problem. And he always taught me a lot more than that. He gave me crucial insights into my own life. Dr Seer was without question someone who had found his passion in life. One of these days, maybe I should ask him how he arrived at his vocation.

He was already standing in the open doorway when I arrived.

Hello. How are you today?

"Hi there. I'm good, thanks. And you?"

He shook my hand, an impish grin playing across his face. I was curious to know what he had in store for me today.

Very good. Thank you. Come in.

He walked briskly down the corridor to our room, and indicated that I should follow him.

Please, take a seat!

"Thank you."

You're very quiet today. Nothing to tell me?

Dr Seer was now grinning broadly.

"Not really. Should there be?"

I had no idea what he was getting at.

You had an assignment, did you not? I'm curious to know how it went. Did you look the woman in the café in the eyes?

"Oh, *that's* what you were referring to! Yes, I did. If I say I'll do something, then I keep my word."

Wonderful! It is not always a given that people are true to their word, you know. So: what happened?

"Nothing."

He studied me for a moment.

What do you mean, 'nothing'? You looked at her, and that was it?

"Yes. That was the assignment, wasn't it? It's not like you told me to marry her or anything."

Nobody's talking about marriage – but do you want to just look at her for the next three years?

"Yes, no… oh, I don't know. To tell you the truth, I've kind of forgotten how one goes about getting to know a woman. But I'm not here because I've signed up for a flirting seminar, am I?!"

Who says you couldn't be? Is there any reason for us not to address this issue here?

On the table in front of us stood a big glass carafe filled with water, and several glasses. Perhaps as a means to give me a bit of time, and to relieve the inevitable pressure that I quite evidently felt when talking about this particular topic, Dr Seer poured some water into a glass and handed it to me. I took a small sip. I'd come to realize that he was only satisfied with the answers I gave if they were honest ones. So I didn't even attempt to respond with anything other than the truth.

"Hm. Perhaps it's my insecurity. I don't want to come across as a failure. What would you think of me?"

Do you really think you can lose face in my eyes? Or diminish your status as a man? Where does this fear come from?

"OK, OK. Never mind. Fine, let's go ahead and do this 'flirting course' then - if you think it's necessary."

No, it's not necessary. But it's something that's crying out to be addressed. Your heart is blocked.

"What do you mean by that?"

If you're worried that you will appear stupid in my eyes then you are also afraid to fail in a romantic relationship. What's more, if your fear of how you appear from the outside is blocking you from pursuing love, then a major part of your personal energy is blocked. This is what we refer to as 'heart energy'.

I took a deep breath, and another sip of water.

"Gosh. And who is 'we', exactly?"

We helpers!

Dr Seer proclaimed this information as though there were no need to for any further explanation. Enthusiastically, he continued.

Have you ever thought about what it means to act from the heart?

"I don't know… sounds quite nice, I suppose."

Do you know what it means?

"To be honest, no, I don't think so."

You base your actions on good feelings, and you trust yourself.

"Hm."

Love is the most powerful feeling that human beings can experience. When you dive deeply into your feeling of love and allow your actions to be led by this feeling, then you won't be worried about doing something wrong. Do you understand?

"Sort of, more or less. I can't quite imagine what it would be like to act out of *love*."

This topic was making me pensive. And all of a sudden, I felt incredibly emotional.

"Do you mean to say that it can be learnt?"

If I weren't convinced of it then we wouldn't be having this conversation right now. And besides: you have already begun to learn it. But take your time! We'll get there. You'll slowly discover your love. You'll feel more self-confident.

He looked at me intensely.

You're already well on your way! THE GOLDEN VIEW is helping you get there.

His words touched me. A quiet sense of gratitude welled up in me. On the one hand, it felt like a huge load of work lay before me. But on the other, Dr Seer showed so much patience and appreciation towards me that I was actually ready to embark upon the 'path' of which he spoke – without having any clear idea of what it might be.

As if he had been following my thoughts he whispered:

THE GOLDEN VIEW will lead you along the path of your heart and your truth. Those who have contributed great things to this world have all acted from their hearts. In our case, we will of course first have to look at what you are able to contribute to your own life. Let us first take a step back – to the lady you are so fond of. To feel attracted to her, to be interested in her, to flirt – what significance does that hold for you?

"What do you mean?"

What do you feel when you see that attractive woman?

"Well... I suppose I think that she's beautiful, how great it might be to get to know her... and that she has a lovely smile..."

And what do you feel?

"Well, to be totally honest: insecurity."

Yes. That insecurity is based on your past experiences, correct? Based on your doubts, my dear Mr Allman. Based on your inner conviction that such an attractive woman cannot possibly be interested in someone like you. Am I right?

"Very probably, yes."

Please sit comfortably, and breathe deeply. Focus only on yourself.

I followed his instructions.

What do you feel in your heart? What do you feel, deep inside, when you look at the lady in the café? What did you feel when you looked into her eyes?

"I don't know."

Feel within yourself. What did it feel like at the time?

"Hm. Perhaps a little warm... and kind of exciting. Yes, it was beautiful. But nothing that could be called love."

Could it not?

"Well, I don't actually know her at all!"

And yet you feel attracted to her.

"Yes, but..."

You feel touched by her – in your heart.

"Well, if that's how you want to put, then OK... maybe."

He was nodding at me, confirming it.

That is already a form of love. Something in her touches your heart, and that's what draws you to her. A very genuine feeling. The more you allow it, the more things can develop, you understand? And that requires courage, of course. Because truly feeling the deepest of feelings and relying on them as signposts to guide your own actions is something very powerful. And one of the keys to creating self-confidence.

Once again I felt touched – touched by this wisdom. His words triggered many things in me. I tried to continue taking deep breaths.

Did you know that one can even see the entire world from the heart?

"That sounds like being in love with everything and everybody, all the time."

In some ways it is very much like that. We'll take a closer look at that at a later point. You'll see how beautiful it is, and how it can change your life!

Dr Seer raised the glass carafe and poured more water into my glass.

Now let's go back to 'flirting school'. Tell me, is there a male person in your circle of acquaintances, let's say a good friend, who you think would find it very easy to speak to the woman in the café?

"Sure. I know several guys like that. For most of them it would be the easiest exercise in the world. Long live machismo!"

Oh, you call it 'machismo'? I see. An exaggerated version of male power and vitality, then.

"Yes. No. I simply mean that many of the men I know would not, as I see it, have the slightest problem looking the woman in the eyes, talking to her, and so on..."

As you see it. Interesting. I wonder if that is also how they see it?

He seemed to like my choice of words.

Now please name a male acquaintance of yours who you think would be able to do it.

"Well, my best friend Andy is a true master when it comes to flirting."

Very good. And how would Andy go about getting to know a woman? What kind of attributes does he have, in your eyes?

In thinking about it, I had to grin. Andy always had been and still is an absolute expert in flirting matters. I, of course, didn't even come close to approaching his expertly charming style. Where such matters were concerned, he and I represented absolute opposite ends of the spectrum, so to speak.

"Andy is incredible, Doc! He's an author and an artist, and women just flock to him. He's relaxed, easy, informal and likable. Most of the time, he's funny, and cool. He has a knack of effortlessly finding the right words, without being shallow. He's such a fantastic storyteller! He approaches women actively, easily gets into conversation with them, and knows how to awaken interest. And to top it all, he's also a great listener. Everyone seems to feel immediately drawn to him. Baffling. How come he has all these great personal skills...?"

That is a very nice description. You have clearly observed things very astutely. Would you say that, for you, he is something of a role model as far as making contact is concerned?

"Yes, definitely. I'd say so! A great role model. And I'm sorry to say that I've nowhere near his level of skill."

Please look at it like this, instead: You are just not conscious of the fact that you also have these personal attributes and abilities within you.

"What do you mean?"

You wouldn't be able to recognize these strengths in Andy if you didn't have the same potential dormant within you.

"Really? Is that so?"

Yes.

He gave me a challenging sort of look.

Well then! Wake these strengths!

"How do I go about doing that, Doc?"

See with the eyes of a role model!

Obviously, the solution was again to be found in yet another perspective. I felt a little confused. What in heaven's name did he mean, 'see with the eyes of a role model'?

Very well. We shall now revisit the situation in the café in our minds. You're sitting at the table drinking a cappuccino. Please close your eyes. Allow your friend Andy to enter your inner field of vision. Imagine yourself slipping, so to speak, into Andy's skin. You're seeing the scene through his eyes. Can you picture it?

"Hang on, give me a second, I'll try."

I closed my eyes and I tried placing myself in the situation. Dr Seer continued to give me further instructions.

Please refrain at this point from thinking about whether you are going to make it or not. Look through his eyes and feel what he feels. You are now him – and yet still yourself. Please describe for me what that feels like.

It took me a little while to get into the exercise. But since I was already fairly practised in following these kinds of instructions, I found it easier than I initially thought it would be. With my eyes closed, I began to describe.

"I'm sitting in the café and looking around. I feel relaxed. The attractive blond woman is also there, sitting not far away from me at the next table. I look into her eyes. She smiles at me, a little shyly – a really lovely smile. I smile back at her. We look at each other for a moment. I feel the impulse to get up and go to her table to start a light-hearted little conversation..."

Very good! Now please take the time to explore this feeling anew, consciously, from within. Does approaching the woman seem easy?

"Yes, it seems very easy! I don't feel any resistance in me."

What do you feel instead?

"Hm. It feels more like joy. A kind of anticipation, the expectation that I'm about to experience something exciting."

And what about courage?

"I don't think I need courage any more! It feels very easy. I have nothing to lose."

And everything to gain?

"Yes. In fact, I've already won, because she gave me such a lovely smile. I feel good."

Very nice! Please take deep breaths. Take your time to come back from your visualization, to return to this room. Come back to yourself.

Slowly, I came back. And I enjoyed that rarest of feelings: a eureka moment.

"Incredible! I've no idea why I was so afraid. Looking through Andy's eyes, everything is so simple – thoroughly enjoyable, even. I wasn't worried at all that it could go wrong. It's not like there was anything really riding on it, anyway. I wish I could be more like him."

Dr Seer smiled.

But you can!

"Ha!"

Yes, you can. You have already felt and experienced it in your visualization just now. 'See with the eyes of a role model!' gives you a feel for certain qualities – and that is enough to enable you to apply these qualities in the situation in question!

"Hm. I've never heard of anything like this before. Are you sure it works? You believe that I can recreate exactly what I just experienced in this exercise when sitting in the café and looking at the woman?"

Precisely! And you know why? Those feelings and mental images that you have just experienced were entirely your own. You yourself generated them within you – you, and no-one else. So when you find yourself in the situation in question, simply do exactly what you did just now. Imagine yourself to be that role model of yours. See the situation through his eyes, and then act!

"So, you seriously think I should approach the woman and talk to her?"

It felt inevitable that I was going to be assigned this kind of exercise again. No doubt about it.

Is there any reason why not?

"No, I don't think so."

Dr Seer smiled in his typical fashion.

Just consider the following for a moment: If you believe yourself to be missing a certain personality trait, but can feel it within you, then clearly you must have it inside you after all. You have just not tapped into it yet. Go ahead! See through the eyes of whatever role model you choose – it doesn't have to be a real person, it could equally be a character from a novel or a cartoon hero! When you apply this perspective, you awaken the dormant potential within you.

"That feels really good! And, thinking about it, if what I'm tapping into is actually my own potential, then I suppose I don't even need the role model in the end, wouldn't you say?

That is very true! Using a role model for orientation is just a tool that helps to demystify an assignment or an event and make it seem possible. This allows you to mentally assimilate the individual steps that you require in order to act with self-confidence in a particular situation. As you imagine yourself as the role model, you consciously realize these individual steps for yourself, which allows you to make them your own. By doing so, you activate within yourself the qualities and skills you need.

"Absolutely brilliant! I'll try it!"

Strangely enough, this daring experiment now seemed entirely possible to me. I had no qualms about daring to give this experiment a go. I asked myself why I hadn't already had the idea to approach the woman a long time ago. Somehow, it seems I've been standing in my own way for way too long. No wonder I so often felt lonely.

You have cooperated beautifully! Come now, you've accomplished enough for today!

"Thank you for the compliments. And thank you for the new perspective. It seems there are quite a few of them."

As usual, Dr Seer accompanied me to the door. He was clearly pleased that I had acknowledged his area of expertise.

THE GOLDEN VIEW is very multifaceted, indeed. Just like life. There's a good deal more for you to learn, dear Mr Allman.

"I'm curious, Doc. Goodbye!"

Goodbye!

7 See through the other person's eyes!

Classic perspective-taking:
the basis of human interrelations

Dr Seer kept me waiting at the door today. I'd already rung the bell twice. I'd been totally immersed in my thoughts all day. Yesterday, I'd finally plucked up the courage to actually speak to the lovely lady in the café and had said 'hello'. And I felt surprisingly good while doing so, although that was as far as things went. Who knows – perhaps if I'd have managed to summon even more self-confidence, a conversation might have developed. But, for now, I was happy to view this experience as a small success on my part. I rang the bell a third time. Finally, the door opened.

Hello, Mr Allman!

"Hello! Why... what took so long?"

What do you mean?

"I rang the bell three times – didn't you hear me?"

Yes, of course. I had even seen you. But you were still deep in thought. I didn't want to interrupt you.

As far as Dr Seer was concerned, this explanation was clearly the most natural thing in the world. Dr Seer was full of surprises.

Please, come in!

After we'd settled into our room, he looked at me inquiringly – as he often did at the beginning of our sessions.

How are you doing today?

"Good, thanks. Nothing special happened. And, before you ask: yes, I did go and speak to the woman..."

Congratulations! And what did it lead to?

"Nothing. And that's totally fine. We exchanged a friendly 'hello', and nodded at each other. She even returned my smile. You said yourself that it's not like I have to jump straight in and marry her or anything."

Yes, I did say that. But we didn't say things had to stop at 'hello', did we. Did you get interrupted? What got in the way?

"No, we didn't get interrupted. It just didn't go any further. I'm totally fine with that."

Wouldn't you have wanted more?

"No. Well, yes. Maybe. Oh, it doesn't really matter."

You don't care?

"No way, that's not what I meant."

You saw things with the eyes of a role model and took the first step towards initiating a conversation. And then?

"Yes, I did. And I'm proud of myself for doing so. That's something!"

You've every right to feel proud of yourself! You did really well!

I hoped that this signalled the end of the discussion of this particular topic. Because, as usual at this point, I felt a certain degree of discomfort.

It is clear that you don't feel comfortable talking about events related to love and partnership. And that is exactly why we have to stick with this topic and work through it.

"Hm."

Dr Seer smiled at me encouragingly.

Behind every emotional blockage there are always experiences that have hurt us at some point in our lives. In order not to re-live the hurt, we protect ourselves and avoid the topic. If, however, we pay close attention to what emotion comes up when we are confronted with the topic in question, and consider what the experience might have been that caused the hurt in the first place, then we can heal the wound.

To this day I still don't know why, but at that very moment I had absolutely no desire to be dealing so intensely with my own issues. But, once again, the Doc took no notice – he was not to be deterred. Sometimes it could all be really exhausting!

So, why didn't the encounter with the lady from the café go any further?

I felt a sense of resistance well up inside me, and grow stronger.

"You've analysed it already – after all, I haven't exactly had the best experiences where women are concerned!"

So the memory of your hurtful experiences stood in the way. You gave your memories more attention than the present situation. It's quite possible that all this happened subconsciously.

I lost it at this point. I couldn't hold back any longer.

"Doc! Is it possible to just have a normal conversation with you? D'you have a few encouraging words you could share with me? Couldn't we just, you know, have a nice chat with each other? Do you have to always ask questions, and persist in digging until you uncover something that I could be doing differently, and better? Everything is difficult enough already as it is. I think that's enough. I've learned a lot, and for that I'm grateful. And now I'd like to end the session."

To my surprise, he was still looking at me with a kindly expression on his face. Clearly, there wasn't much that could irritate him. Least of all my anger.

I understand you!

'Oh great, now he's even being all understanding about it. Sure, probably because he's zoomed out and taken the bird's eye view, or something', shot through my head. Crazy as it sounds, it would've in fact been much more satisfying for me if Dr Seer had been insulted, for instance. But my words seemed to bounce right off him. That made me even angrier! So I tried to provoke him.

"You don't really give a shit what I say, do you. The main thing as far as you're concerned is that you're always right, and can make a great show of your wisdom!"

What on earth was going on with me? I had no idea where this frustration was coming from. All I knew is that I was fed up with everyone always knowing better, and with me always stuck in the fool's role. I felt affronted, and was in no mood to continue playing the fool for some know-it-all.

It's not very nice to be made to feel small and to be driven into a corner, with the feeling one is being picked on.

"Great, I'm pleased you see it like that. But that's exactly what you just provoked."

This feeling originated in you. Our conversation triggered it in you. The way we interpret someone else's words is always our own inner choice – and it's the same with the emotions that arise as a result.

"Fantastic. Naturally you have another smart explanation for everything. And, as ever, I've only got myself to blame, right?"

It's not the blame that lies with you, but the responsibility. And taking responsibility for ourselves is in no way a negative thing – on the contrary, it is wonderful that we are able to control how we feel, is it not?

I'll let you in on a secret: The better you get to know yourself and the more conscious you become of your own issues and how you deal with them, the harder it is for unconscious emotions and deep-seated, hurtful experiences to control and determine your behaviour and experiences. You will be able to live increasingly in tune with your heart's desires. You will get closer and closer to attaining this state if you genuinely decide to continue along the path. But you don't have to decide right now whether this is something you. We'll talk more about it later.

For today, I'd like to make a suggestion. We'll put the whole 'love and flirting' topic aside for now, and instead use this situation to impart a very important lesson. Please have faith in what I say – you will get something very precious out of it. Do you have the patience to continue for just a few more minutes?

"To be perfectly honest: no, I don't!"

I went too far. My behaviour towards the Doc today had not been very polite, but I just couldn't keep a lid on things. To be fair, it was in fact part of his job to deal with people and their frustrations. But despite this, I now felt guilty.

"I'm sorry. I didn't mean to be so frosty."

Dr Seer really didn't seem to take offence at anything I said or did.

It's all right. Don't worry. I understand you very well. You have gone through a lot! But please, take a little longer to consider THE GOLDEN VIEW.

He nodded at me, in a bid to cheer me up.

The perspective that you'll learn today is: 'See through the other person's eyes!'

"Hm. Alright then, if you insist. But through whose eyes?"

Through mine!

"Through… yours? I'm supposed to see through your eyes?"

Yes, see through my eyes! You made several assumptions regarding my intentions during the course of our conversation. These assumptions in turn

73

triggered certain reactions and emotions within you. You assumed that I was out to make you feel small, and wanted to force you into a corner. I invite you to see through my eyes and put your assumptions to the test!

There was undoubtedly something about this exercise that appealed to me very much. But the feeling of being overwhelmed was definitely stronger. This was turning out to be such a tiresome session. I hadn't expected anything like it before coming here today.

"Err... but you see, the issue is... well: I don't know you. This is completely different to thinking my way into my "flirt role model" Andy's head. I've known him for years, and we've shared loads of experiences together."

That doesn't matter. For this view, there is a very simple and effective tool that will help.

"OK then, I'm curious now – let me guess, does it involve me putting on your non-existent glasses?"

This made us both laugh. But Dr Seer got straight back to focusing on what was important.

Actually, that's not a bad idea at all. But I have another suggestion – we swap places.

"You mean, I go and sit in your big chair, and you take my place?"

Yes, exactly. It might sound a bit strange, but with this perspective it is very helpful to physically assume the position of the other, too. It enables us to detach from our own position, and switch to that of the other person. Shall we? I'll explain more when you're sitting in my chair.

"It sounds kind of fun. OK, I'm ready."

And so we swapped places. As a matter of fact, everything suddenly did look different. The room seemed a little darker, because the windows were now behind me, and the space also felt a little smaller. For the first time, I noticed that there was a picture hanging on the wall behind my usual chair.

It was of a large, golden eye, with a pupil that looked like a white star. An unusual picture. As unusual as the Doc's name, really. The picture was the only personal item in the room. There wasn't even anything to write with on this side of the glass table – unusual, for a counselling environment. The Doc truly was a peculiar person. How could he possibly remember everything he was told? I'm sure he had many more clients apart from me.

Dr Seer was gazing at me peacefully.

You are looking around the room and wondering what kind of person I am, am I right?

I felt caught out. This was probably not the aim of the exercise.

"Hm. And that's not what this is meant to be about, I suppose?"

No, no. It's totally fine. Use all the information available to you! In order to see through the eyes of another person, anything one can see from the position of the other can be helpful. Please now also look at the seat in which you were sitting before.

The chair, currently occupied by Dr Seer, was made of light-green leather. It looked very new and, to my surprise, not in the least bit worn. It looked very comfortable, as I knew that it was. A chair designed to make sure its occupant feels truly at ease. It was placed in the room in such a way that one could easily look out of the window and see the green foliage outside. There was box of tissues positioned within reach – probably for those that felt the need to cry, as I had done. Under the chair there was a thick white rug. This place looked like it had been arranged with a lot of thought and care.

Do you like 'your spot'?

"Yes, very much. It looks comfy."

And what was my intention in making it that way?

"Hm. Most likely you wanted your clients to feel safe and secure. And for them to be comfortable."

Very good. I'm glad you can tell! Now, please try to put yourself in my shoes and see things through my eyes. From my perspective! Think back to the beginning of our conversation. Why do I ask all these questions that are sometimes unpleasant for you? What is my intention in doing so?

What exactly did Dr Seer hope to achieve with this? To my surprise, the answer came to me very easily. Sitting in his chair it just burst out of me.

"You... why, you want to help me, of course. You'd like me to be successful. For me to steer my life in a positive direction. You want me to fall in love, and make the most of every opportunity. You'd like me to grow, and gain insight. You want me to feel good. You'd like to share your knowledge with me."

He was listening to this flood of words gushing out of me, and beaming.

You truly are seeing things through my eyes!

"A man – me – is sitting in front of you, completely paralysed by his inertia, someone who chickens out and shuts himself off from others. And you're not giving up on him. You see what he's capable of and you believe in him. You want to help him overcome his personal obstacles. And for that you even endure his insults."

It was crazy! My anger and frustration had completely evaporated. It felt like the proverbial scales fell from my eyes and I understood: There was a completely different intention behind his intense line of enquiry. My perception had been wrong.

"Oh dear... Goodness Doc, I'm so sorry! You really have the best of intentions, and you're totally motivated – on my behalf. And here I am wallowing in self-pity, wanting to crawl into some hole in which to hide. The experiences and disappointments of my life have so much control over me that my interpretation of everything that happens is utterly coloured by them. And I don't even catch on when somebody is trying to help me!"

76

Dear Mr Allman. Thank you for your kind words of appreciation. I congratulate you on your insight! But please, don't put yourself down. It was understandable that you were angry. And it was actually very good that things happened as they did. Only when we allow our emotions to come to the surface can we look at them and, ultimately, heal them. I am happy about what happened today, and I see that you've made some new discoveries – such as how to see things through other people's eyes, for instance.

"Oh yes, that's definitely true! I'm totally speechless! I think I can use this perspective on a daily basis."

Visibly content, Dr Seer winked at me.

This perspective always provides instant understanding of another person's position. I'm happy for you!

"Thank you, thank you SO much! I'm deeply appreciative of all you've done… particularly for your incredible patience and understanding!"

My pleasure!

I was fascinated, and found that my curiosity was aroused yet again. And I felt an even stronger willingness than ever before to continue working on my problems and inadequacies with Dr Seer, and to have him accompany me on my journey.

"Please tell me something, Doc: Is there a perspective for every imaginable human situation? I mean, is it always possible to take a different perspective on things? And are certain perspectives applicable only for certain situations?"

These are important questions! There are of course innumerable ways of looking at things. THE GOLDEN VIEW can be divided into precisely 23 separate perspectives, covering the entire spectrum of human experience. In other words, it covers the complete range of life questions and human problems – from profound, emotional issues to everyday decision-making and the big spiritual questions in life. You will come to know all the new perspectives, should you so wish, Mr Allman!

"I would like to, yes!"

You can tackle nearly every single earthly problem using THE GOLDEN VIEW. The perspective you need depends on the situation, topic or individual problem, as well as the predominant emotion involved. You've experienced this vividly for yourself, haven't you.

"Yes, indeed. And I'm very impressed. Why is it that I've never heard about this method before?"

The notion of changing one's perspective has been around forever, however the multiplicity of the perspectives and the secret, so to speak, behind each one of them has never been explored in this form before. THE GOLDEN VIEW represents the first ever matrix of mental perspective taking that can be completely and comprehensively implemented and embedded into the context of human life.

Dr Seer looked at me meaningfully.

What we have here is a complex system. And once you have experienced how well it functions you can then internalize THE GOLDEN VIEW intuitively and with ease.

Spellbound, I listened to him.

And I'll tell you another secret: Each new perspective that you encounter and apply will help you become a more conscious human being. That is the path I was talking about.

"I... have visited you seven times now, not counting our first meeting. Does that mean that I can come and see you at least another 16 times? Which would make 23 of these golden perspectives?"

If you are willing to do so, then yes.

"Yes, absolutely! I'd definitely like to continue!"

Then I look forward to your next step. Trust yourself. Each situation, each experience, each emotion – your entire life, the entire picture – can change.

"Though it's also quite strange."

Yes, it often is, in the beginning. And in the end, one is always amazed.

"An amazing strange change!"

Dr Seer laughed, and I did too. He had a brilliant sense of humour, and I grew to like him more and more each time we met – even though at times I felt a little 'dazzled'.

Part II

BECOMING CONSCIOUS

8 Look from within!

Recognizing and living your true needs

As I made my way to see Dr Seer today, I realized that things felt different. For the first time, I carried an inner certainty that I was finally making strides towards finding solutions to my problems. Sure, I could never predict what the Doc was going to focus on during each session – the end result of the work we did always surprised me. But today, more than ever before, I felt certain that everything was connected, and that I had already made quite a few changes to myself and to my life. I really was starting to look at everything from a different perspective! And in many situations I *behaved* differently as a result, acting with more self-confidence and assuredness. Maybe I'd become emotionally stronger. The nagging feeling of being a victim of circumstance in my own life had receded into the background. Yes, and now I was more curious about my options.

Dr Seer joyfully shook my hand as he welcomed me.

Please come in, THE GOLDEN VIEW awaits!

Without pausing for a response, he politely yet purposefully led me in a different direction to the one we normally took.

Today we're going to a new room.

The human being is a creature of habit, so this change unsettled me, a little.

"Why?"

Because you are now a step further! You have accomplished a good deal, Mr Allman, and I'm very proud of you! Perhaps you've noticed over the last few days that, with the help of THE GOLDEN VIEW, you've already made quite a few changes in your everyday life? Or rather, that you've made changes within yourself?

"Yes, I have noticed that! As a matter of fact, I realized it just a few moments ago, on my way here."

You see! You have become more aware of yourself. Do you remember how I told you that THE GOLDEN VIEW would help you to become a more conscious person?

"Yes, you said that the last time I was here."

Dr Seer opened the door to the room where today's session was evidently going to take place. This room was quite a bit bigger than the last one. Here, too, the wall-to-wall carpet was white, and the room felt very bright and spacious. The two armchairs stood out: both were leather-covered, one cherry red and the other chestnut brown in colour. Between the two chairs stood a small, square metal table. It featured a peculiar mix of colours and materials, but in conjunction with the whiteness of the room, the overall effect was aesthetically pleasing.

Today we shall go further. Or rather, deeper.

Dr Seer nodded at me.

Which chair would you like to sit in?

Without thinking, I let myself fall into the red chair.

"What do you mean, we'll go deeper? I thought we'd already been taking an in-depth approach."

Yes, we have. And now you're going to begin an even more intense period of self-reflection. We'll look at your life more closely.

I felt a simultaneous mix of joyous anticipation and a sort of queasiness. What the Doc had planned for me sounded like hard work.

Do you remember when you cried as you stood in front of the mirror? The tears came from your innermost core. But you weren't crying because of a 'real' situation. Nor were the tears triggered by merely gazing at your own reflection. Instead, they came because...

83

"… I had made contact with my innermost core, yes. I felt that very clearly!"

And that was quite evident at the time! And now you're going to enter into a true dialogue with yourself. When you really get to grips with your innermost core and closely examine what is hidden there, you can alter and heal troublesome memories.

"You mentioned that before."

Focused, Dr Seer continued:

We shall look at everything very closely over the course of our next sessions: the deep pain that keeps resurfacing, caused by past experiences; violations that you have never been able to forget and have never properly processed; accusations you make towards yourself, consciously or unconsciously, about decisions you made at some point; desires that you have not yet realized and that have now become tormenting or suppressed thoughts; behaviour patterns that may be manifesting on an unconscious level and that are keeping you from being the man you really are and aspire to be.
What's the real cause of your loneliness? What lies deep within your core that prevents you from believing in yourself? Why is it that often even your simplest intentions don't seem to work out as planned?

He paused for a few moments, as if wanting to give his words time to percolate and reach me on a deeper level.

"Whoa, that sounds like a lot of work!"

Don't worry, we have all the time in the world! THE GOLDEN VIEW has already helped you in many everyday aspects. And it will guide you further on your path and throughout your life. It will support you, step by step, in your search for clarity. And confidence. You're well on your way already!

Dr Seer winked at me in his familiar, inviting manner.

Please take a few slow, deep breaths – as you've learned to do – and then we shall begin. I expect you're somewhat curious about what comes next, am I right?

Given how sure I'd been about wanting to carry on last time, I couldn't chicken out now just because I didn't feel entirely comfortable. After taking a deep breath, which did indeed make me feel lighter, I answered:

"Yes, true. OK, it can only get better."

Wonderful! First, please answer the following question: How do you relax?

"You mean, after work?"

Yes, for instance.

"Hm. I guess I do what people normally do. Most of the time I go out for a drink with my colleagues. Sometimes even for two or three."

I see. And how well does that relax you?

"I don't know… quite well, I guess. It's a way to unwind. Admittedly, most of the time the conversation is still about work, but at least the mood is more relaxed."

I had no idea where the Doc was going with this.

Do you feel good doing it?

"Doing what?"

Well, when you let your hair down with your colleagues after work by going for a drink, or two, or three.

"No idea; that's just what you do."

And how do you feel when you get home afterwards?

85

"How do I feel then? Well, the day is over. I'm tired. I'm always glad to be able to go to bed. Sometimes I watch television for an hour to tune out."

To tune out, I understand. And do you feel completely relaxed? Do you feel good, physically, when you do that?

His questions irritated me.

"I think so. I'm tired by then, at any rate. How do you define relaxation?"

Dr Seer moved forward to sit on the edge of his chair, so he was closer to me. As if quoting from 'The Book of Truth', he offered the following emphatic explanation:

When a person is completely relaxed, then body, mind and spirit are in harmony. They feel inner peace and calm. Their energy reserves recharge.

I had to clear my throat.

"Um… well, in that case, I have to admit that the description doesn't quite match what I experience during these relaxation phases."

How does it feel to you, then?

"Hard to say."

He looked at me, and waited.

I'm here to help you! THE GOLDEN VIEW will help: Look from within!

"Err… and how do I do that?"

You visualize the situation – in our case, the moment when you get home after your working day or after your evening get-together with your colleagues. And you examine how this situation appears INSIDE you. Use the following tool to help you: Imagine you are a miniature version of yourself, equipped with a flashlight, and that you enter inside your head to have a look at the thoughts you're having. Then send this 'mini-me' wandering down into the heart region, which, in the holistic sense, is the central seat of your emotions. And then send him deeper into the belly area, where even more emotions reside. The miniature you shines a light on all these areas, before finally travelling through your body to see what kind of physical sensations are present.

"Sounds kind of strange."

Indeed, it is. And at the same time it's very revealing. Would you like to try this perspective?

"But how is that going to work – a miniature version of myself, traveling through me?"

I'll show you.

"OK, why not. Alright, I'm ready."

As always, Dr Seer was happy when I showed willingness to learn.

Wonderful. Please make yourself comfortable, breathe deeply, and close your eyes.

I let myself sink into the chair, and Dr Seer began to issue instructions:

Please visualize yourself in the situation we're interested in: you're just arriving home after a long day. To relax, you went out with your colleagues for a drink after work. Can you imagine yourself in that moment?

"Yes, it was like that only last night. OK, I'm there."

Good. Now imagine that you, as a tiny version of yourself, are going inside your own head – the head of Mr Allman – as a miniature man with a flash-light in his hand. You shine the light from inside and look at the thoughts that are present there. You can see each thought, symbolically speaking.

I had to grin. It was a funny notion, stepping inside myself as a miniaturised person.

So, what thoughts do you see when you look from within like this?

87

"Hm. There are lots of thoughts here. It's all pretty chaotic. It's all about how stressful the day was. How my colleague Carl is always repeating the same old story about his never-ending quarrel with his other colleagues, something that's been going on for months. Then there's thoughts about the next day, too. Telling me how exhausting it's undoubtedly going to be. But, thankfully, I know how helpful it is to look at things from above – I've gotten used to adopting this perspective now. It helps me quite often in my daily routine."

I am glad to hear it! Would you say that, as things currently stand, the situation looks relaxed inside your head?

"No, I wouldn't, actually. There are way too many thoughts."

I understand. Now proceed, as a miniature version of yourself, down into the area of your heart, which is the symbolic centre of your feelings. And please, don't forget to breathe deeply as you do so. What are the feelings you find there?

"OK. Right, the feelings. Uh, yes. That might take me a little while."

Just take your time. Shine a light into every corner of your heart, from the inside.

"Alright, I will. Just give me a moment. OK, here goes. There's this feeling of being restricted by everyday life. But, equally, I'm also glad that I'm home at last. What's more, I'm looking forward to my bed. Obviously I feel more at ease than during the day, probably thanks to the alcohol."

From your viewpoint, is this a state that could be called emotionally relaxed?

"Good question. Hm. No, I don't think so. It's too dulled or too muted for that, I'd say. I imagine that true relaxation feels much more pleasant. More like happiness, maybe. Strange, I've never seen it like that before…"

Dr Seer chuckled out loud.

You have also never looked at things from within quite like this before! Now please let your 'mini-me' travel through your body. Examine your body from within. As before, please remain in the same situation – the moment when you get home after having been for a drink after work. How does your body feel then?

"OK, so I'm wandering through my body with a flashlight. Uh oh, perhaps I'd better not look too closely at the liver right now. Just kidding, I don't think it's all that bad... Hm. My body is tired. My back is tense from always sitting. I can still feel the remnants of the mild stomach ache I had on and off all day, as is so often the case. There's a slight buzzing in my head from the alcohol. I feel exhausted and sleepy."

Seen from within like this, does your body feel relaxed in this situation?

"No. It feels tense and tired."

Good. Please remain within yourself for another minute or so, and then slowly come back to us here, in this room. When you are ready, open your eyes.

I took another moment to fully inhabit the feeling, and then opened my eyes.

"Wow, what a brilliant method!"

Dr Seer looked at me intensely.

Have you discovered anything?
"You bet!"

Please describe it for me!

"I've realized that my definition of relaxation has been completely wrong all this time! I've just realized that going for a drink with my colleagues after work – this being what I do for relaxation – doesn't actually relax me all that much."

Aha. An important realization!

"Yes."

Dr Seer gave me a little more time to ponder this discovery before continuing:

Now we can approach the matter from the opposite direction and ask: What do you really need in order to relax? Let's obtain the answer to this question by adopting the view from within again. Please try to enter into a state of true relaxation. Allow your fantasy to help you to imagine your very own personalized, ideal and truly relaxed scenario.

Observe closely what happens within you!

Intuitively, I first took a deep breath in and out, closed my eyes again and transported myself to a state of ideal relaxation. To my surprise, it wasn't difficult at all. Immediately, the image of lying on a beach on one of the South Sea Islands appeared in my mind. I felt the sun on my face and heard waves lapping gently in the background...

Are you now in your own personal visualization of a truly relaxed situation?

"Yes."

What's it like inside your head when you are relaxed?

"It's quiet inside my head. There are no thoughts whatsoever, and I don't want to speak... I'm day dreaming..."

And what does it feel like in your heart when you are relaxed?

It was hard for me to answer because I was so deeply immersed in this wonderfully calm state.

"Hm... I feel absolute tranquillity; I feel detached, at ease, free... and also safe..."

Very good! And how does your body feel when you are relaxed? Look from within!

"I'm breathing deeply – yes, it's safe to say my body is suffused with oxygen. My heart is beating calmly and regularly. My body is enjoying the rest. My energy reserves are filling up and my body is recharging."

You are doing very well! Stay on your South Sea Island for another minute or so. And then come back, slowly.

I opened my eyes and tried to orientate myself.

"Oh, did I refer to a South Sea Island?"

No, but it was quite plain to see!

Dr Seer waited a moment, and smiled at me.

Let's examine the results of adopting this special 'view from within', Mr Allman. As looking at things from within has shown you, the things you usually do to relax do not in fact induce a true state of relaxation at all. What might be an alternative? What could you do instead that would relax you in a similar way to what you just experienced on your South Sea Island?

"Well, what I find totally surprising is that it seems I actually have to be alone in order to relax. And that I like to do so outdoors, in nature... it doesn't necessarily have to be a South Sea Island."

Yes. What might that look like? What could you do to accommodate these aspects? You also mentioned that your body was full of oxygen, and was recharging.

"Hm. I always used to love going for walks, especially in the evenings. At some point I stopped doing it because I was afraid it would drag my mood down if I wandered around aimlessly on my own like that. But, actually, I'd love to go for regular walks again. I'm guessing you would approve of that, right?"

Dr Seer grinned at me.

My part in this is not to evaluate what you do. For me, everything centres on showing you that often people do things that are not actually beneficial at all. These habits are not a good fit for you, and they are the wrong choice for achieving what you are trying to achieve by practising them. People often stick with behaviour patterns, personal habits and rituals because they think that by doing so they are taking care of important needs. But because they have not defined or even recognized their true needs, they become dissatisfied and lose energy.

To get to the heart of the matter, you can look from within to recognize what you really need on the one hand, and discover the ideal modes of behaviour to satisfy your need on the other. Relaxation is a relatively harmless example. You can use this perspective to deal with many more complex issues in life. Taking the 'view from within' helps you discover if what you are doing to achieve a certain goal actually fulfils what is truly needed within. In addition, this view helps you to find an alternative that is better suited to you and comes closer to meeting your real needs.

"Yes."

Another indication that a certain activity doesn't truly harmonize with one's inner core is when it's somehow hard to get done, or motivation is completely lacking – without there being a plausible explanation for why this is so. In such situations, one should definitely take a look from within, to discover and select new alternatives.

"That actually makes logical sense."

Do you realize that today you have made a very important discovery?

"That going for walks by myself would relax me much more than going to a bar with my colleagues?"

Yes, that's one. And the other is that you just redefined being alone. For you, being alone is actually relaxing. What does this mean for you? Remember what you felt when you stood in front of your own reflection.

"Hm. I felt lonely... I believed that I always feel lonely when I'm alone. That's the reason I go out after work with the others as often as possible. OK, so it's with my colleagues... But relaxing alone just now didn't feel lonely at all. On the contrary! It was more like you described it: a feeling of being in harmony with myself!"

That is a very good insight, Mr Allman! To be 'alone' does not necessarily mean being 'lonely'.

"Yes, I've never looked at it that way before. It's good to know!"

Dr Seer smiled and nodded at me.

Just so you don't misunderstand me: In no way do I want to dissuade you from going out with your colleagues for a drink or two or three, as you put it. Companionship is very important for every human being! I would merely like to bring you more closely in touch with yourself so you can better recognize what it is you really need. And so that you become aware that you have the freedom to decide what to do.

"I understand. I never had a particularly clear idea of what relaxation actually means for me. And now, if I really want to relax, then I'll go for a walk. And on the way I can perhaps see if 'looking from within' helps me address any other issues. Things I do that don't make me feel particularly good."

Do so! Keep your eyes open to what is going on within you!

"I find myself doing that more and more anyway since meeting *you!*"

I know. And that is the whole point.

"How do you know all this, Doc?"

What do you think?

"I don't know. It's clearly something you're passionate about. And I'm sure you've taught **THE GOLDEN VIEW** to hundreds of people, right?"

He gave me a meaningful look, but didn't say anything.

"I suppose this method would actually help everyone, right? Take the whole 'looking from within' thing, for starters! If people knew of this method, then a fair few would probably recognize that they've been doing things that don't benefit them at all – don't you think?"

That is true, without doubt! THE GOLDEN VIEW can help everybody, because it grants us new awareness. Just like what is happening to you right now. Now I suggest you head home. You've learned quite a lot today, and it will take some time to sink in. This process is called 'integration'. It means that you'll internalize the newly acquired perspectives, fresh insights and feelings, and incorporate them more and more into your daily life. This will, of course, require some time.

"Yes."

Wouldn't you like to take a little detour by heading towards the lake nearby and going for a little walk?

"Oh yes, I'll do that!"

Satisfied, Dr Seer offered me his hand.

Yes. It will do you good. Goodbye, Mr Allman!

"Thank you, Doc. Goodbye!"

9 Look at the decisive moment!

Making the right decision –
intuition will ultimately provide the answer

Tonight I went back to the lake to get my head straight. For days now I had been preoccupied by a particular issue that I hadn't yet discussed with the Doc. After finally agreeing to the salary increase I had been hoping for, my boss had now even gone so far as to offer me a new position. And I felt completely overwhelmed. I couldn't decide whether to accept this offer or remain in my old job. And this inability to make a decision left me feeling uneasy. At the same time, I kept recalling Dr Seer's encouraging words – that I was no longer at the very start of my journey of self-discovery. What's more, I knew that I was already putting a number of the golden perspectives into practise successfully. With all these helpful tools at my disposal, you'd think I'd be able to make the right decision!

Sitting on a bench in the evening sun, I stared at the surface of the water and tried to 'look from within'. What did my head say, and my heart, and my body? Unfortunately, there was just way too much swirling around inside me, and all of it was so chaotic that it seemed to be getting even more muddled. I was also lacking the necessary peace of mind to properly go into myself at this point in time. I found no clarity at all. The problem was that my boss wanted an answer by tomorrow morning. So, slowly but surely, I felt a sense of despair begin to spread through me, in part also because my next appointment with Dr Seer wasn't for another four days.

I tried to imagine what the Doc's advice would be. He'd probably tell me to start by taking a few deep breaths. OK, fine: I slowed my breathing and did my best to calm the thoughts going round and round in my head. And sure enough, I started to feel a little more relaxed. At that point I realized that I was using the 'see through the other person's eyes' technique – seeing through the eyes of Dr Seer, in fact. So I looked at myself from his perspective and gave myself advice as though I were he. In so doing, I suddenly saw how important it was to him that he was there for me whenever I was in desperate need. And that's when I felt the urge to spontaneously go and visit him. Without thinking, I got up from the bench and set off. When I got there, he opened the door in the blink of an eye.

Ah, there you are! Good evening, at this late hour!

"Please forgive me, Doc, but I… well, it's kind of an emergency!"

It's fine, it's fine! I can see that it's urgent. Please, come inside! You know the way – please go on ahead! I'll just fetch you a glass of water.

Despite feeling guilty about turning up uninvited, I was very happy that he evidently had some time for me. While I walked briskly down the corridor, past all the mirrors, I realized that the one with the white wooden frame – in front of which the Doc had taught me to 'look in the mirror' – was no longer hanging on the wall. I hadn't noticed it was missing before.

Dr Seer handed me the glass of water.

Incidentally: We see that which we are willing to see.

I took a big sip of water.

"Doc, I have an urgent problem! Please forgive me for showing up here totally unannounced. But I had a feeling it would be OK."

Your feeling was absolutely correct. Tell me, what's troubling you?

"I have to make the right decision, and I don't know what to do. My boss has offered me a new position – a promotion, so to speak – and he wants to have my answer by tomorrow."

And you don't know if you should accept the offer.

"Exactly! It's a superb opportunity, of that there can be no doubt!"

So what are the reasons against accepting it?

"Hm. It would definitely be very stressful. I don't want you to think I'm shying away from the challenge. It's more that I'm quite content with my old position – especially now that I've just received a pay rise, as you know."

I'm aware, yes. And I can see that you are very confused.

"You can say that again!"

What is it exactly that's confusing you so much?

"It's the fact that there are advantages and disadvantages to both – that's why I can't decide."

Dr Seer breathed slowly in and out, taking deep breaths as though doing so on my behalf because I was so nervous. Funnily enough, it did actually help a bit.

Good. Please try to relax. Let's take a look at it together. So, we have two alternatives, A and B. A is your old job, B your new one. Please begin by describing for me the advantages of option A.

"OK... the advantages are that I've known my colleagues for a long time already, and even know some of them quite well. Well enough that we sometimes go for a meal or a drink together after work. Then there's the fact that I'm confident in my role and know what I'm doing. The salary's also fine, particularly since I now get paid more."

I understand. And what are the advantages of option B?

"Well, the new job would definitely pay much better! And what's more, they would provide me with a company car – something I've never had before. The new job would certainly be interesting, and I would have to travel a lot, which would get me out and about more. That being said, it's also bound to be more stressful."

Good. Now please tell me what disadvantages you see where option B, the new job, is concerned.

"Well now, let me think... I don't know the people in the team, and rumour has it that they're rather difficult to get on with. I'd obviously also be under a great deal of pressure to perform, since I'd first have to familiarize myself with my new field of work. Yes, that would definitely be very stressful."

And what are the disadvantages of option A, if you were to stay in your old job?

Again, I had to think.

"Well, I'd certainly feel that I'd missed out on a good opportunity. And, of course, I'd be staying in a familiar area, which could become boring at some point."

Dr Seer waited for a moment, as he always did when something was important.

Let's now take a look at the bigger picture. The defining characteristics of the decision you're facing are that it is urgent, has a direct impact on your life, and has a certain complexity.

"What do you mean by 'complexity'?"

You find yourself in a dilemma.

"Meaning what, exactly?"

It means that in your line of argument the advantages of A are directly connected with the disadvantages of B, and vice versa.

"What do you mean by that?"

In option A, you know your colleagues; in B you don't know anyone. Pursuing option A gets you less money, option B more. You are already familiar with the work you'd have to do for option A, in option B you'd have to get used to a new set of responsibilities.

"Yes, that's right."

This is the why listing the pros and cons wasn't helping.

"Oh really?"

And I'll let you in on another secret: no 'right' decision is ever made on the basis of a list of pros and cons! Itemizing the advantages and disadvantages is purely a way of dealing with the problem intellectually. But the decision itself is ultimately made on a different level.

"You mean something like intuition?"

I still didn't know where the Doc was going with this. He was looking at me, expectantly, which made me feel a little impatient, somehow.

"You won't believe how often I've tried to tune in to my intuition in order to work out what to do. I'd concentrate really hard, and even make sure I was taking deep, slow breaths. People are always saying: 'Just listen to your feelings!' But how am I supposed to do that? My feelings don't seem to want to communicate themselves particularly clearly to me. At least not in this case. I've also tried looking from within. But that didn't get me any closer to a decision, either..."

I almost got the impression that Dr Seer was withholding the solution from me for some reason, although I fully expected him to have the 'decisive' perspective up his sleeve. But I noticed my mood had worsened considerably because I was disappointed in myself for not being able to choose. I could feel the pressure building up inside as well, given the urgency of the situation.

It only took a split second for the Doc to notice my discontent.

Dear Mr Allman, please bear in mind the following: Whenever a decision takes more time than one would like, there is always a rhyme and reason. Don't blame yourself! Whenever the right decision remains hidden, the situation represents a learning opportunity for you. I know this probably sounds a little strange, but if the decision is taking a long time then there is always a deeper reason for it. It's even possible that there's some significant insight to be gained.

"Yes, that's all well and good, but the thing is I really don't have the time to go around gaining big insights right now! My boss wants my definitive answer by tomorrow!"

I know. And that's why we're doing this right now. You will leave here with a decision that is right for you, I promise you that. If necessary, I'll free up the entire night so I can help you. However, there is one condition – one that will apply to all future decisions that you will have to make in life.

"And that would be... what?"

Don't put yourself under pressure! Practise calmness! Naturally, that doesn't mean things can't also happen quickly. But the pressure has to go so you can make your decision with clarity.

"Easier said than done."

He fixed his earnest gaze on me.

Mr Allman, I shall now proceed to tell you a secret that applies universally, given how eager you are to know more: If there are aspects of your life that you don't seem able to manage, or if you keep trying to achieve something but it refuses to work out, or if you need to make a decision and you just can't do it, then realize that none of these things happen because you are too stupid, slow, inconsequential, incapable or anything like that.

"But why, then?"

Because it corresponds to your current inner situation! The blockage you experience indicates that there is something in you that wants to be examined. It's highly likely that there's something underlying the matter that requires attention – a bigger problem, or issue, that can be resolved upon closer examination. Do you understand what I'm trying to say?

I felt calmer, and like a burden had somehow been lifted off my shoulders – although I couldn't define precisely what that burden was.

"I think I understand."

When we cease blaming ourselves, or even punishing ourselves when things in our lives don't quite happen the way we want them to, then a tremendous power is released within us. We can use this power to first of all accept the situation for what it is.
Then we can look deeper and identify what the situation is trying to tell us. Behind every blockage lies huge potential! Once we recognize the real issue underlying the obstruction, we grow beyond it. And this gives rise to totally new possibilities within us that allow us to solve the supposed problem!

His words moved me. Once again he exuded a sense of limitless benevolence that touched me very deeply. I have never experienced this in another human being before. Dr Seer clearly always saw the positive in a person, without restriction.

He gave me a very kind smile.

Some things simply take time – often inexplicably so. Time is needed, even when one expects things to happen much faster. But, perhaps as a direct result, it ultimately produces a better outcome! If you trust in the fact that time is working for you, then you can take a lot of pressure off yourself.

"It feels really good to hear you say that, Doc. Thank you!"

I see that you're growing calmer. That makes me very happy. And, by the way, it won't take us all night for you to reach your decision.

I had to laugh. I liked his sense of humour.

THE GOLDEN VIEW will guide you to the right decision.

"Yes."

Do you have any idea why you haven't had a clear feeling for the answer yet?

"No."

Then please pay close attention to what I am about to explain. Feelings, or intuition, speak only in the NOW. So far, you've always tried to make the decision by imagining both possibilities along the lines of 'what would happen if'. You've been weighing up one alternative after the other, taking it in turns to consider option A and then option B, and so on. However, both choices, one of which you need to opt for, are intermingled within you, as I explained earlier. The positive aspects of A reflect the negative aspects of B and vice versa. In your thoughts, imagination and feelings, both options are connected with each other. And so far that has kept you oscillating between the two, unable to move forward. And that's why you were unable to find the right answer, because you could neither think nor feel your way to the solution.

I hardly dared speak. I'd never heard anything like it before. How could a person possibly see things so clearly? As usual, Dr Seer waited to make sure I had absorbed all he had said.

The 'right' decision is made on the basis of intuition. And the secret of how to free your mind and create a clear path through which to access your intuition is as follows: Imagine yourself in the very moment, the NOW, of just having made the decision. Explore this 'decisive' moment from every angle.

"That doesn't sound all that straightforward!"

But it is! We are not trying to project ourselves into possible future situations – it's not about trying to imagine what it would be like if you were already in the new job, or had kept your old one. We are entering the moment immediately after you have said YES to one alternative, a mere three minutes after you reached the decision – and it is from that viewpoint that we look more closely at what is happening within you. We repeat this process for each individual option. We transport that moment of decision into the NOW, and allow your intuition to speak.

"Brilliant! I've never heard of making decisions like that."

Of course not. You are still learning to use THE GOLDEN VIEW. I'm now going to take you to a place in which your intuition will speak clearly. Are you ready?

"OK, just a second."

Previous experience told me that I needed to concentrate and relax myself as best I could. I got comfortable in the chair, and automatically closed my eyes.

Dr Seer noticed, and was pleased.

I'm proud of you, Mr Allman – your cooperation is excellent! I know it's not always easy for you. But you are making significant progress!

Dr Seer then proceeded to take me through 'Look at the decisive moment!', which he explained was the golden perspective I should use when making decisions.

Please imagine that three minutes ago you made your final decision and chose option A. You have just called your boss and told him that you would like to remain in your old job. Please focus completely on this scenario. Imagine yourself in some familiar location, perhaps sat on your sofa, at home. Tune in to this picture, and feel!

"OK, just a moment, I'm imagining it…"

Take your time.

A pleasant sensation spread through me. And to my own surprise, a feeling of great relief.

How does it feel?

"To be honest, it feels pretty good, Doc! Liberating, somehow!"

Good. Please stay with this feeling for a moment, and commit it to your internal memory. It's all about feeling it, not thinking about it or analysing it. Breathe deeply. And then return to a neutral state within yourself. Can you manage that?

"Yes, I think so."

After a while he gave me further instructions.

Now imagine that you just decided, three minutes ago, to go for option B. You have just called your boss and told him that you would like to take the new position. Place yourself once again in some familiar location, tune in to this situation, and feel.

For some reason, I found this much more difficult.

Are you there yet?

"Hang on, I'm trying to regain my concentration."

Again, the Doc gave me time.

How do you feel now, having just decided to take the new job?

"I… I don't know. It feels a bit oppressive, somehow. How strange…"

Don't begin to evaluate it yet. Simply observe what you are feeling after saying 'yes' to the new job.

It didn't take me long.

"No, it doesn't feel good at all! It puts me under pressure! It's completely clear to me. No, it's not what I want."

I understand. Please stick with it for another minute or so. And then open your eyes!

"Goodness me! Why on earth did I agonize over this for so long?"

Mischievously, he looked at me.

Well, because you weren't aware of this perspective until now, and so didn't have the right tools to help you make the decision! Because your intuition was unable to speak clearly! I imagine that comparing your two emotional reactions is not particularly challenging anymore, wouldn't you agree?

"You're right. My feeling in regard to option A, remaining in my old job, was totally good, and felt right. The decision to take the new job didn't feel good at all. My intuition is clearly telling me that I would like to stay in my old position. Hm, that's not what I would have expected!"

Dr Seer listened to me attentively, as always.

"What I mean by that is, it doesn't make logical sense! The new job would definitely bring me greater prestige within the company, more responsibility, much more money, a company car, and so on and so forth."

Intuition doesn't follow the laws of logic, my friend. Nor is it possible to influence it with strategies that make sense to the mind.

"I've never seen it so clearly before."

Consider the following connection:
Your mind knows what you want. Your soul knows what you need in order to feel good. The soul only speaks in the now. And intuition is the messenger of your soul, or, put another way, of your heart, of your deepest, innermost desire.
Therefore, whenever you are faced with a decision-making situation in which it is not clear what the right move is, then simply look at the decisive moment! Visualize the now as it would be immediately after the decision has been made. And then see how each decision feels. Your intuition will soon tell you which step is right.

"Fantastic! I find this perspective incredibly helpful! Now tell me something, Doc: What would happen if, instead of imagining the moment immediately after the decision has been made, one were to picture the situation, say, three months down the line?"

You can do it like that, yes. However, you run the risk of distorting your pure intuition. For one thing, it's possible that you can't really imagine the situation – in this case the new job – because it's an experience you haven't had yet. Also, your intellect is not completely shut off during the process of imagining, so your intuition may become obscured by thoughts.

"I see. That makes sense, yes."

Take a mental journey into the moment immediately after you have made the decision, because that is the most effective method of accessing your feelings for instant clarity about what would be best for you. Do this for any future decision dilemmas you have. The current one, of course, you have just resolved.

Dr Seer smiled in his unique way.

"Yes, exactly. I feel so happy now, knowing that I'm staying in my old job. I'll let my boss know tomorrow. It feels absolutely right! And to tell you the truth, I don't care in the slightest what my colleagues will say about it. I'm just so relieved!"

As he often did, Dr Seer allowed his gaze to rest on me. Today I perceived this as very pleasant. It felt as though it was recharging my batteries.

My dear Mr Allman, do you think there might have been a deeper significance to your inability to make a quick decision? What would have been different if you had decided faster?

"Good question. I would have made the decision whilst feeling pressured, and suffering a lack of clarity. Under those circumstances I'd most likely have made the wrong choice! I would have taken the new job, because I would have allowed myself to be guided by the thought that one shouldn't let an opportunity like that slip by. And ultimately it would have made me unhappy, because prestige and status symbols are not at all important to me."

Spot on! And let me tell you something else: It was also about you discovering how to access your intuition!

"Ah, yes! I see."

Once someone recognizes what they truly need, as opposed to what they think they need to do, then they are able to follow their own true path. They no longer find themselves following a random path. You will instead follow your own unique path. You recognize what it is you are longing for the most. And what you truly, deeply desire.

"Yes."

But we shall examine that more closely on another occasion. Take a look at the clock.

Dr Seer nodded at me. It was midnight.

"Heavens! I sincerely hope I've not taken up too much of your time!"

Look at it this way: Time is relative. And when viewed from afar, it was just a moment. You made the right decision to come here unannounced. That, too, happened because you followed your intuition. Maybe you were just not conscious of it. So that means you made two good decisions today. Congratulations!

He gave me his hand, laughing.

I wish you good luck for tomorrow! Goodbye!

"My heartfelt thanks, Doc. Thank you. Goodbye."

10 Stare into space!

When you are stuck...

I was feeling downright exhilarated today! The very next morning after my session with Dr Seer, I spoke to my boss and informed him of my decision to decline his offer and remain in my old job instead. And his reaction was completely positive. It's amazing, the feedback and reactions you get from people when you are in true harmony with what you say and do. The effect is almost unimaginable – it has to be experienced to be believed.

Today was Friday, and I had been able to get out of work a little earlier than usual. I still had a good two hours until my session with Dr Seer, so I went and sat in my favourite café again. The nice blonde woman who so often attracted my attention, and to whom I had at least managed to say 'hello' in the past, was nowhere to be seen, unfortunately.

Instead, I bumped into my old friend Andy, who I had not seen for several weeks. He often frequented the café to gain inspiration for his novels by observing people – at least, that's what he always claimed. Andy was delighted to see me. However, something about his appearance immediately gave me the impression that he wasn't doing so well. Even though he instantly engaged me in lively conversation, in his usual eloquent and amusing way, I sensed that, today, his behaviour was more of an act. Under the surface, his mood seemed very different. This struck me as an unusual observation to make, so I wondered whether there really was something the matter with him today, or if it was just that my perception had changed. Perhaps my work with Dr Seer had already sharpened my powers of perception – or perhaps refined my sensitivity to these things?

After chatting to him for a while, I couldn't help but ask Andy if everything was alright. To my surprise, his response was one of relief, and he immediately began pouring his heart out. He told me that for days now he had been struggling with writer's block. He was currently working on a story about relationships, a kind of romance novel. I knew of the project; he'd been working on it intensively for several months now. After all, Andy is and always has been an absolute pro when it comes to love and romance! But today he was clearly feeling far from great.

There was an air of desperation about him as he described his problem to me. At the moment, whenever he sat down to write, his flow of ideas would simply stop after a few lines. This made him feel that he was running out of inspiration; he found the formulation of his sentences awkward, and didn't really like what he'd written. Most of the time he'd just delete the sentences immediately after writing them. The worst part was that he felt himself becoming intellectually tense and restricted. And, as every author and artist knows, this usually kills the creative process. He kept losing sensitivity and a sense of connection to his story, and at the same time felt like he had run out of energy for his project. Writing a love story under these circumstances was absolutely impossible! It was obvious that Andy had no idea what to do. He even spoke of dropping his current book project.

I listened to what he had to say. Occasionally I would respond with statements such as 'I understand' or 'I can see that', upon which I smiled to myself, because I realized I'd obviously picked that up from the Doc. I thought long and hard about what I could suggest to my friend. I went through all the perspectives I had learned so far in my mind, hoping to find a solution. But none of the perspectives in my repertoire seemed suited to this particular problem. So I secretly decided to dedicate today's session with Dr Seer to my friend Andy.

Since I hadn't told anyone, not even Andy, about Dr Seer or THE GOLDEN VIEW, and I intended it all to remain a secret, I simply told Andy that I wanted to take some time to think through his predicament. I said I'd call him when I had some ideas. Dr Seer suddenly popped into my mind – it occurred to me that he would have insisted that Andy should not put himself under such pressure. So when we parted ways, I advised Andy to relax, and take the pressure off. The fact that I cared enough to say this clearly moved him, and lifted his spirits. I left him in the café and made my way to Dr Seer's house.

Hello there. I'm curious to see what you have brought for me today!

He opened the door for me with an inviting smile. I felt overcome by a sudden wave of guilt. Was he expecting a gift from me? For all his wonderful help, perhaps?

"What do you mean? What I've brought for you?"

Well, I can see you come with a specific question in hand. But please, come in.

After we had settled into the room with the red and brown chairs as usual, he initiated the dialogue.

Now, what would you like to ask about today?

"You're right, I do indeed have a question. But first let me say hello – I didn't greet you on my way in, did I. As for my question… well, this time it's not for me, but for a good friend of mine instead. Andy – you remember? I told you about him."

Ah, yes. The author who knows so much about love.

Dr Seer smiled.

Is he suffering from heartache?

"No, I don't think so. But he's not doing so well, Doc. He's writing a novel at the moment; a love story, in fact. He was just telling me how he's been struggling recently with a weird sort of writer's block. He's trying to make headway with his novel, and says that often he can't get any further. He's no longer able to come up with any original ideas, and is now thinking of giving up on writing the book altogether."

I understand. And you would like to help him with this problem.

"Yes, but I can't take on the role of co-author! I'm a total catastrophe when it comes to creative writing. If you knew how difficult it was for me back in school, when we were forced to write essays with titles like 'My most memorable holiday experience'… awful! I'm simply no good with the written word. I admire Andy for earning his living with it."

Now, the act of writing can be valuable for a multitude of reasons. Not only for authors. It can help you to voice your innermost concerns, or clear your mind and clarify your thoughts. Writing can help you focus. And it can help you to fortify your own desires so you can manifest them in reality. Did you know that?

"Um…. no, I wouldn't have seen it that way. For me personally, writing is mostly about composing to-do lists and filling in official documents. It has more of a functional purpose, for me."

Yes. You'll broaden your horizon in that respect too, my friend. You'll see. But let's get back to your current concern. Did you know that your friend Andy is actually very fortunate?

"Why?"

Because he has you as his friend. And because you really want to help him. What do you think his problem is?

"Well, the writer's block, of course. He never used to have it before. On the contrary, he was always overflowing with ideas."

And what is his love life like at the moment?

"What a question!! I don't actually know for sure. But it's bound to be good, I'm certain of it! Andy always has… well, let's say that he's quite the Casanova. That's why he can write so well about these things."

So you don't feel that there may be an emotional problem underlying his writer's block?

"Doc, you're the expert here, not me!"

And you're well on your way…

"Well, I certainly noticed straight away that he wasn't doing so well. I asked him about it, too. He says it's because he feels stuck."

Please examine the following correlation: Very often, we find hidden psychological issues behind intellectual blockages. Perhaps he is unable to concentrate because he doesn't truly believe in his novel, and so does not really believe it can be a success. Maybe there is also an emotional problem

111

at the root of it all; perhaps he is very lonely, in spite of – or maybe precisely because of – his image and 'Casanova lifestyle'.

"Hm. You think so? I've never thought about it like that."

And there's no need to do so today, either. Take these thoughts as inspirations! We are free to choose which way to look at the issue! I suggest that we take the simple approach today. You would like a strategy for resolving creative blockages. And so that is what we'll look at now. I'd like to make a suggestion: Let's take this issue and expand it to include blockages that can arise within any kind of results-oriented activity.

"Oh. OK, great!"

It's not just artists and poets who encounter these kinds of obstacles, you know. They apply for every human being, and can be felt during any kind of activity. Suddenly there is the feeling of being stuck and unable to move forward. It doesn't matter if the task in question is building a shelf, repairing a car or writing a letter. One ruminates about a concept, something that urgently needs to be carried out, and finds oneself unable to move forward. Some key part is missing; the inspired idea, the perfect formula.

The Doc was looking at me, and smiling. He was obviously enjoying today's topic.

What kind of situations do you know of, Mr Allman? Have you experienced this 'getting stuck'?

"Yes, I have. It's a problem I often encounter when I have to write an official letter. As I said, I'm not very good in written communication. I write something, and then immediately delete it. I start thinking about it… and then somehow begin to feel increasingly unproductive. I stick with it out of a sense of duty, very often under time pressure. At some point the whole situation starts to frustrate me, and I feel uncreative and muddled. I can imagine how Andy must feel. Although I can't presume to know how bad it must be for an author.

112

You have described it very well! Incidentally, you will be surprised to discover how well you can write. When you are emotionally touched by what you want to express, or when you want to convey a message, then you can definitely write, you'll see! I only mention this in passing.

I had no idea what he meant. But meanwhile I had grown used to such moments with him, so I was not irritated. I knew that, at some point in time, an explanation would follow. I couldn't have known at that moment that this remark related to a much later point in my life.

Let's get to the heart of the matter. The typical problem with these blockages is that the more one mulls over the issue at hand, the less one achieves. The more one tries to produce something good, imaginative or successful, the less effective one is. Actively trying to force it generates ideas that are less and less suitable.

"That's terrible! We fixate on the need to come up with the right idea, and because of that, no ideas come to us at all. That's crazy!"

Dr Seer's eyes twinkled.

That's exactly the point, Mr Allman: People get stuck in to something, and can't let go! Fixation occurs. Things stop flowing. Let us look to THE GOLDEN VIEW to see what can be done.

"I can't wait to find out."

Stare into space!

"I beg your pardon?"

Would you like me to repeat myself?

"No no, I heard what you said. But... were you being serious?"

What do you think?

"Hm. You probably were, yes."

Indeed. Completely serious, even if the name of this perspective might raise a smile. You see, the secret is letting go of any expectations about the outcome. There are different ways to approach creative work. Sometimes the entire work exists as a finished idea in the mind, and needs only to be executed step by step. Sometimes progress is made by trial and error – until, at some point, it works. One idea gives birth to the next. But there is also an aspect of creativity that takes place when it seems like one is doing nothing at all.

"Yes, I know exactly what you mean. That moment when a good idea suddenly pops up from nowhere! And it's true – that often happens just when one it is least expecting it."

You see! When inspiration simply refuses to strike whilst writing, or when the next step towards the solution fails to appear, the reason is often that one has become fixated on the notion that an idea has to come! As your flow of thoughts stagnates, you become insecure and put yourself under pressure. Symbolically speaking, the channels through which the good ideas and right impulses flow become narrower.

"Really?"

Dr Seer continued with his explanation, unperturbed.

And this is the key to solving the problem! Let me use another image to explain: Imagine that we do not actively generate ideas and impulses, but that they come to us instead, flowing into our minds from a great 'sea of ideas'. By thinking about it, all we do is clog the flow of ideas.

"An interesting thought!"

When we experience a mental blockage, the most important thing is to enable the stream of ideas to start flowing again. Or, with other activities, to allow the impulse for the next solution-oriented step to surface of its accord rather than to actively work it out!

"OK, so how does one achieve that?"

He snapped his fingers as if wanting me to pay particular attention – or to demonstrate how simple the method was.

By staring into space!
When you find yourself stuck, proceed as follows. First, take deep breaths, in and out. Let go! Let go of the content, the work, and the longing for a good idea, for the completion of the project.
Stop obsessing about what you're trying to achieve, and focus purely on yourself.
Look up from your paper, avert your gaze from the screen, look away from the shelf you are building. Put down the pencil. Don't leave your hands hovering over the keyboard – rest them on the table either side. Let go of the activity you are currently stuck trying to progress. Don't force yourself. Take a break!

"But what if you're under a lot of time pressure?"

So much the better. Then we just stop time!

"Ha! That's easy for you to say!"

Yes, and I mean exactly what I say. Ultimately, using this method will even gain you time. Our key sentences for the moment are: If I sit here doing nothing, my creativity will come back. I let go! The solution will come to me.
Whenever you experience a blockage or get fixated during any activity, just stare into space! Let your eyes roam around the room without fixing on anything. Gaze into the air – you're invited to stare. The only thing you are to focus yourself and your attention on for the moment is the air itself. It represents the 'non-solid', the free, the not-yet-defined from which every-thing can originate. Provided you allow it without trying to control the process for a while.
You will begin to sense what this is all about. When you let go of your thoughts and drop the compulsion to write something, or the need to finish the activity you are currently stuck in, then an energy starts flowing towards you with which you are able to generate new, useful ideas. Let your thoughts come and go, let them flow through you without evaluating them. The air now represents the creativity pool!

115

Empty your mind, or just think nonsense – the main thing is to achieve a certain degree of mental relaxation. Stare holes into space for a moment! These holes symbolise the entry portals for your desired ideas. Inspiration strikes not when you try to ease its passage, but when you leave it alone. What do you think?

"Hm. Makes sense, I guess. It feels good."

You will sense the moment when the blockage shifts. The right impulses will come, and you will be able to continue working. You will be able to concentrate on your work again – and you'll notice that, suddenly, it will all be much easier!

The Doc's explanation was pretty easy to picture, and I liked the imagery he used. Nonetheless, I still doubted that it could really be that easy.

"But wouldn't it be hard not to slip into 'waiting-mode' while staring into space?"

Indeed, it requires a definite readiness to give oneself up to emptiness and incompleteness, to let go of rationality and structure, and to give up the usual strategies we apply when we're working.

He looked at me intensely.

It works immediately if there's a genuine willingness to do it. And, as a matter of principle, that applies to every perspective of THE GOLDEN VIEW. You have experienced this already.

"I most certainly have."

So, try it out! For any activity, whenever you reach a point where you get stuck, let go and stare into space! You'll be surprised by the impulses that come to you. When you let go and move away from intellectual fixation, you create space. This allows ideas to form, such as who you could ask for advice, or what small step you need to take next. Try to be open to unusual impulses and approaches!

"I understand. Thank you, Doc!"

My pleasure! Please share this perspective with your friend Andy! And thank him, because it was he who provided the inspiration for today.

"I'll do that!"

By the way, it's a good idea to continue keeping your experiences of THE GOLDEN VIEW to yourself for the time being.

"Oh, you're aware that I'm not sharing it with anyone?"

What do you think?

"That you can see it?"

You're getting better by the minute.

Dr Seer smiled, pleased.

And one more thing: I was not expecting any sort of present from you, of course. Your trust in me and the fact that you continue to come are wonderful gifts in their own right.

His words touched me.

"What have I done to deserve your generous help?"

You have been yourself, my friend. By trusting that your life will steadily improve, by setting out to walk your own path and live your life more consciously – nothing more, nothing less.

"I can't thank you enough."

You'll see, there are many more experiences around the corner that will feel like presents for you. Goodbye, my friend. See you soon!

"See you soon, Doc! Goodbye!"

11 See with the eyes of a child!

Invigorating day-to-day life

There are some things in everyday life that have to get done – even if you absolutely don't feel like doing them, or consider them completely pointless. And simply ignoring them is obviously not the answer. A conscious human being, one who walks his or her own authentic path, as Dr Seer would put it, deals with such situations differently. But how?

Although I increasingly noticed how much *THE GOLDEN VIEW* and the sessions with Dr Seer were changing my life for the better, today, it has to be said, I was in a really bad mood. The kind of bad mood I get in when forced to do something that I don't really see the point of doing – like fulfilling certain social obligations. In this case, it was a corporate event. Work was celebrating a company anniversary tomorrow, and the mere thought of it was enough to trigger in me a strong sense of aversion and the desire to flee.

As it happened, I had a session scheduled with Dr Seer this evening, the night before the event, and so this irritating issue needed to be addressed today.

Why hello! I must say, you don't look especially pleased today.

"Good evening, Doc. Yes, I'm sorry to say that's true."

Without saying anything more, Dr Seer ushered me into our room.

How can I help?

"Hm. That's a good question. I'm not sure that you can. I'm afraid there's no getting out of it."

Out of what?

"Oh, it's this company event I have to attend tomorrow evening. And, put simply, I have absolutely no desire to go."

In fact, just talking about it annoyed me, something I couldn't hide. Dr Seer, as always, remained benevolent and focused.

I understand. That doesn't sound particularly pleasant.

"'Not particularly pleasant' is putting it very mildly! It's utterly horrible!"

He looked at me without speaking, and we fell into an extended period of silence. I was trying hard not to let my resentment get the better of me. I breathed deeply in and out. And suddenly, out of nowhere, I had a brilliant idea.

"Doc, I've got it! Now I know what to do! I'll just approach it with the tiger's-eye view!"

He continued gazing at me, in silence. Taking this as encouragement, I grew more excited.

"Yes, that's it! I'll spend the evening seeing with the eyes of a tiger! Why didn't I think of it before?!"

So, this event requires you to have strength and courage?

His question puzzled me.

"Um… well, actually no, not really."

Smiling, Dr Seer began to speak.

My friend, you've realized that the way to resolve this unpleasant situation is to take a different view of it. You want to go into the situation with a new perspective, and that is absolutely the right approach! But what makes you choose the tiger's-eye view?

"Well, because seeing things that way makes me feel good, and invincible. Those feelings would definitely help me get through the tediousness of it all."

Ah, so that's the problem! You're dreading the boredom you associate with such events.

"You have no idea how pointless these corporate events are. Getting through the entire evening is torture. You have to listen to a bunch of dreary, longwinded speeches, after which everyone stands around with a glass of bubbly in hand and tries to survive the evening by making superficial small talk. The whole situation feels tense, and forced. It's always the same, and nobody really enjoys themselves. To be honest, I'd much rather just skive off. But that's impossible."

Why?

"Because it could negatively affect my job. My boss wouldn't appreciate my not turning up, and I could end up damaging my reputation in the company. No, it's not worth the risk. Much better to bite the bullet, and go."

I understand.

"You know how it is… long-serving employees get presented with certificates, and hymns of praise are sung in their honour. It's the same drill every year, and they always trot out the same old clichéd phrases. I reckon that now, after the talks we've been having, the meaninglessness of it all will be even more apparent to me."

Why is that?

"You know what I mean! It's not like *you* waste your time on such dull activities!"

Dr Seer's expression remained unchanged. Step by step, and with great patience, he guided me, as he always did, through my feelings and thoughts.

What exactly can't you stand about this event?

"It's the fact that I don't get anything out of it! It's a waste of time! At least five or six hours of my life that I'll never get back – lost time during

120

which I also have to feign interest, and pretend to be fascinated and enthusiastic! I already know how dull and drawn-out the evening will be."

What would you need to be able to cope with this situation better?

"Good question. A heavy cold would be ideal! Although... I suppose that wouldn't really be the answer either."

With that 'solution' you would actually just be harming yourself.

"Exactly. So, what do I need? I don't really know."

Could it perhaps be a different feeling about the event?

"Hm. Yes, I'm sure it'd feel totally different if I hadn't ever been to an event like this before, and went in there as a 'newbie' without knowing what to expect... then I'd probably find it quite exciting. But how could I induce that feeling? Is there some sort of drug I could take? Sod it, I reckon I'll just get drunk when I'm there, to make it more tolerable."

Dr Seer smiled a knowing smile, yet seemed to be taking things very seriously.

Do you want clarity and consciousness – or distraction and self-deception?

"What do you mean?"

Do you want to watch as your life flits by, or do you want to live consciously? Do you want to plod through life without really knowing where it's going, or do you want to determine your own path and realize your true potential?

"I want to realize my potential, of course!"

You see! And that is only possible if you have your eyes wide open, if you are alert, and see things clearly! Numbing yourself to make an unpleasant situation seem more pleasant might feel like a helpful solution in the short term, but it won't help you to move forward. Ultimately, it won't be any use to you at all – on the contrary!

"Yes, you're probably right."

It was obvious that getting this message across was very important to him. I felt a bit of an idiot for coming up with the stupid idea of trying to get through the evening by consuming large quantities of alcohol. It seemed I was still a long way away from being the kind of conscious person the Doc often alluded to. Naturally, he noticed my irritation.

You are much closer than you think! What else might help to make this compulsory function seem more pleasant and easy going? You've already mentioned it, as it happens!

"You're referring to the idea that I should find it as exciting as if I'd never been to a function like it before?"

Dr Seer nodded at me, confirming my suggestion.

Exactly! What would you feel if that were the case?

"Hm. Anticipation, perhaps? Or… curiosity?"

At that moment, my mood lifted and I began to feel better. I was amazed, once again, to see where the Doc was leading me.

You've got it! THE GOLDEN VIEW refers to it as: 'See with the eyes of a child!'

"Oh. I'd never have come up with that one. How could I? Seems that I was a bit wide of the mark, suggesting the tiger's-eye perspective."

What we're talking about here are the pure, fundamental qualities. The tiger stands for courage and strength, the child for curiosity and impartiality. Go on a journey of discovery!

"Do you mean that I should approach this company function like a journey of discovery?"

Exactly.

"That sounds like it might almost be a laugh, I have to say."

And it is! To a certain extent, this journey happens inside you. And that can indeed turn into a very amusing way of entertaining yourself. When you see things with the eyes of a child, you tap into your own natural curiosity. Before attending the event, put yourself in a state of joyful anticipation. You have no idea what's coming – only that you are totally up for making new discoveries! Like a child!

"And you think that might really work?"

Just try it! Consider this for a moment: By expecting the evening to be boring, you are already programming your perception and experience for that to be the case – and chances are that the evening will indeed turn out to be very dull.

"Yes, I guess that's true."

Children have a few habits that put them in a better position than us adults. A child lives completely in the moment. It makes discoveries and does not pass judgement. It approaches each situation with an open mind.

Dr Seer's explanations sounded very promising to my ears. But I wasn't ready to be quite so easily convinced.

"But a child would find it even more boring! They'd hate having to sit around for hours without moving!"

It's not about imagining the child as a real person, Mr Allman. You wouldn't take a real, live tiger with you whenever you need courage now, would you? It wouldn't have been fair on the animal or beneficial to your negotiations if you'd taken the tiger along to the meeting about your pay rise. You see with its eyes, figuratively speaking, in order to connect with the intrinsic qualities of the animal. And you do exactly the same when you see with the eyes of a child. You approach the situation with a childlike attitude of curiosity and innocence.

Slowly, I was beginning to warm to this way of seeing.

When you are faced with something you absolutely don't feel like doing, and there's no way round it, then see things with the eyes of a child! Imagine you are experiencing the situation for the very first time, and that it is full of new and exciting discoveries and experiences.

"I've never tried anything like that before!"

The Doc was smiling.

Of course you have, you've just forgotten it. When you were a little child, this view was completely normal for you.

Let's practise it now, using our imagination. Please close your eyes and think about the event tomorrow evening. Try to assume the curiosity and complete impartiality with which a child would approach such an event. What might you discover there if you were seeing everything with the eyes of a child?

I closed my eyes and allowed myself to indulge in a bit of free association.

"Hm. I could observe more closely the reactions of the people receiving their certificates, to see whether they're truly happy about it or not. I could try to find out how the other guests are feeling – after all, everyone is in the same boat, having to attend the same boring event. I could also listen more carefully when people are speaking to find out what they are really trying to communicate, or to establish whether, ultimately, it's all just hot air. Another option would be for me to just look at what people are wearing."

Very good! What else might there be to discover?

"I could strike up a conversation with totally different people than I usually would – for instance, I could talk to those I'd only encountered briefly in the lift. I could ask more personal questions, and make an effort to take things beyond the small talk we usually engage in when stood around with our glasses in hand. I could talk to them about genuine topics, about things that move me personally."

Well, this isn't sounding quite so boring any more, is it?

"No, not at all. It's actually good fun, and a refreshing break from the norm."

Wonderful. Give it a go! You will always find something new to discover!

"I'll definitely try it!"

Good. You may now open your eyes again. That was just a practice run, designed to attune you to this particular perspective.

Suddenly, we both had to laugh. I felt so much more at ease now, and in a much better mood. Dr Seer had the knack of making clear that one always has a choice when deciding how to approach difficult situations, day-to-day problems, and life as a whole. The Doc seemed to believe that every challenge has a silver lining that can help us to grow – one only has to be willing to find it. As if he had once again read my thoughts – I had started to believe he could actually *see* them – he continued to explain.

You are free to choose how you want to view a certain situation. You can opt to find it boring, or exhilarating, interesting and instructive. It is totally up to you! In this way, you can actively influence what you experience and determine how you feel.
First, be aware of the thoughts and emotions that prevail within you before you attend an event or appointment. And then decide if and how much you want to change what you are thinking and feeling at that moment. Do you feel any fear?
If so, it's time to see things with the eyes of a tiger! Is there prejudice and antagonism? Then see with the eyes of a child! And I'll tell you something else – 'seeing things with the eyes of a child' enables you to do even more. With this perspective, you can revitalize your entire everyday life. You'll be able to experience and evaluate your routine activities in a new light. Your senses will heighten, and because of your unprejudiced attitude you will discover something new every day. On top of all this, your relationships with your fellow humans will also be rejuvenated.

"I think I understand! To be honest, I'd even like to try seeing things with the eyes of a child on my way home."

Well then, do it! Why not?

I had to laugh. I really liked Dr Seer; I enjoyed his patience, his sense of humour and the surprises he always had up his sleeve for me.

"I'd probably discover so much new stuff that I'd never want to leave that state of wonder and amazement."

Then stay there!

"True, it's not that much longer until tomorrow night, anyhow."

When you are in a state of amazement you are in the NOW. And – do you remember?

"What? When I was a child?"

Dr Seer winked at me.

We'll be taking a look at your childhood at a later point, too. THE GOLDEN VIEW shines a light on everything. But I mean something else. Do you remember what can only happen in the NOW? We've had this before.

"Oh, yes, of course! You said that intuition only speaks in the NOW. As a clear feeling."

Quick as a flash, I understood another completely new connection.

"It's only logical. When you're without prejudice then there are no critical thoughts in the mind, and that makes it possible to *feel* with greater clarity. This provides the foundation for being able to approach a situation without reservations – and through that, the situation can turn out to be eventful and remarkable."

Very well observed! Go into the NOW! Discover! Feel and allow yourself to be guided by your intuition – not by prefabricated, negative expectations! Absorption in something has much to do with intuition. You are open and allow yourself to be guided – by what you perceive, by what the moment provides, by what you are really interested in. No matter whether there is a rational reason for it or not.

"Thank you, Doc. You're helping me to see life in a whole new way."

He gave me his hand, smiling.

All you have to do is to experience it! THE GOLDEN VIEW will guide you! And now: have fun! Go on a journey of discovery! Goodbye!

"I'll do that! Goodbye!"

12 Stop right there!

Breaking destructive behaviour patterns

I didn't usually arrive early for my sessions with Dr Seer, but today I got there with ten minutes to spare. I wasn't sure whether to ring the bell or not, so I lit a cigarette to kill some time. I should have known by now that my early arrival would not have gone unnoticed by the Doc. With a welcoming gesture as always, he opened the door for me, taking me by surprise. I immediately threw the cigarette to the ground and stubbed it out with my shoe.

Oh, you smoke? Hello, Mr Allman!

For some strange reason, I felt like I'd been caught out – although his was by no means a particularly personal question. I think I even blushed.

"Ahem, yes…"

Dr Seer gave me his hand in greeting.

Very well. Please come in! You know the way.

Not only did I know the way, I also knew Dr Seer well enough by now to suspect that he would turn his observation into the topic of today's session. He liked to incorporate spontaneous events into our sessions and use them to illustrate fundamental principles of life. I think it must be quite self-evident by now how much this approach has benefitted my personal development and what a wealth of insights each and every meeting has given me. *THE GOLDEN VIEW* has helped me in so many situations. Like at last week's company event, where seeing with the eyes of a child enabled me to really enjoy myself. But now I felt strangely uneasy. Could this perhaps be a lingering psychological after-effect of applying that perspective? After all, I had felt very childlike just now, when the Doc asked me about my smoking habit. Kind of like a child who had been caught by his father secretly puffing on a cigarette. As we sat down in our room, Dr Seer looked me squarely in the eyes. The fact that he was smiling didn't really do much to ease my nervous apprehension.

Why did you smoke just now?

He asked his question in a very friendly voice, and yet I still felt like I was being scrutinized.

"Well, to tell you the truth, I've never asked myself that question…"

Then it's about time, surely!

"I have no idea why I had a smoke. I just had a few minutes to kill."

His intense gaze made it difficult for me to explain.

"I was here a bit early. So I just lit a cigarette."

I understand. So whenever you arrive early for an appointment, you just fill your spare time with smoke.

"Ouch, Doc! That doesn't sound too clever at all!"

No, I don't suppose it does…

"Alright, OK. You're right, it isn't good. And I should definitely stop, because it's bad for my health and so on and so forth…"

He listened to me attentively while his facial expression remained friendly.

Mr Allman, do you remember I once told you that I don't judge you?

"Sure, I remember."

Well, you have just judged yourself in a negative way. That indicates that there's an unresolved issue within you that needs addressing.

No doubt about it, the man's observational skills were second to none. And just as he had done time and time again over the last few weeks, he read me with impressive accuracy. Resistance would have been futile – and almost childish.

Are you ready to take a closer look at this issue?

"Then I guess today will be about smoking, right?"

Let us examine the situation. There's much more to it, you'll see!

He nodded at me encouragingly.

There's no need to worry, my friend. I have no intention of dissecting you under the microscope. You'll do a much better job of that yourself.

Now I had to grin. Deep down, I knew that, ultimately, taking a close look at my psyche, my experiences and my behaviour was good for me. And so I tried to overcome my initial resistance. Dr Seer noticed the glimmer of my growing desire to participate, and began to explain.

You see, we are dealing with behaviour patterns that are automatic. Behavioural patterns that you repeatedly demonstrate in certain situations without having any real awareness of why you act that way – and without having any choice in the matter.
Behaviour like this always follows a specific pattern. And smoking mostly falls into this category.
Once we find out which situations trigger such automatic patterns of behaviour in us, we can uncover the hidden objective that lies behind it. Because, Mr Allman, the motivating factor is always an unfulfilled subconscious desire!
In the next step we can then understand how to break these patterns and discover what action we could take in their place. Then we can consciously select a behaviour that truly fulfils our hidden desire, and so contributes towards our wellbeing. Do you follow what I'm saying?

"Not quite, to be honest."

Let's go back a step. You said that you smoked a few minutes ago because you had arrived too early and had a few minutes to spare.

"Yes. Exactly."

In what other situations do you normally smoke, and how much?

"Well, I guess there are quite a number of situations… For instance, whenever I go for a drink with my colleagues, we all tend to smoke. Sometimes I'll have a cigarette with a cup of coffee in the morning. And, of course, I always have a smoke when there's lots of stress at work, as a way to take a break. I normally smoke on average about ten cigarettes a day. If I go out in the evenings, then it's usually a few more."

I see. So, one of the main reasons you smoke is when you need a break. What purpose does smoking serve for you in these kinds of situations?

"As I said, it gives me a way to escape the stress for a while."

So smoking gives you a feeling of temporary relief?

"Yes, something like that, I presume."

Tell me, do you sometimes feel the need to smoke a cigarette during our sessions, too? You've never mentioned it so far.

This question perplexed me. He was right, I'd never smoked at Dr Seer's. The idea of doing so had never even entered my mind. Despite spending hours on end here, I'd not once felt the need to interrupt a session with a cigarette break.

"No, for some reason I don't."

Why do you think that is?

"I… hm. I don't know."

The Doc rested his gaze on me, which automatically caused me to become more focused on the question. Why did I never feel the need to smoke a cigarette here? The question was gnawing away at me. Suddenly, I felt as if I'd almost touched on the answer – without being able to explain exactly what it was. I started babbling, purely to break the silence.

"Almost all my colleagues smoke. And when we're on a smoke break outside, we can talk about things that would be inappropriate for us to discuss in the office."

131

Dr Seer kept looking at me, and somehow his constant gaze helped my thoughts to flow and allowed me to freely associate. I continued thinking about it. Was it perhaps also possible to connect smoking and the 'path to the more conscious human being' that he was always talking about? Did I not feel the need to smoke during our sessions because I was so preoccupied with myself and my journey? Or was the reason simply that I was removed from my daily routine and all the associated stress whenever I was here?

Finally the Doc started speaking again.

Do you like to smoke?

"Hm. You know, I don't actually find that it tastes that good. Sometimes my stomach even feels a bit queasy once I've had a few cigarettes."

And how did it all start in the first place?

"Oh, that's a long story... The habit crept back in after I started smoking again due to a personal crisis, for want of a better word. I used to smoke when I was younger, during my apprenticeship, but I managed to quit and didn't smoke for years after that. When the crisis came along, it simply became habitual again."

I had to sigh deeply.

"To be honest, it was quite a crappy period back then, five years ago."

Yes, I can see that. What happened?

"Oh, you know, the usual. My ex-girlfriend left me more or less overnight, after an almost seven-year relationship. And things with my job were not going so well, either. It was all a bit much. And that's when I took up smoking again. But I don't think I'm addicted to nicotine."

Hang on – you said you entered this crisis some five years ago. And when did it finish?

"Well, the really difficult phase lasted about half a year."

Aha. You started smoking because of this personal crisis, and then you continued to smoke once the crisis was over?

His insistent line of inquiry made me feel uncomfortable. Or maybe I was just experiencing some final form of inner rebellion before facing the personal truth that was causing this oppressive feeling in me. I'd experienced this phenomenon here several times before.

"Doc, that's just how it is. A habit, pure and simple! I know *you* don't have any vices!"

Why?

"Well, because you see everything so clearly, and because you're wise!"

I'm absolutely certain that it was in no way his intention, but I suddenly felt small and incompetent. Dr Seer, on the other hand, appeared happy about what I had just said.

Mr Allman, you're so much closer to your moment of realization than you think! So you are assuming that a wise person who sees everything clearly wouldn't smoke?

"Yes. No. I don't know. I don't even know why I said that."

All right then, let me tell you something. If you make a conscious decision to smoke, then do so, by all means! Provided the profit is greater than the loss.
The thing to remember is this: Personal insight – or seeing things clearly, as you put it – means understanding that one has freedom of choice. It means freely deciding what to do, and why – and being conscious of one's true needs.

"Oh, right."

You, my dear Mr Allman, never got to freely decide to take up smoking! You were subject to an automatic impulse. At some point you reached for a cigarette because, unconsciously, you assumed that smoking could alleviate psychological stress. And that may well be the case. It provides short-term relief.

And that's the very nature of the dilemma. Smoking doesn't resolve the emotions lying beneath the current feeling of stress – the very emotions that caused the tensions in the first place. Nor does it ultimately free you from the stress itself; on the contrary, it keeps you trapped in a vicious cycle of non-functioning coping mechanisms. Smoking has become a behavioural habit to which you compulsively succumb in certain situations, such as when your job pushes you beyond your limits. Chances are it's a habit that you would prefer to get rid of because it does you more physical and psychological harm than good.

"You're absolutely right."

Consider the following, my friend. Habits that have not been consciously chosen by us but that we have more or less slipped into adopting over the course of time cost us a lot of personal energy. Often this is something we can actually sense. Only very few people who smoke cigarettes regularly would actually say that smoking makes them happy and contributes to their wellbeing.

To break such habits and regain your energy, you have to uncover which emotions and needs triggered the habit to develop in the first place. What is the inner mechanism that supports this behaviour?

When you admit to yourself that you are dealing with automatic behavioural patterns that you have to disrupt, then you have found the lever with which you can erect a stop signal. By analysing the deeper emotional causes, you gain another lever with which to better dissolve the behaviour pattern at its core.

All this sounded very plausible. At the same time, I felt overwhelmed. But Dr Seer continued speaking, undeterred.

What we're looking at today is strictly speaking not a new perspective, but a neat and effective little method that I like to call 'Stop right there!'. It's a kind of formula that encourages us to metaphorically shake off our automatic behaviours – and with that to choose freedom and consciousness. Can you follow me?

"More or less."

He looked at me, probingly. It was absolutely impossible to hide anything from him.

Do you feel a little stressed right now?

"Yes… I don't quite know what's going on with me."

Would you like to go for a smoke?

Even in my wildest dreams, I'd never have expected him to make such a suggestion.

I'll come out and smoke with you, if you like!

"Pardon me?! But… but you don't smoke at all!"

No, but I've decided that I want to, right now.

I tried to collect my thoughts.

"Well, OK then… why not?"

No sooner said than done. And so I found myself standing with Dr Seer on the veranda behind the house. Cigarette breaks usually have a kind of bonding effect for the people involved, and this time was no different. I found it pretty cool that he actually came outside and smoked a cigarette with me. It made me feel like we were buddies.

"Tell me something, Doc. Why is 'being conscious' and 'living consciously' so important? For whatever reason, I still don't fully get it."

Taking those first drags on my cigarette triggered the familiar high, stimulating my brain and getting my blood pumping. I became very animated as I continued to explain my thoughts to Dr Seer.

"Because, well – it's all the same, isn't it? *You* making a conscious decision to smoke, or *me* smoking purely because I'm stressed – the victim of an automatic impulse, so to speak – ultimately, the result is the same. We're both having a smoke. So, the way I see it, in the end it doesn't actually matter whether the smoking happens consciously or due to an automatic habit. So why do we need to be conscious all the time?"

Dr Seer puffed on his cigarette with obvious pleasure, and listened to what I had to say. His answer, unsurprisingly, came in the form of a question.

Why are you here, my friend? Why do you think you keep coming to see me?

"What does that have to do with smoking?"

He was not to be deterred.

Just take a moment to calmly give it some thought. Why do you come here?

"I want to feel good; I want to solve my problems. I just want to be happier."

A moment of silence followed. Dr Seer stubbed out his cigarette.

Becoming conscious is the only way to get there!

At this point in time I wasn't able to fully understand what the Doc meant. However, I could sense the truth in his words. I'd reached the end of my cigarette, so I let it fall to the ground and stubbed it out with my shoe. The Doc disposed of the cigarette ends in a metal bucket at the other end of the veranda.

We returned to our room for the last phase of today's session. When he began to speak, his words sounded like an official announcement:

Would you like to be free of your smoking behaviour pattern?

"Yes, I would."

Do you know how automatic behaviour works?

136

"Yes. What you explained earlier is absolutely true! I don't even think about it when I reach for a cigarette. I don't really want to smoke. I've been trying to quit for over a year now, but it's not working."

Why do you think it hasn't worked yet?

"Perhaps because I've only really been trying half-heartedly?"

That's one way of looking at it, yes. Your reason for quitting was that it would be healthier to stop. But the decision didn't come from your inner-most self, or from a deep, inner sense of conviction, nor did it come from your awareness. And this precisely illustrates the point I am trying to make: strictly speaking, it's not a question of deciding AGAINST smoking, but of opting FOR a more conscious and happier life. The decision should come from your heart, and not from your mind.

He nodded at me.

And, if you recall, you had actually already made this fundamental decision when you came to see me the first time.

"Yes."

Let me explain things more explicitly, so you truly understand the connection. If we don't take good care of ourselves and consciously deal with whatever is happening on an emotional level inside us, then we find that, when faced with recurring difficult situations, the subconscious takes over. Stress is a prime example. Whenever this happens, we inevitably move away from ourselves and thus lose sight of what would benefit us and contribute to our personal growth.
Our main concern here is finding a way to put your decision to live a more conscious life into practice, so that you are able to take responsibility for yourself and consciously choose what you do, in order to reach and main-tain your inner equilibrium. You will not only be more conscious and more emotionally and physically balanced as a result, you will also find that you have more energy at your disposal.

"Yes, that's what I want Doc!"

Great. What we need now is a specific signal, something to remind you to 'stop right there' whenever you find yourself about to slip into a destructive behaviour pattern.

He reached into his jacket pocket and pulled out a small, orange-coloured rubber ball. He handed it to me.

Here you are! It's a gift: your own personal 'stop right there!'

Somewhat confused, I took the little ball and stared at it. Dr Seer chuckled.

This is the signal that will remind you that you decided to live consciously. And it will remind you of something else as well: that you are free to decide what you want to do – even if what you want is to light up a cigarette. Or not!

"Right, OK…"

So, in future, whenever you feel the need to go out and smoke a cigarette at work, for example, please first reach for the orange ball. Stop for a second, and ask yourself: What do I feel? What do I really need now?
Now let's review your automatic responses again. Why do you smoke? You already identified the reason.

"I mainly do it when I'm stressed."

And what is it that you actually need instead?

"Relaxation."

What else might it be? Try to connect it to the insight you gained about attaining consciousness, and look a little deeper...

"Hm. Maybe there's an underlying desire to find my inner balance. Yes, and that would explain why I don't usually feel any desire to smoke when I'm here with you. Because I'm always able to connect with myself when I'm here!"

Excellent! You have hit the nail on the head. Whenever you feel the desire to smoke a cigarette, first ask yourself what it is that you need. In most cases, the answer is relaxation and inner peace. Ultimately, it is in your power to make the conscious decision whether you want to smoke a cigarette or would rather do something else to relax. What might that be, for instance?

"You would probably recommend taking three deep breaths. Or going outside to get some fresh air for a few minutes."

Dr Seer smiled.

Those are all very good ideas! Deep breathing, of course, brings you closer to your inner self within seconds. And it's certainly relaxing, as you know. Going out for some fresh air or taking a short walk is also helpful. As you discovered before by looking from within, a walk is a great way to relax the body. Incidentally, another option would be to drink a glass of water and think back to our conversation from today while you drink it. What did we say was the only way to achieve happiness?

"To get there, we have to become conscious."

I felt a bit like teacher's pet, but didn't let it bother me.

Wonderful! Then let's make that our motto: 'To become happy, we must become conscious'. And your personal 'stop right there!' will prompt you to remember this motto. What do you think?

I was really beginning to like this method.

"So every time I feel the need to smoke, I should reach for my orange ball instead – my own personal 'Stop right there!'. This reminds me that I can decide freely, and that I would like to live consciously. And then I remember the motto: *'To become happy we must become conscious'*, and ask myself what it is that I really need at that moment. Most of the time the answer will be 'relaxation', 'a short break', or 'to regain my inner balance'. That's when I decide whether I still want to smoke, or if I want to do something else instead – something more appropriate to helping me to relax, like popping outside, drinking a glass of water, or taking some deep breaths."

You've got it! Spot on! And please don't beat yourself up if it turns out that you still want to smoke a cigarette. Because, in this case, it will have been a conscious decision.

"I have to say, Doc, that sounds really smart! But I can't imagine I'd still want to smoke, at that point."

All you have to do is experience it as your very own, personal conscious moment!

The Doc seemed happy. After a short pause, he continued to explain:

Everyone has the ability to recognize their own automatic behaviour patterns, and can break through and dissolve them by becoming conscious. We all have unconscious habits that control our actions and behaviour. For example, there are situations that prompt us to react aggressively over and over again, even when it's not what we want.
Every kind of addiction is an automatic behaviour pattern. If physical dependency is added into the mix, then the situation becomes even more complex. An addiction can be healed – but only through the process of becoming conscious of the mechanism behind it, and breaking this mechanism through deep, sincere intention and a strong impulse to 'stop right there!'. In addition, we will also understand what's really behind the unconscious behaviour or addiction, and be able to see the true needs that we've been trying to satisfy.

"That sounds very plausible!"

There are a number of behaviours that can develop into automatic behaviour patterns if the individual has an unconscious need to alleviate a burdensome emotion. Eating, for instance, is a habit that can develop in this way.
There are people who eat excessively when they feel troubled. They do it because they are looking for a way to feel better, and eating more than their body requires gives them the impression of filling a need. But this is an

unconscious process. Not only do they experience the alleviating effects for no more than a very short time, the relief is not genuine – the increased food intake can't heal their sorrow. The great hunger for love, so often hidden deep in the heart, cannot be sated through physical nourishment.

Let's look at an example. Imagine a middle-aged woman who is deeply emotionally distressed. She might find herself going to the fridge countless times to take out something to eat, even though she isn't actually hungry. But at some point there might come a time when she closes the fridge door without having taken out any food.

That would be the moment to pause for an instant and ask herself: Why do I eat so much? What's going on inside me, on an emotional level? What is it that I really need?

After experiencing this conscious moment, chances are the woman will first feel the need to cry. Then she might feel compelled to call somebody close to her, in order to open up and talk about her sorrow. The realization might finally dawn on her that things can't go on like this, and that she has to do something in order to regain her happiness. In taking this step, she has mentally stepped out of her behaviour pattern. In this moment she has become a more conscious human being.

I listened, spellbound, to Dr Seer's reflections. He was so good at telling stories.

This woman now has the ability to make a real change, and is finally in a position to be able to approach and process the issue that is making her sad and psychologically distressed. At the same time she can now address and change her eating habits, and be kinder to herself. She has told herself to 'stop right there!'. One way she could help prevent herself from succumbing to the mechanism in future would be to post this message as a visible signal – somewhere like on the refrigerator door, for example. The signal doesn't represent prohibition, but rather serves to remind her of her intention to live consciously. It could take any form – perhaps a green sign with: 'Stop right there!' printed on it, or another symbol – a yellow laughing sun, for instance. Anything, provided it is a symbol that motivates her personally and makes her feel good.

This description touched me.

'We all have behaviour patterns and not-so-helpful habits that conceal something completely different. And evidently, each of us has the ability to achieve self-knowledge', I thought to myself.

Very often, our unconscious needs are hiding unseen emotions, distress, pain, unresolved sadness or a weakened self-esteem. That is completely human! Telling ourselves to 'stop right there!' brings us much closer to healing these emotions. We'll look at that deeper emotional level at some later point in time.

The Doc was nodding at me encouragingly.

If you take your personal 'stop right there!' seriously and make it part of your everyday life, you will already be making excellent progress! It means that you are a significant step closer to a happier life. You'll see.
It is important, however, that you associate something positive, both mentally and emotionally, with your 'stop right there!' symbol. It's the only way to ensure the effect is motivational and invigorating.
Stay with it and don't be too hard on yourself if you occasionally slip back into the old behaviour pattern. Every change in behaviour requires constant repetition and practice. The new consciousness in your life also manifests itself through actions.

I threw my orange ball high up in the air and caught it again with one hand. We both had to laugh.

"That's what I'll do, Doc! And by the way, orange is my favourite colour – but you knew that, didn't you. The ball will live on my desk or in my pocket. From now on, it goes wherever I go!"

Then your life will soon consist only of conscious moments.

"Just like yours, I suspect. Am I right?"

We walked down the corridor to the front door together. Chuckling, he gave me his hand.

'Consciousness' is my middle name. Goodbye, Mr Allman.

"Goodbye! I feel much lighter. Thank you!"

Holding my little 'stop right there!' ball firmly in my hand, I left Dr Seer's house and walked briskly down the paved pathway towards the street. I was just about to go through the large gate when the Doc called out.

Mr Allman, your cigarettes! You forgot your pack of cigarettes!

The Doc stood in front of the door, waving his arm with my half-full pack of cigarettes clutched in his hand.

"Oh, please throw them away! I don't need them anymore!"

Good, my friend. You decide! Goodbye!

He was smiling as I left.

13 Look into your past!

In-depth understanding and resolution of emotional burdens

Are you ready to look even deeper today?

Dr Seer got straight down to business. And because I was probably staring at him in total bewilderment – we had only just greeted each other – he added:

You have to really want it, of course.

I knew by now that he never asked a question without a reason, and that there was bound to be something significant lurking behind it. But I had absolutely no way of telling what he had in mind for me for today.

I am not allowed to persuade you, you see.

"What do you mean, 'you're not allowed'?"

Your free will forbids it.

"Oh, I see."

I noticed that my pulse was beating faster now, and I began to get a little nervous.

Dr Seer gently pushed me along the corridor towards the room where we had spent the last five sessions. Before we had even reached the door, the words burst out of me:

"Doc, I think I'm ready for it. I want to go even deeper!"

Very good, my friend! Now is the right time.

He looked at me intently.

Have trust! Trust in yourself – even if looking deeply within seems unpleasant. You'll feel much lighter in the end, you'll see. Please take a seat.

I was glad to let myself fall into my familiar chair. Dr Seer handed me a glass of water.

How has the smoking been since our last session? Have you smoked in the last few days?

I took a big gulp of water.

"Oh, I'm glad you asked! No, I haven't smoked a single cigarette since then! I was tempted a few times. But then I recalled our conversation. I'd made the conscious decision to take a few deep breaths every time I felt the urge instead. 'Stop right there!' makes a big difference."

Very good!

"I really hope I can stick with it. Besides that, I've been feeling quite strange this past week, Doc. Lots of feelings have been surfacing. D'you think it might be connected to stopping smoking?"

That is quite possible. What kind of feelings were they?

"Hard to say... It felt a bit like... sadness. A familiar sense of loneliness, something I've not felt for a long time... it was almost like..." A sudden thirst came over me, so I reached for my glass and drank almost all the water in it. Dr Seer watched me with an expression of kind concern, which made me feel a little calmer. I tried to collect myself.

"... it was kind of like lovesickness, you know?"

Yes. I can see it.

And after a short pause, he added:

I was expecting these feelings to arise in you. That was the reason I began by asking if you were ready to take an even deeper look today.

Once again I was moved by his gentle way of guiding me. His considerate nature was clearly one of his key attributes. He gave me some time.

Last time you said that you started smoking some five years ago.

"Yes. When my girlfriend at the time left me…"

Would you like to tell me more about it today?

We both knew that the topic of 'love and relationships' would come up again at some point – not least of all because the Doc had announced several times that we would be dealing with my emotional life more intensely. I'd never experienced psychotherapy or life coaching before, so had no idea what to expect from this kind of analysis. But everything seemed completely different from the norm where Dr Seer was concerned, anyhow.

"I'm not quite sure. It might be a good idea, yes."

I had to swallow. There was suddenly a lump in my throat.

"Well, we … Sarah and I were together for almost seven years. We wanted to get married. And then she just upped and left me, overnight."

I noticed that my palms were sweaty, and I found it increasingly difficult to speak.

"She fell in love with somebody else. She said it wouldn't have mattered anyway, because the energy was gone between the two of us. But it didn't feel that way to me… I didn't share her take on things."

I understand. She broke up with you.

Dr Seer took a long, audible breath.
It was very painful for you at the time.

"Hm."

Would you still want to be with Sarah today?

His question made me think. It was something I hadn't asked myself for a long time. When it finally came, my answer surprised me.

"No, I wouldn't, actually. We don't actually make that good a match."

Dr Seer kept probing, as he was wont to do.

That means you now accept the situation as it is? This lost love is not an issue for you anymore?

"That's right. I think it's no longer an issue."

He let his gaze rest on me for a good ten minutes or so – it felt like an eternity.

But I see that your pain is still there.

I took a deep breath, and sighed.

"Hm. Yes, it still hurts to talk about it."

As I spoke, I put my right hand on my chest.

"It always feels like there's this inner pressure, pushing its way up to the surface."

At that moment, I realized that I'd never spoken to anyone about this sensation, even though it had become so familiar to me over the last few years.

"Sometimes this feeling nearly chokes me, Doc."

Dr Seer nodded. I could sense that he understood me completely. He sat on the edge of his chair, moving closer so he could look at me more directly, and whispered:

What feeling is it?

Tears welled up in my eyes, and I made no attempt to hide them.

Please let yourself feel it. Feel it fully.

"It... it's the feeling of having been abandoned..."

A solitary tear broke free and cascaded down my cheek.

"… by someone I love."

It's good that you are crying. Allow it, my friend.

Patiently, the Doc listened to me, radiating kindness and respect. My tears were flowing freely now.

You have been abandoned once before – earlier, as a child?

For a few minutes I was unable to reply. I couldn't say anything at all. After a while, I tried to collect myself. In that moment I realized that these strong emotions were putting me under huge strain. Dr Seer handed me a tissue, and I blew my nose.

"Do you plan to dig up my whole past with me now?"

No. That is not the point. I would like you to take a healing look at your past.

Reassuringly, he nodded at me.

THE GOLDEN VIEW will show you how you can heal your pain, which is connected to experiences buried far back in your life history. By no means do we want to dig up your entire past, or go indiscriminately looking for old, painful experiences.

He spoke very slowly, with particular emphasis, clearly wanting to make sure I took in every word he said.

The perspective I would like to show you today is called: 'Look into your past!'

"Hm."

Please try to follow me as I explain how it works. It's like keyhole surgery. Minimally invasive, but highly effective. First we examine which painful emotions we're currently feeling and the thoughts that are connected with them. We reflect upon the causes of the unpleasant emotions being experienced now.

Then we look to the past to search for and locate the principal emotional root causes of the current pain.
In the next step, we recognize and understand the psychological reasons for why we felt so bad back then. This understanding enables us to gradually begin letting go of the original issues and the hurtful emotions connected with them.

"Sounds great. But does it really work?"

That depends on how willing you are.

He looked at me with an encouraging smile.

And you've already started.

"Why do people always insist one shouldn't 'suppress' anything? Has that got anything to do with it?"

Well, it's like this. Whenever we suppress an experience, we ban it from our consciousness. We do so unknowingly, to prevent the painful emotions that the experience would otherwise trigger. The pain gets pushed out of our sphere of awareness, as it were, because we perceive it to be unbearable. However, these experiences and the intense emotions connected with them remain stored in our subconscious, where they prevent us from freely creating new positive experiences. This is a constant drain on our personal energy reserves, and prevents us from accessing our inner power. Please try to internalize the following principle: Emotional pain can only be alleviated and dissipated through becoming conscious. We have to take a good look at the experience in order to understand what lies at its core and to change the way we feel. Doing so allows us to integrate it into our consciousness in a healthy manner. Our personal energy, which was blocked before, is now released. Do you recall our motto from last week? 'To become happy, we must become conscious!' This applies here as well, in every sense. To become happier, we must first become aware of everything that makes us unhappy. In so doing we are then able to open ourselves up to new impulses in our lives, and can heal and grow.

149

"Wow, I've never looked at it like that before. I always thought we had to carry our old wounds around with us. I didn't believe it was ever really possible to disentangle ourselves from certain negative events and painful experiences."

This seemed to be very important to Dr Seer.

THE GOLDEN VIEW teaches us that it is possible to heal even very old psychological pain. Furthermore, it shows us that it's not about digging up our entire past as part of some therapeutic exercise to go searching for supposed suppressed experiences. It's the other way round: We look at what matters and what hurts in the NOW, and identify the emotional patterns that are present. Then we seek out the original cause, and find a way to dissolve these emotional patterns.

"What do you mean by 'emotional patterns'? Emotions that come up automatically?"

That's one way of looking at it, yes. We identify those situations that repeatedly cause us pain, or sorrow, anger, or sadness. We always react to such situations in the same way because of the emotions that are triggered automatically. If one is not aware of the underlying pattern, one has almost no choice regarding one's own behaviour.
By going back into our own personal history and seeking out the causal events, the all-important key incident that produced this emotion in the past, we are able to heal it in the NOW.

He filled my glass with water and was silent for a moment. Then he got up from his chair, went to the window and opened it. When he came back he looked at me pensively.

Who abandoned you when you were a child?

As if a switch had been flipped, I suddenly found it very difficult to speak again. It was as though I had lost my voice.

"My... my father."

150

I swallowed. I hadn't spoken about this episode in my life for years, if not decades.

"My father left my mother when I was six years old. He walked out on her to be with another woman."

A sudden coughing fit took hold of me, causing my eyes to tear up again.

"It was a nightmare. My mother cried nonstop for months and months. She was completely beside herself."

How did you feel at the time?

"Me? I felt totally alone. Abandoned. Lonely, I guess. Yes, I was lonely. It felt like…"

I had to stop myself. Indescribable pain rose up in me, trapping the words in my throat. I found myself having to use the tissue I had been clutching for a second time, as I broke down in tears once more. The Doc gently touched my shoulder.

How did you feel back then – as a child?

"… like… nobody was there for me. That nobody loved me, cared about me, was interested in me – that there was no-one to give me a hug and provide stability. I didn't understand why my father abandoned us at all. I even thought it was because of me… that I wasn't good enough for him as a son, or something like that. That I wasn't important to him. That I wasn't worth staying for…"

Stay with it, my friend.

"OK, Doc."

What was going on inside me was incredibly painful. But I felt that I was in good hands with Dr Seer. He waited a while, to give me time.

After a while he softly asked:

Was it a similar feeling to when your girlfriend left you so suddenly?

"Yes. I think so. Yes, it felt very similar."

I blew my nose and felt a momentary sense of relief.

You see? Your lovesickness over Sarah was closely connected to the pain in your childhood.

"What do you mean?"

Take a closer look at it all. As a child, you were abandoned very suddenly by a person whom you loved. You have not yet overcome this pain. As an adult you were abandoned in a similarly unexpected way by your partner – and the sadness it caused was even more intense. Why? Because your childhood experience of being abandoned merged with the way you perceived the break up, even though the latter took place much later in life.

"Are all these things really so intertwined within me, Doc?"

Quite evidently, yes.

"All these years I've been asking myself why the separation from Sarah hit me as hard as it did. Separating from someone is a painful process, no question. But I had no idea that it could hurt so much!"

Yes. And now you know why.

Dr Seer nodded at me with compassion.

I know that 'Look into your past!' is a very strenuous perspective to work through, Mr Allman. Do you still want to continue?

I did indeed feel as though I'd been put through the wringer, emotionally. Nonetheless, I didn't feel in the slightest inclined to break off the session. I knew that the things we were working through right now were enormously important. And besides, I was already in the thick of this retrospective view of my past.

"Yes, of course."

You are making very good progress!

"Thank you, Doc, for guiding me through all this so patiently."

I am merely accompanying you. The rest you are doing yourself. THE GOLDEN VIEW is your guide. So now let us continue to look further into your past. Please try to understand that you have stored a childhood trauma deep within yourself: the trauma of being abandoned. Now, with the support that you need and the inner strength that you have, you will be able to free yourself from this trauma. By becoming conscious of this experience, you are already changing it as we speak.

Dr Seer indicated that I should stand up.

Please go over to the window and take a few breaths of fresh air!

Feeling a little awkward, I rose from my chair and went to the window. The sun was just beginning to set, and the sky was bathed in orange light. It was a beautiful evening. The air was scented with the fragrance of late summer.

How bizarre that I was only now, somewhere approaching the middle of my life, confronting myself with my childhood pain. I suppose it's a point that we all arrive at, sooner or later. What I had finally understood is that you have to truly allow yourself to go there. Only then is it possible for us to alleviate our negative experiences. These things don't heal by coincidence, nor do they heal without action on our part.

I returned to my chair while the Doc waited patiently. I was certain he was following my thoughts – though goodness knows how he managed it.

Your part involves becoming aware of your emotions and the experiences that caused them. Choosing to face them, and to take a closer look. And that's what we're doing right now.

"Yes."

As a child, you were helpless. As an adult, however, you have various strategies at your disposal to help you deal with hurtful experiences. You are able to take responsibility for the situation. As a child, you had no alternative but to surrender to the hurt – in this case, the pain of being abandoned. As a grown human being you can take responsibility for yourself. You are in charge of designing your life. At some point, your relationship with your previous girlfriend stopped working. Today, you recognized that the separation was actually good for you. This awareness means you can disengage from the pain caused by the loss. And if that has not yet happened, you can do it right now. It's never too late for emotional healing.

"Yes."

In addition, you now have the opportunity and the strength you need to heal your inner child, the one that was hurt in the past.

"How do I do that, Doc?"

By understanding why things happened the way they did and by shouldering personal responsibility now. Doing so will enable you to transform your emotions. You will even be in a position to learn something very valuable and gain new insights. Please try to be receptive towards the following ideas. Life brings with it joy and love, but also pain – that is the nature of being human. No-one is born into a life that is completely free of painful experiences. The decisive question is: How does one deal with it, and what can one learn from it? When we dare to open up to our pain, and consciously and lovingly work through it, then, ultimately, we can only benefit from it.

"I've never seen it that way before."

My friend, life is first and foremost about experience. We all have scars, both physical and emotional ones. It's not a question of erasing pain, or of belittling a painful experience, or of suddenly finding it enjoyable. We all have to undergo our life experiences, and that inevitably brings with it the possibility of being hurt. However, we always have a choice when it comes to dealing with these experiences – we are free to make peace with the hurtful events, to understand them and use them to further our own personal growth. Viewing things from a higher level of consciousness allows us to heal every painful experience and shape the NOW in a new and positive way. Do you understand what I mean?

"I think so."

Dr Seer's endless wisdom impressed me time and time again.

Shall we continue?

"Yes, definitely!"

Good. Let's turn our gaze back to the separation from your girlfriend. I know it may not be easy, but please try to recall how you felt when Sarah left you.

"OK, I'll give it a go."

Feel free to close your eyes. Remember the feeling. Let it come, even if it hurts.

Once again I felt an agonizing lump in my throat and a heavy sort of pressure on my chest. But today's session had already begun to change things within me, and I felt a willingness to face my past.

The Doc spoke with a firm voice.

Take a deep breath, and stay with what you're feeling – remain within yourself. You will now look into your past with full consciousness! Please make yourself comfortable and try to open yourself to my words – allow yourself to be guided by them.

"OK."

Imagine your life as a path – a yellow, sandy path leading through a land-scape. You yourself are 'hovering' above this path on a higher plane. Your elevated self observes Mr Allman as he moves along this path. It collects all his experiences, everything he learns and all that contributes to his personal growth. This higher self sees his entire potential. Now return to your experience of the separation from Sarah and look down on it from this

155

meta-plane. View yourself and your experience from the viewpoint of this second self. Yes, you look at the scene from above, as you already know how to do.

Why did it happen the way it did, back then? Why didn't the relationship last? What does the clear view of your own past show you? Take as much time as you need.

I imagined myself in the scenario Dr Seer described. Images from my past appeared before my inner eye – moments from the relationship I had lost, and the sharp pain I felt when we said goodbye.

"I think my former girlfriend just wasn't happy. Being with me didn't make her happy."

Were you happy, with her?

"I... don't know."

Please stay on the meta-plane and retain the higher perspective it affords. Take a long, considered look, and ask yourself once again: Were you happy in the relationship?

I tried to reconnect with the feeling from back then, but couldn't get a clear sense of how it felt.

"It's hard to tell if I was happy with her."

I understand. If I may be so bold: If you find it so difficult to say for certain, then I suspect you weren't happy.

"Hm. In any case, I never felt I was enough for her."

You spent seven years with Sarah and were considering getting married – and yet you never felt that you were enough for her?

"In the beginning I did, of course. You know how it is: you're in love, and in the first few months of a relationship everything is totally different anyway. But after that, she often gave me the impression that she found me somehow boring. That I was too normal."

Please hold that feeling. Do you see anything else?

"Hm."

Could it be that you created this impression yourself?

"What do you mean?"

Look at it like this: Feelings always originate inside ourselves. Exterior circumstances or the behaviour of others can only function as triggers. It is we alone who unconsciously generate our own feelings – through our perceptions and interpretations of situations and relationships.

"I loved Sarah very much, you know! She was incredibly attractive, and not the sort of woman who would necessarily go for someone like me. You get what I mean, right?

You're really belittling yourself there, aren't you!

I'd never seen it that way before. I'd always thought that assigning yourself to a particular category in terms of attractiveness and the likelihood of acquiring potential partners in life represented a healthy kind of realism. As far as I was concerned, I considered myself to be somewhere near the middle of the range.

It seems that this relationship was not particularly beneficial to your feeling of self-worth.

"That may be so, but that didn't stop part of my world collapsing when she left me. I thought I'd never manage to be with a woman like that ever again."

The kind of woman you feel inferior to?

Dr Seer's remarks became increasingly annoying. I opened my eyes and went to drink some water, but found I couldn't swallow. I guess I was too muddled. The Doc remained focused, as always, and continued to ask questions.

What is love about, Mr Allman?

"It's about not being lonely, about having someone around who is there for you…"

Yes, that's certainly desirable. And do you also happen to know what it's really about?
A loving relationship is about appreciating, respecting and desiring each other, and about helping each other to grow. True love does not have any conditions. It is purely one person trusting in their own value and uniqueness to the other. Love gives both partners strength, which makes them feel empowered and secure.

A loud sigh escaped my lips. I had definitely never experienced this kind of love.

And you are worthy of being truly loved!

Once again I found myself welling up. Dr Seer got up from his chair and came to stand beside me. He laid his hand on my shoulder, like a protective father-figure. After a while he asked, in a whisper:

How do you feel when you are here, during our sessions?

"Well, it can be pretty strenuous at times to be dealing with my own issues so intensely. But I always feel very well taken care of. You are very kind to me, and also very patient."

I faltered. I hadn't even said the most important thing yet.

"I… I've never experienced anything like this before."

What haven't you experienced before?

"The feeling of being so unconditionally accepted by someone else. To be accepted exactly as I am. To know that I can say anything. And that you still like me in spite of it all – that you're even prepared to help me, even though I behave like an idiot sometimes. You… you do like me, don't you?"

Dr Seer was smiling.

I don't only like you, I see you and value you for who you are! You are a priceless and very lovable human being. You are worthy of being loved – exactly as you are!

I had never received a compliment like that before, and it touched me more deeply than I wanted to allow. Awkwardly, I dabbed at the corners of my eyes with the tissue.

"Thanks so much for saying so."

Gently, he moved away and walked back to his chair.

What you are experiencing now is how it feels to be truly accepted for who you are. Keep hold of this feeling and assume the elevated perspective once more. Now please take another look back at your past relationship and the separation experience. Do you see anything else now?

Immediately, I realized that I felt much lighter inside and could breathe more easily. The feeling of inner pressure was nearly gone.

"If I look at it that way, then it wasn't true love at all. At least, not the kind of love that you described. Our relationship didn't have much to do with cherishing one another and 'helping the other to grow'."

Lost in thought, I let my eyes drift towards the window.

"I adored Sarah very much. But in worshipping her, I guess I belittled myself. I kept getting smaller and smaller beside her. I'm sure it's not what she wanted... And, if I'm completely honest, from the very beginning I was afraid of losing her."

Dr Seer looked at me without saying a word.

"Doc, suddenly I see with absolute certainty that it wouldn't have done me any good to stay in that relationship. Even though it hurt like hell when it ended. But then came my contemplative phase, when I started searching... for the meaning of life, or whatever. I may not have gotten very far yet, but who knows: maybe I wouldn't have ended up meeting you if things had turned out differently back then..."

Everything is connected. Much more so than people realize.

"Essentially, it was because of the separation that I asked myself, for the first time, if and how I could change my life. And what I actually want in life..."

You had already started out on the path to finding yourself. Your journey began before you met me and THE GOLDEN VIEW entered your life – you just weren't aware of it. And through learning to look into your past, you are now becoming aware of it. As such, you have actually uncovered something precious behind this painful experience – do you see?

"Yes."

And, incidentally, we encountered one another the very moment you were ready for it. Even that wasn't a coincidence. How do you feel now?

"I feel freer, somehow, and more relieved. Yes, liberated. The pressure on my chest has gone!"

Good. We should take a short break now, as we still have a little more work to do today.

"What else is there to talk about?"

Well, we've looked at the pain that the relationship caused, and have eased the residual feelings by integrating this experience into your consciousness. What we still have to look at is your childhood pain in relation to your father.

"Hm."

Or would you prefer to work through it some other time? It's your decision.

"No, I think we should do it today. Now that we've come this far, I want to see it right the way through."

Wonderful. Please go and stand by the open window for a few more minutes and breathe some fresh air. Allow your thoughts to flow freely, and let yourself relax. I shall leave you alone for a few moments in the meantime.

He winked at me and slipped out the door. I made an effort to breathe slowly and deeply, and returned my gaze to the evening sky, losing myself in the moment. After a while, the Doc suddenly appeared next to me again. I was so lost in thought that I hadn't even noticed him re-enter the room.

You should eat something. It's going to be a long session today.

With a small nod of the head, he held out a plate with a sandwich towards me.

With French cream cheese – just as you like it, am I right?

Somewhat taken by surprise, I took the plate from him. As I did so, I noticed that my stomach was rumbling loudly. I was really hungry.

"Oh, thank you very much. And yes, that is indeed my favourite cheese. But this is hardly necessary…"

Even though his kindness made me feel a little uncomfortable, I could hardly restrain myself from wolfing down the sandwich straight away.

Of course it was necessary!

I settled back into my chair, plate in hand, and savoured my sandwich while listening to the Doc's words.

You've already worked on yourself a great deal today. The past can't be healed in twenty minutes, you know. That's why it's important that you fortify yourself. Physical needs should not be neglected when the mind is so active.

With my mouth full of sandwich, I managed to squeeze out a mumbled: "True!" in response.

161

And it wasn't just your mind that was active – you had a lot going on at an emotional level, too.

He waited, and let me finish my sandwich in peace. When I was done, I put the plate on the small table and let out a contented sigh.

"Thanks, Doc – phew, that feels better!"

I'm glad. Then we can continue.

"I'm ready!"

He looked at me with a searching expression.

Tell me, what is your relationship with your father like today?

"It's… well, I don't have any contact with him. I broke off all contact entirely when I was about twenty years old."

Why did you break off the contact?

"You want the honest answer? Because he's an asshole, and always was! He screwed things up with us back then, plain and simple."

I understand.

My pulse began to race. I felt an extreme kind of rage rise up within me.

"Sorry, but there's no other way to say it. My father made a huge mistake in abandoning us. And he never put it right. He never even tried! I don't think he gave a damn, one way or the other. He got in touch with me when I was about twelve years old, out of some pseudo sense of duty or something. We'd had pretty much zero contact until then. After that, I saw him two or three times a year, but it always felt really superficial, and never really achieved anything. He didn't know me and had never really been interested in me. When I moved out of my mother's house, he came and asked, out of the blue, if I might like to move in with him. I wrote it off as some kind of sick joke! Suddenly playing the caring, considerate father, after all these years! That's when I ended it once and for all, and never contacted him again."

You're still very angry with him, aren't you?

"You bet I am!"

Have you ever told your father how you felt as a child? How much hurt he caused you?

"No, never. How could I? He doesn't even listen properly. He was never really interested to hear what I had to say. I... I'd almost say I hate him for that!"

That I can see.

"I can't imagine it's all that difficult to see, in this particular case."

I could sense the entirety of my anger – all the deep resentment I felt for my father, and the wound in my soul that he inflicted on me when I was a child – I felt all of it activating at the same time inside me.

You're right. But this makes it all the more difficult to uphold your own energy levels while carrying hatred and anger within.

"What do you mean?"

Any negative emotions that we feel about other people primarily harm only ourselves. They drain our energy reserves. And they destroy our inner peace, upset our emotional equilibrium and prevent us from loving ourselves.

"Hm. So what should I do? I wouldn't mind the opportunity to get rid of my anger. But that would require him to apologize to me first. And that's never going to happen."

My friend, I'm now going to tell you another secret – the secret of how we can heal old emotional pain without receiving an apology from the people who have hurt us.

Dr Seer waited for my reaction.

"Well, I can't wait to hear it."

The secret is forgiveness. Look into your past and forgive those who have hurt you!

"Seriously? I don't know... you're saying that I have to forgive my father, even though *he* was the one who behaved like an asshole?"

It's not about doing your father a favour, but about ridding your psyche and your own energy system of the hatred you feel, and freeing yourself from your negative emotions. That's how you will be healed.

"Hm. I'm not so sure I can manage that!"

I think you can. Please come with me!

Dr Seer signalled that I should get up and follow him to the far end of the room, which was completely empty. The white walls and white ceiling made a very clean, almost sterile impression. The term 'blank page' came to mind. The Doc stopped in the middle of the room.

Please come and stand here.

He stood opposite me, about one meter away.

Please take deep breaths, and allow yourself to calm down. Take your time!

"I'll try."

Dr Seer looked at me with a serious expression.

I am now your father.

"Oh, just a second. Let me get my head around the idea first."

Clearly, this exercise wasn't exactly going to be a walk in the park for me. So I gathered all my courage, and tried to concentrate.

"OK. I'm ready."

Dr Seer kept his eyes fixed on me.

I am now your father. Please look me straight in the eyes and tell me what you felt as a child.

I found the whole situation really quite difficult, even though it was only staged. It all felt extraordinarily realistic to me.

Please continue to breathe deeply in and out.

I stopped thinking, and let myself go. All of a sudden, I was that little boy who had been abandoned by his dad and for whom the world no longer made any sense. I let it all flow out:

"I was so frightened – you were gone so suddenly. Mum was crying all the time, and I had no idea what I was supposed to do. I was all alone, with no-one to help me."

My eyes filled with tears. And all at once, with unexpected intensity, I felt the familiar and excruciating pain I knew from my childhood. As if in a daze, I heard Dr Seer's voice at my side, speaking softly to me.

Tell your father what you wanted back then, when you were a child.

He then resumed his previous position, standing opposite me so I could address him face to face.

"I wanted you to at least come and apologize to me. In the beginning, I kept hoping you'd come back to us. But after a while, all I felt was disappointment. I just couldn't understand how you could abandon us like that! I simply couldn't get my head round it…"

All of a sudden, my perception changed and I felt a little dizzy. Perhaps it was all a bit much, and was starting to affect me physically – or my circulation was playing up as a result of all this drama bubbling up inside me, finally seeking release after I'd carried these emotions around for so long. I perceived a soft hissing sound at first, and then I heard the characteristic voice of my father, a voice I had not heard for over twenty years. I couldn't tell if it was real, or imagined. Dr Seer began to address me, speaking in the unmistakable voice of my father:

My son, I know what I did to you, and I now feel more sorry than you'll ever know for how I acted back then. It was very painful for me too, but at the time I felt I had no choice… I knew of no other way to deal with the situation. I made a big mistake, and I should have taken much better care of you. You were only a child, and none of it was your fault – you were merely a victim of it all. I'm deeply, deeply sorry. I know it must be very difficult to believe, but I love you, and have always loved you. I was never able to show my love for you because I was afraid of weakness.
It was all too much… more than I knew how to handle, at the time. I know that I've failed you as a father. And I wish I could somehow put it right.

It was as though time stood still. For what felt like an eternity, my father's words echoed within me. I heard Dr Seer's voice as if from far away.

Are you able to accept what your father has told you?

A strange sense of relief flooded through me. I felt like I was dreaming, and yet at the same time I knew I was just standing there, in this white space – in nothingness, in a kind of vacuum, ready for a new beginning. After a while, a pleasant and peaceful feeling washed over me. How much time had passed? Hours, or minutes? I heard myself answer:

"Yes."

Then please tell him that now.

I felt overwhelmed by what had just happened to me and within me. I tried to find the words.
"I accept that, dad."

Dr Seer gave me a soothing look and gestured for me to take a few deep breaths.

How do you feel?

"Good."

This is what forgiveness feels like.

"Yes."

To forgive does not mean that you endorse the way people have behaved towards you in the past. It only means that you see their behaviour from a place of love and acceptance.
Try to approach the past with understanding and a sense of goodwill, and assume that these people did not want to hurt you. Your father did not want to cause you pain. He was insecure and full of fear, and that is why he was unable to treat you as a loving father would. You don't have to excuse his behaviour. But you can make peace with him.

"Yes, I'd like that."

You'll learn more about looking with love at a later point. You'll discover how to see people with your heart. You'll learn how significantly this perspective can change everything in your life. Come, let's sit down again.

We went back to our chairs. Dr Seer refilled my glass with water, and handed it to me.

So, at the end of what has been a very important day, let's observe the following: There are two poles in the human body that are the root of all feelings and emotions – love and fear. In the past, as a child, fear sprang up inside you: the fear of being abandoned. And, strictly speaking, your parents should have created the opposite pole for you as a means to help you combat this: the love pole. But this wasn't possible. Your father was gone, and your mother was caught up in her own pain. As an adult, you now have the opportunity to look at that fearful situation in your past from a new standpoint: with love. You can infuse it with love, and so heal the past situation.
If you forgive the person who inflicted the pain upon you, you present that person, and especially yourself, with love. This allows you to dissolve your

167

own fear and the negative emotions connected with it. You will become stronger, and freer, and will be open to new experiences. The pattern of fear will relinquish its power over you, and you will attract love into your life. Give yourself an imaginary hug, and thank yourself for handling this difficult experience so well.

Please give yourself a little more time, Mr Allman. Healing the past takes time. You will now find yourself going through a process of transformation. You have invested a lot towards this today. Who knows – perhaps you will actually want to speak to your father one day. You will know when the right moment comes, in any case.

I felt empowered and strong, and yet completely relaxed. And so it was that I felt the sudden impulse to give Dr Seer a hug. I stood up unexpectedly, and hugged him. I think he was moved by it. Like a loving father, he hugged me back.

"Thank you so much, Doc."

Thank you for keeping up so well. Allow everything to settle into place at its own pace, in peace – everything that has happened today. You've made huge progress. Now I suggest you go home. Rest! It's already quite late. Come, I'll accompany you to the door.

"Thank you."

Still a little dazed, and simultaneously very relieved, I followed behind Dr Seer as he moved down the dark corridor. With an acknowledging smile, he opened the door for me and said goodbye. It was dark outside – and the night felt soft and peaceful.

14 Look into your inner sun!

Drawing new strength

Having immersed myself intensively in my past in a way I'd never experienced before, I spent the first few days after our session feeling that there couldn't be many more new insights left to gain. Naturally that wasn't the case – and I still had a long stretch of that much-discussed path ahead of me. But without doubt, a huge burden had been lifted from me. I felt so much lighter, and freer.

This taught me another important lesson taken from THE GOLDEN VIEW: When dealing with issues that make us sad or weigh us down, or problems that we have not been able to solve, the most important thing is to look at them consciously, and to see them for what they are. Turning to face a painful experience can be enough to trigger a process of change within. I can free myself a little from my painful feelings purely by making myself aware of them.

I'm sorry to say that I wasn't in the best of moods as I made my way to see Dr Seer today. I was troubled by the one question that I was unable to answer despite all the breakthroughs I'd made in recent weeks: How to deal with negative issues that I'm powerless to change. The ones that crop up in everyday life all the time and drain my energy, but that I can't alter, no matter how hard I try, because they're outside my sphere of influence.

I arrived at Dr Seer's door, at which very moment the heavens opened and a mighty downpour began. Dr Seer opened the door for me with a cheery expression, as always.

How are you today, Mr Allman? Oh, you seem to have had a lucky escape! he said with a smile, pointing at the sky.

"Hello, Doc."

He could tell straight away that something wasn't quite right with me.

Hello! You don't look all that happy about it, though. Please, come in!

I stepped inside, into the corridor I was now so familiar with. And see there – unbelievably, *'my'* mirror, the one with the white wooden frame, was back and hanging in its original spot. Without hesitating, Dr Seer positioned me in front of it so that I had no choice but to look at my reflection. Just as he had done a few weeks ago when I learned to 'look in the mirror', he came to stand beside me and looked in the mirror with me.

Now, how are you?

"I'm not doing too badly. Can't complain, really."

In his usual way, he allowed his gaze to settle on my reflection, and probed further.

Please take a closer look!

I sensed that pretending that nothing was wrong would get me nowhere, so I tried to adopt a more cooperative attitude. When I looked at myself again in the mirror, I had to concede that my expression did not exactly paint a very relaxed picture.

"OK, I admit it: I'm stressed. But my stress has nothing to do with my being here."

For some reason, I felt slightly uncomfortable about being in a bad mood in the presence of Dr Seer, especially given all that we achieved in our last session. And besides, the cause of my stress seemed far too trivial to be worthy of discussion as part of our session.

Look closely. And don't evaluate. Just observe!

My tension increased even more now that I had pinpointed it. I couldn't hide it – something that wasn't possible around the Doc anyway!

You are free to talk about anything that is preoccupying you, my friend.

"Yes, perhaps we should talk about it."

Dr Seer nodded at me.

We shall address whatever it is that is troubling you in detail in a moment. But first tell me what else you see in your reflection, right now?

"It's… I'm almost embarrassed that I'm so grumpy today. Particularly as you're being such a huge help, and I was so convinced that I was making good progress working my way through the golden perspectives."

Dear Mr Allman, you are aware of your current state, which proves that you have indeed made great progress already! You are able to describe your inner situation to me very well indeed. You were immediately certain that your mood has nothing to do with the fact that you're here. You don't just succumb to the emotion, Mr Allman, you reflect upon it, in every sense of the word.

He raised his eyes, and smiled at me in the mirror.

And that is the key: your awareness.

"But it doesn't feel good. And what's more, I can't shake off my bad mood. I've been feeling this way since yesterday."

So you think that adopting the perspectives of THE GOLDEN VIEW means you always feel good? That it means feeling emotionally invincible?

"Actually, yes. That's true, isn't it? In *your* case, I'm sure that nothing and nobody could adversely affect you."

We are not attempting to become immune to all life's difficulties, obstacles and challenges, but rather to live our lives consciously.
THE GOLDEN VIEW helps you to understand and change everything that you encounter in the world, life in general and your day-to-day experiences. Adopting new perspectives allows you to acquire new positive impulses for the next steps on your path. Yes, and ultimately that will have a positive influence on your feelings.

"I do understand that. And yet there are some things in daily life that are just stressful, however you look at them."

Good. Now please come with me, and we'll take a detailed look at it all!

171

To be honest, I was relieved to finally step away from the mirror. As helpful as this perspective was, I found the process of 'self-diagnosis' very strenuous indeed. We began discussing the matter as we took our seats.

So now, tell me: What is it that you find so stressful?

"Well, to tell you the truth it's actually something so simple and daft that I feel our time is too valuable to be spent discussing it. But I'm hugely irritated! I've had a building site in front of my house since last week. They dug up the road and the pavement, and are redoing absolutely everything. It's non-stop noise, all day long, and it's driving me crazy! And it's supposed to go on for another two months, so I've been told. Two months!"

I understand.

"I presume THE GOLDEN VIEW can't be applied in these sorts of situations, eh?"

Why not?

"Well, because it's not something that can be influenced. I can't do anything about it."

Think back to the 'Look at the situation from above!' technique. You applied that particular perspective when faced with a packed subway carriage, didn't you. Did you have a direct influence on that particular situation?

"No, strictly speaking I guess I didn't."

What effect did looking at things from above have back then?

"Well, I remember that it enabled me to shake off my negative mood a bit, and helped me to perceive the situation differently. I stopped being so annoyed by it all."

The Doc seemed satisfied.

Very good! So the first step is to change your own perception of the situation. This then allows you to change your mental attitude and your emotional reactions to it. Incidentally, you actually influence every single situation that you are a part of, even when you're in a crowded subway. Because if you're calm and relaxed, then you will inevitably have a positive impact on your fellow passengers' mood, even though your influence may not be immediately obvious.

"But there's absolutely nothing I can do about a construction site in front of my house now, is there! Or are you saying I should go upstairs, look down on the builders and hey presto, they'll automatically make less noise?"

Out of nowhere, I felt anger boiling up inside me, and suddenly felt like picking a fight with someone. As always, Dr Seer registered every detail of my shifting emotional state, but remained calm and collected.

What exactly is it about the building site that makes you so angry? There's the noise, and probably the mess that confronts you whenever you look out of your window. But what else?

I sighed a deep, weary sigh. 'It's incredible how even the most trivial things in life can consume so much energy', I thought to myself.

"Oh, I just find it extremely unfair that of all the houses in the street, the building site has to be right in front of *mine*!"

Ah, I see. You feel personally affronted.

"Yes, I suppose I do, in some ways. I have a demanding job, and I need peace and quiet when I get home. As things are at the moment, I have to put up with their crashing and banging until well into the evening, and I even get to listen to it on Saturdays."

He looked at me with a searching expression.

"I seem to recall you saying that everything is connected with everything else, Doc! So that means that, one way or another, this unpleasant situation has *got* to have something to do with me personally."

My dear Mr Allman, that there are higher connections of great significance criss-crossing each human life is definitely true. However, if you take as a personal affront an occurrence in the outside world that does not, in fact, have anything to do with you, then you are creating the problem within yourself. It indicates that there is something going on inside you that demands closer examination. You evidently don't feel that your need for peace and relaxation is being respected when you get home from work. You feel that you are not being 'seen'. This is linked to your sense of self-worth. And that's something we're going to continue working on, one step at a time. Please believe me when I tell you that you are no longer at the beginning! The closer you get to being able to view yourself as valuable and worthy, the less you will jump to the conclusion that you are being personally attacked. So yes, in that sense you could say that everything is connected. Do you see?

Let's spend today focussing on ways to help you better deal with the situation that's draining so much energy – this building site of yours, in front of your house. One of the first ways to solve the problem is to bear the following in mind: You yourself decide how much energy you want to invest. Getting angry about the whole situation actually costs you quite a lot of energy!

I had to let all that sink in before I could respond. I should have known that, as ever, the responsibility for solving my building-site problem would lie with me – something that struck me as an almost preposterous notion as far as 'managing circumstances beyond my control' was concerned. I don't need to mention that the Doc immediately noticed my struggle. He was unable to suppress a characteristic grin.

Mr Allman, I promise you that THE GOLDEN VIEW will provide you with a solution to this problem, too. Let's go back a couple of steps and take a slow-and-steady approach.

"OK."

Now, let's look at it from an entirely matter-of-fact point of view: What we've got here is a situation that you find very stressful and that you are clearly unable to influence through any kind of action on your part. That is

174

to say, there's nothing you could actively do to make this situation more tolerable. Am I right?

"Yes, exactly! I could, of course, try to sue the construction company – or whoever is responsible - because the builders are working way too late into the night. But firstly, assuming that my complaint is even processed, I suspect that it wouldn't be dealt with until long after all the construction work is finished, and secondly, my chances of actually getting anywhere would be very low. Besides which, going through all that would definitely stress me much more than it's worth."

Can you think of anything else you could try?

"No, I can't do anything! I could take it up with the site manager, but that wouldn't help either."

Alright. So, to sum up: We're dealing with a situation that you are unable to change into a more a positive one by means of any actions on your part.

Dr Seer's patience had already lifted my spirits a little. At any rate, I felt that I was able to take his reflections on board more easily, and I sensed my frustration diminishing.

Now for the next question: Is it possible to physically remove yourself from the situation that is tormenting you? Could you live somewhere else for the next two months?

"I'd thought of that too, but I don't think it's an option. The only person who could potentially accommodate me is Andy. I'm sure he'd offer to put me up in a heartbeat – we've been friends forever. He only lives a 10-minute walk from my house. But it wouldn't be such a good idea."

Why not?

"Because, to be honest, staying at his place would be an even bigger inconvenience. As you know, Andy is busy writing his romance novel at the moment. Which, by the way, is going really, really well! Thanks to your advice and THE GOLDEN VIEW, he was able to overcome his writer's block and is now back on track. And that's fantastic! I'm happy for him, absolutely. But one of the things about Andy is that he has a totally different sleep rhythm to me, particularly when he's in one of his writing phases, and so we'd end up disturbing each other a lot. He sometimes writes through the night, has "breakfast" in the afternoon at a café and starts writing again in the evening. And he needs peace and quiet when he's working. I'd have to sneak around the flat being quiet as a mouse. What's more, he likes to invite people round for spontaneous parties at his place. And that can happen any time, even in the middle of the week, which is less than ideal for *my* sleep patterns."

Alright, then. So physically removing yourself from the situation is not a realistic solution for you either. Let's summarize what we know. You're faced with circumstances that are having a negative impact on your mood and nervous system, but you cannot change these circumstances themselves, neither can you escape from them. So what you need is a strategy that will help you to more comfortably bear the situation and to reach a state in which you don't waste so much energy on it any more.

"You sure know how to get right to the heart of the matter, Doc."

Dr Seer grinned at me.

What do you think I'll tell you to do first?

"Hm. Breathe deeply in and out?"

Precisely. Please do so now, and allow any tension you feel to leave your body. We're close to finding the solution.

"May I open the window, please?"

Of course, by all means!

I went to the window and opened it. The air smelled of summer rain, and the room filled with a pleasant coolness. As I walked back to my chair, I was suddenly struck by an idea.

"Doc, if I were to view the situation through your eyes, then I wouldn't be so inconvenienced by it, right? I mean, if I needed an example of a role model through whose eyes I could see things, then it goes without saying that the role model would be you! And I'm sure you wouldn't be in the slightest bit bothered by things like a stupid construction site."

He listened to me, smiling.

What makes you think the situation wouldn't inconvenience me?

"Well, because you'd be above it."

That's actually a very useful thought. It brings us back to the point we mentioned just now: the first step to resolving the problem is to decide how much energy you are willing to let it cost you. You can make the conscious decision to stop feeling angry and to devote as little energy as possible to this issue!

"That's easier said than done."

Your idea to look at the situation through the eyes of a role model – me, in this case – was quite a good one.

He looked at me with a mischievous twinkle in his eye, and we both burst out laughing.

"*In this case*' – nice one, Doc! You're *always* my role model!"

A sudden strong gust of wind pushed the window wide open and swirled through the room. Dr Seer jumped up to close the window, and returned to his seat, laughing.

You're on the right track, my friend! Look at it this way: Rising above unchangeable, stressful situations is possible thanks to the following factors. First of all it's about taking a conscious approach. Recognizing the situation for what it is and the impact it triggers. This you have already done. Second, it's about not letting the circumstances annoy you too much, and not mentally focussing on the unpleasant aspects. Do you accept personal responsibility for this?

"I think so."

177

Good. Third, one must apply a strategy that helps to maintain one's own energy levels and that is not connected to the external stressors. An inner strategy is called for.

He gave me a bold look.

THE GOLDEN VIEW calls it: 'Look into your inner sun!'

"Hm. Sounds kind of esoteric."

I prefer the term 'mysterious'. The 'inner sun' is a secret that only few people make use of. It's a metaphor for the source of power within us, from which we can draw energy by using the power of imagination. But we have to do it actively! In doing so we are able to recharge on a spiritual, psychological and mental level, and thus protect ourselves against external influences.

"That all sounds very plausible. But the construction site won't disappear as a result."

Dr Seer now spoke with a serious tone in his voice.

What have we learned, Mr Allman? If we are unable to change a difficult situation affecting us from the outside, then we strengthen ourselves on the inside! 'Look into your inner sun!' makes this very clear, telling you to use your inner strength whenever your power to influence external factors is limited. Gain new strength from within, instead of giving it away to the outside world!

I was feeling a certain discomfort.

"Is the whole inner-sun approach a bit like a meditation technique, Doc?"

Don't worry. We'll get to that a bit later. Looking into your inner sun is more like taking a little mental journey, to your own inner sun. It doesn't have to be a sun per se; the sun is merely a symbol for your inner source of strength, your visualized place of power. And every one of us has his or her own unique imagined representation of this. Maybe you'd like to visualize your South Sea Island again, and use that as your destination. Do you remember?

"Yes, that was when you taught me to look from within."

And you found that pretty easy! Are you ready? Because congratulations: You are now getting to know the next golden perspective. And I think you're going to like it.

"OK. You've convinced me. Just give me a second!"

I found it incredible how Dr Seer managed to motivate me to open myself up to new perspectives time and time again. The fact that deeper truths were also revealed to me at each step along the way was something I'd almost gotten used to.

I made myself comfortable, and closed my eyes.

Take your time, and take deep breaths.

After about a minute he began to issue instructions.

Observe your breath, and imagine you are slowly entering your mental world. Your eyes are no longer looking outwards, you are looking deep into yourself. Your inner world will show you images.

It was astonishing how fast I could relax and lose myself in the exercise.

Tell yourself: 'I'm now making a journey to my inner sun, my inner source of strength.'

I repeated his words, whispering them softly to myself. About two minutes passed – or was it twenty? – and I concentrated on breathing deeply, and not thinking about anything but my inner source of strength. I found this much more difficult than at the beginning of the exercise. Suddenly, images of my apartment and the construction site began popping up in my imagination. Somewhere in the midst of it all, my mind threw in the stubborn demand that I simply *decide* not to allow the construction site to cost me any more energy. And this thought blocked me.

Dr Seer, as usual, was following my inner processes.

Let go of all those thoughts! Let them pass you by like clouds. Don't put yourself under pressure! All is well, and all is as it should be. The work you are doing right now proves you have already decided to use your energy for yourself, and that you won't waste it on anything that is not beneficial for you. Breathe deeply and prompt yourself once more by reminding yourself: 'I'm now making the journey to my inner sun.'

It was a huge help having the Doc there to catch my initial blocks and guide me through so patiently. I kept my eyes closed and tried to open myself to what was happening within me. After a few moments I relaxed.

Now visualize a door. Allow a door to appear in your imagination!

I began to picture a door, a beautiful, massive wooden door, and after a few moments I could see it quite clearly. But the door was tightly closed, and was obviously not going to be opened all that easily.

Behind this door lies your place of strength, which we will now call your 'inner sun'. It is a place where you feel good and where you can recharge.

Dr Seer went along with what I was imagining.

Now open your door! You can do it! Concentrate on the door, and open it!

Open, sesame! All of a sudden, there I was, inside my inner world of strength. It amazed me all over again to discover how much I could do using my fantasy.

What do you see now? Where are you?

I had to clear my throat in order to answer. I felt very far away from our actual conversation. I could only manage a whisper:

"It... it's the beach again. My South Sea Island!"

Ah! And what does it feel like, being there?

"Oh, it feels wonderful. Warm. I'm lying in the sand, enjoying the sun and recharging."

Please try to experience it with all your senses! What do you hear?

"I hear the ocean. The rhythmic sound of waves in the background."

What do you smell? What do you taste?

"Hm… There's a fresh breeze, and I can smell seaweed, and the ocean. And there's a slightly salty taste in my mouth."

Enjoy it.

It was a delightful feeling to be in that visualization. I screwed my eyes tight shut.

And what does it look like on your South Sea Island?

"I'm on a long, spacious beach with sparkling white sand. Looking around I see turquoise waters in front of me, and a few coconut trees and some hibiscus bushes with big flowers behind me."

Even with my eyes shut, I had to grin.

"Sounds kind of tacky, doesn't it?"

I was certain Dr Seer was also grinning from ear to ear. I couldn't see it, but it felt like he was.

That is your inner sun. And it's not at all tacky – it's wonderful, and loaded with energy!

"And the sun is shining here! If you could only see how tanned I am already, Doc!"

It suits you! Please stay there a little while longer and enjoy the strength it is giving you.

"OK."

I continued to concentrate on my South Sea Island scenario. It relaxed me and gave me strength at the same time. It felt like my batteries were being recharged. After a few minutes I was given further instructions.

Allow this image and the feeling that goes with it to be deeply embedded within you. Say to yourself: 'I now know my inner sun and I can always come back here whenever I need strength in my daily life'.

I whispered the sentence to myself, and for a fraction of a moment it seemed like a farewell. I didn't want to leave this marvellous fantasy world! A short while later I heard Dr Seer speak, more loudly this time.

Are you sure you can always find your way back there in order to recharge?

"Absolutely."

Very good! Then slowly come back, please. Say goodbye to your inner sun, and return to this room.

As I expected, it was not easy to leave that place. I'd never experienced anything like it before – I had no idea that it was possible to dive so deeply into one's imaginary world. When I finally opened my eyes, it took me a few moments before I could focus on the Doc and see him clearly.

He nodded at me encouragingly.

Very well done! Please look into your inner sun regularly. Ideally do so every day. This will give you the energy you need in order to find your balance again. And immutable external circumstances will then no longer have the power to affect you so strongly.

"I'll do that! But can you please explain how it's even possible that one can gather strength from one's imagination?"

It works because you feel good when you create that visualization. The mind doesn't distinguish between real experiences and things that you vividly imagine. When beautiful feelings and positive associations are tied to the mental image, then it will immediately boost your current energy level and your general energy supply. In order for the method to work you need to apply it regularly. You will definitely feel the difference – your nervous system will benefit from it enormously. Find the right moment and the right place in which to apply it – in the evenings, for instance, when it gets quiet. Use this method regularly, and dive in and recharge your batteries!

"I will, I promise! From now on I shall look into my inner sun for at least 30 minutes every day."

Laughing, Dr Seer gave me his hand.

Well, five minutes would also do the trick. Shall we agree on five minutes? You see, it's important that the time and the mental energy involved doesn't seem too much. Otherwise keeping it up becomes too difficult over a longer period of time.

I shook hands with him, promising that I would practise this perspective regularly. The Doc accompanied me down the corridor of mirrors towards the front door.

You can thank the difficult external circumstances for leading you to discover your inner sun!

"You really know how to put a positive spin on everything, don't you!" I said, teasing him.

That is what I'm here for, my friend! Look, good fortune strikes again!

Gesturing in the same way as he had done when I arrived, he pointed towards the sky. The sun had come out, and was shining brightly on my face. How fitting!

"Doc, you're incorrigible! Goodbye!"

Goodbye!

15 Look at yourself with kindness!

Revealing and reversing negative self-judgments

"Tell me, Doc: Why are so many people not in a good place, emotionally? In fact, most people don't seem to be happy at all... how come?"

That is an extremely important question.

Dr Seer looked at me knowingly.

And the answer is both complex and simple, at one and the same time. What do you think the reason is?

"Maybe it's because they haven't found their path?"

That's one way of looking at it, yes. And what does it mean, to have not found one's path?

"Hm... that they're unsure of themselves?"

I actually quite enjoyed it when Dr Seer challenged me to find the answers to my own questions. It made me feel like I was a student at a secret school that taught the truths of life. He gave me a searching look.

What does this insecurity stem from, do you think? What's it about?

"I think many are searching for something without really knowing what it is."

Dr Seer rose from his chair and walked over to the door of the room. It was already late evening. We had taken our seats and started talking as soon as I arrived, and had left the door to the room open. Closing the door as he spoke, Dr Seer continued.

Let us look more closely. For many people, feeling emotionally unwell is the status quo. They perceive it as normal. Sometimes they feel better, sometimes worse, but they would never claim to feel truly 'happy'. Often they believe that the reason for this is that they don't have all the material goods they want, or that they consider themselves unfairly treated by others or by life in general. But the real cause is unresolved pain. People carry within them experiences that have yet to be reviewed, processed and integrated into their consciousness – and that therefore still cause pain and cost energy deep inside. You have experienced this yourself.

As he returned to his chair, he gave me a meaningful look.

Now comes the crucial point: This pain is connected to a pervasive fear of not being important. Most people don't feel valuable, deep on the inside. Their feeling of self-worth is weakened. They feel an inner emptiness. And thus they are lacking in self-confidence. Anyone who feels unworthy is unable to trust in and rely on themselves. In essence, people are unhappy because they don't trust themselves.

"But why? Why don't they trust themselves?"

In most cases, they had an experience at some point in their life that weakened their self-worth and shook their faith in themselves. It need not have been a conscious experience. Frequently such experiences take place in childhood.
They involve experiencing that the love received from caregivers is dependent on how you behave. And so fear was able to enter in, as it were – the fear of not being loved. This led to a pattern of self-judgement whereby the self is evaluated in relation to the amount of love received. Always accompanied by the fear that this love, the emotional life force, could disappear at any time.

As he spoke, Dr Seer took a lighter from his pocket and lit a tall, white candle that stood on the metal table between us. The room took on a special atmosphere.

When a person experiences unconditional love, a vast force becomes active within them, and this gives that person confidence. Unfortunately, few are lucky enough to experience such love during childhood and to go through life carrying it in their hearts. Despite its rarity, this experience is the prerequisite for being able to share love. Parents who themselves did not experience unconditional love when they were younger carry fears within themselves that have never seen the light of day. Likewise, their innermost feeling of self-worth has, to a certain extent, been lost – and has not yet been rediscovered.

So it often happens that these parents, even though they want the best for their child, make their affection dependent on conditions. Consequently, the child's trust in life and in his own creative power is compromised. And the cycle continues until the moment when it is finally interrupted.

A lot of people have always felt weakness, inadequacy and a fear of failing deep down inside, and have found themselves unable to withstand the judgments of others or have felt afraid of being abandoned. Consciously or unconsciously, most people are constantly judging themselves.

I reflected on what he had said, and realized that his words seemed familiar to me. The concept was not entirely new. And yet a new idea slowly began to form: Had we perhaps all come into this world with unlimited self-confidence, and had simply forgotten how to feel it? Of course, the Doc had already read my thoughts. Gently, he leaned forward slightly towards me.

Today I'll tell you another secret, my friend: Every human soul has huge potential in terms of its abilities and possibilities. Each is connected to the great source that is 'unconditional love'. Linked to this is the deep sense of self-confidence and interpersonal love – and the knowledge that we are all connected, and are all of equal worth.

His green eyes flashed, and for a brief moment I was a little taken aback. Every now and then, Dr Seer had something about him that made it seem like he was from another planet. Today this effect was very pronounced. Maybe because it was late at night and the room was poorly lit.

In its original state, the soul knows that it is so, but each individual under-goes experiences that lead them away from this trust in themselves. They experience fear instead of love. Do you remember? We spoke of this before.

"Yes."

The particularly fatal thing about all this is that it takes place in your head, because 'those judgmental other people' don't exist in reality! Your fear of failure and of not being loved shapes the image that you have of yourself. Even when you know that you are capable of doing several things really well, your feeling of self-worth is still not firmly anchored. You don't look at yourself with kindness.

"And so that's why people feel lousy most of the time?"

Do you think that you have control over what happens in your life? Over how you feel and what you experience?

"Yes, I've come to understand that that is the case."

So let us now consider the following: When you don't trust yourself, you make yourself small, and enormously restrict your own possibilities. The unconscious fear of failure, of not being loved or of being abandoned, literally causes your energy to contract and – figuratively speaking – you make yourself smaller.
This directly affects what you feel, how you act, and – following the laws of logic – what you experience... that is to say, what resonances you get. You feel worthless, and often find yourself in situations that reflect this very feeling. And even if you do receive recognition from others, you can hardly accept it, because you don't really believe it to be true.

Suddenly feelings of uneasiness and anger welled up inside me. I had visited Dr Seer many times and had understood and learned so much. And yet, again, I recognized myself in what he was saying. Had I won back so little of my self-confidence? Was I a 'bad student'? With a casual gesture, he interrupted the spinning carousel of my thoughts.

What's irritating you, Mr Allman?

"I... I just feel as though you're talking about me. You think I'm one of those people without any self-confidence, don't you? Who've lost it, and who are basically beyond saving."

I have said no such thing.

187

"I suppose not. Um... sorry."

It's important that we understand what is happening inside you. Let's take a closer look!

"Should I go and stand in front of the mirror?"

Would you like to?

"No, I think it should work without it. I reckon that I've become a bit more practised in the meantime. In, you know, the art of self-reflection, or whatever you call it."

I noticed that Dr Seer was struggling to suppress a smile, and I now found the situation a little strange. I tried to sort through my thoughts, and sat up straight in my chair. The Doc waited.

What happened just now, inside you?

"I... I recognized myself in what you said. I think that I still lack inner self-confidence, a lot of the time."

What exactly is so unpleasant about this realization?

I was mildly astonished to realize that my anger had already vanished, and I was able to look at myself from a distance.

Dr Seer winked at me.

You see! It's quite evident that you're no longer a beginner! You consciously deal with the processes going on inside you. You have already stepped out of your emotions and are able to observe them from afar. Congratulations! You are a very good student, if that's what you want to call it. Please, describe your earlier feeling to me.

"Thanks, Doc. So on the one hand I was annoyed when I thought you were referring to me when you talked about people who are lacking in self-confidence. On the other hand, I have to say that I do still devalue myself a lot of the time, it's true. And then I was angry about the fact that I've been coming to you for weeks and weeks, and still haven't rid myself of this problem."

And now look: You have just devalued yourself again this very moment.

"What do you mean?"

You direct negativity towards yourself and use up a lot of energy, particularly when you reproach yourself or feel angry, as you put it. You cut yourself off from positive experiences, because you doubt yourself, feel guilty and focus on your supposedly weak or negative sides. Through feeling dissatisfied with yourself, you fail to create the space for successful experiences and feelings of happiness and self-confidence to resonate.

"Hm."

If you believe something, either consciously or unconsciously, and give it your attention and energy, then you create reality. Did you know that?

"No, I can't say that I did."

Dr Seer seemed very focused, almost serious. Once again, it seemed extremely important to him that I understand what he was saying.

When you believe that you always fail and that other people might reject you because of your shortcomings, and if you give potency to these beliefs in the form of negative feelings, then you create the corresponding experience. You literally attract failure and dissatisfaction into your life. A fundamental sense of discomfort, sadness and discontent spreads through you.

"Sounds reasonable. But what's the way out? Permanently, I mean..."

He pulled the lighter out of his pocket again and flicked it on. Holding the flame a few inches in front of his face, he looked at me through the flame.

You know the answer!

"Let me guess: there's another golden perspective involved, right?"

189

Now, what kind of perspective might we need, here? Which viewpoint could you adopt to make yourself feel happier and more valuable, and to enable positive experiences to unfold for you?

"Hm. I could just try and see everything in a positive light?"

That would undoubtedly be wonderful – if you truly felt it was so. The solution we are looking for, however, is not about tricking yourself or not taking your own feelings seriously.

"I see. So I have to see myself as genuinely worthy?"

Correct! And you must feel it!

"Alright. But how do I do that?"

By being kind to yourself! The key is to look at yourself with kindness!

Dr Seer seemed to brighten, now that we had arrived at another golden perspective. And I was curious to know more.

"Should I look at myself a bit like how you see me? You're always kind to me!"

That would also be a fairly useful tool to use. But you don't need my point of view for this. Let's completely focus on you.

He winked at me in encouragement.

Today you will look at yourself through your own eyes. And with kindness, too! THE GOLDEN VIEW will help you do it. Let me show you how it works.

"I'm excited."

For a minute he sat silently in front of me.

Do you love yourself?

"Pardon? What a question... I don't know, I've no idea."

It is what lies at the core of this perspective. And, fortunately, it is also its consequence.

"Does that mean I can use this perspective even if I'm still not sure whether I love myself?"

Of course! If you look at yourself with kindness, you will find your way back to self-love! And to self-confidence. And it is for precisely this reason that you will learn this view today.

Quite unexpectedly, I felt emotions rise up inside me. I actually had to fight back tears. Dr Seer seemed unsurprised by my reaction. As he so often did in such situations, he handed me a tissue.

You're closer than you think! Make yourself comfortable. I will now tell you about the perspective that brings back your self-confidence.

I was glad that he gave me time to collect myself. It was unbelievable how many different kinds of emotions I kept experiencing here. With a firm voice he began to explain:

'Look at yourself with kindness!' has three components: self-forgiveness, focusing on your own positive qualities, and building confidence in yourself and your life.
First of all it is about forgiving yourself. You have already seen what a relief and how powerful it is to forgive people who have hurt you in the past.
To sincerely forgive someone is not easy and requires a high degree of willingness to be emotionally open. Self-forgiveness is even more difficult, because we are usually more critical of ourselves than of others.
Try to let go of self-blame, guilt and self-devaluation – and also the supposed mistakes you committed previously. All these punishing feelings will never lead to anything positive unless they are constructively transformed into insights, and thus have their negativity resolved.

What kind of issues could you forgive yourself for?

What have you repeatedly blamed yourself for?

What do you currently consider to be false steps you have taken along the way? Are there any mistakes that still weigh you down – any supposed errors that rob you of energy whenever you think about them?

Do you blame yourself for something?

What comes to mind when you hear these questions?

I was just about to blow my nose. I should have known that things would get down to the nitty-gritty sooner or later.

"Oh, I think of all sorts of things. For example, I blame myself for hardly ever achieving the goals I set myself. And every year on New Year's Eve I make new resolutions and then never actually keep them – things like wanting to lose a couple of pounds, and do regular exercise."

I understand.

Dr Seer stared at me intensely – as he so often did when he was guiding me towards a new realization.

As soon as we stop blaming and punishing ourselves for things in our lives that do not work out as we imagined they would, then we release tremendous power within ourselves. We can use this force to first of all recognize that the situation is as it is. And then we can look deeper and recognize what it is that those things want to show us. Behind every personal blockage there is hidden great potential! This came up before. Do you remember?

"Yes, you told me that a while ago."

When it comes to those unkept resolutions, what might you say to yourself if you were to look at yourself with kindness?

"Hm. Perhaps I'd say that there must be an internal reason for my not yet having managed to exercise and lose weight?"

Quite right! It's not that you haven't managed to do those things yet because you were too stupid, too slow or too inconsistent. It's because there was something in you that complicated things, and made it hard to implement these projects. There was a feeling blocking you – and that feeling needs to be taken seriously. And it seems like there was also a lack of self-confidence at the time.

"That's right. And despair, I think. For years and years, I had this underlying feeling that there's no point working on myself, as it doesn't change anything anyway. Added to which there was the force of habit, too. But... when I think about it, that feeling has changed over the last few weeks. Ever since I started coming to see you."

As you have often experienced in recent weeks, we are ready for change in and of ourselves when we become aware of our emotional states and internal connections – if we look at them, understand them and then treat them with love and compassion. The good news is that on any day, at every hour, and every minute, we can start over. All change is possible in the NOW. The failed attempts of the past mean nothing in the current moment – they are irrelevant.

My friend, without doubt there are quite a few memories in you that you have not yet forgiven yourself for. And in each instance, the following applies: You acted as you did at the time because, subjectively, it felt right or like it was the only way to go. You would act differently today because you are now at a different level of development and consciousness. So it is not about blaming and judging yourself, but about learning from the experience.

"Yes."

Look at it this way: Life is learning. We all need to learn to forgive ourselves, for life also means development. There is no one on Earth who has never committed an 'error' – and in any case, what constitutes a mistake is always a question of perspective. The wonderful thing is that by assuming a new perspective, we can recognize why we might deem something we did or didn't do to have been a mistake in retrospect. And this insight can be very valuable.

"But what if you hurt other people? How can you forgive yourself for something like that? How do you draw something valuable from that?"

Look at yourself and your behaviour with kindness! Try to understand why you acted the way you did. What was your intention back then? How did you feel at the time?

He smiled and nodded at me.

You don't have to answer now. Let it sink in and the answers will come.

This guidance reassured me a little. There was so much starting to churn up inside me that I could never have put it all into words.

Your thoughts are revolving around the idea that you were not always kind to others. You are thinking of a specific person that you have hurt on an emotional level, am I right?

"Yes."

How did it come about that you hurt this person? Did you want to hurt them?

"No, absolutely not! But sadly I suspect that my actions were probably taken that way."

If that is so, then please acknowledge that it was not your intention to hurt this person! Tell that to the person, in your mind. Explain to them why you acted as you did. And furthermore, recognize that it was the right way for you. You felt the way you did, and therefore it seemed right at the time.
It's possible that you also regretted your behaviour, but there was definitely some reason that made you act the way you did. It seems that you were also afraid. You felt helpless. Perhaps overwhelmed. Whatever the situation was, at that time it was your way of dealing with things. Recognize this, and accept it! Be compassionate towards yourself!

"Hm."

Obviously you would behave differently today. So now let's find out: What would you do differently now, and why? What can you learn from this? Please look closely! Because this is how you hone your awareness! Perhaps there is an important realization waiting for you within!

"Well... I..."

As much as I tried, I found myself unable to string a clear sentence together.

You don't have to respond. Allow it to work in you. A useful method is to write a letter to the relevant person. You don't have to post it. As we discussed, writing has a cleansing effect in and of itself.

Dr Seer slowly rose, stepped closer and then crouched down beside me, right next to my chair. With a gentle gesture he took my right hand and placed it on my chest.

Please take deep breaths, and close your eyes!

I continued to follow his instructions, and suddenly felt dizzy. Old memories flew through my mind in a confused jumble. Various events that had been seared into my memory were now presenting me with a dramatic slideshow of all my previous mistakes.

Take a deep breath. And smile as you do so. Please smile at your inner self! Show some sympathy for yourself!

I now heard his voice as if from a distance.

You have given your best at all times, my dear Mr Allman. You are allowed to make mistakes and to learn from them. Even if in hindsight you see your own behaviour as morally unsound and inexcusable in your eyes, you can still ultimately consider it a valuable experience. When you let go of your anger and look at it from a higher level of consciousness, you may even find that this 'grave' error is what helps you to take a big step forward in your growth. Smile at yourself, and be compassionate. Forgive yourself, learn from it, and allow yourself to open up more!

Several minutes passed, during which I just sat there and let it happen. Dr Seer's words flowed through me. Then I had to sigh, a deep and strong sigh. I felt relief, and I realized that what was now happening within me felt good. I uttered a timid "thank you, Doc", and gradually heard his voice sound from what seemed a normal distance. I opened my eyes. The Doc was sitting opposite me, nodding at me.

I thank you! Give yourself a little more time. I'll now let you have a few minutes alone. And when you're ready, then follow me!

"So, we're headed back to that mirror after all, are we?"

As I said: you're getting good at this.

He laughed, and disappeared through the door.

A short time later I did indeed find myself once more in the corridor of mirrors in front of 'my' mirror, the one with the white wooden frame. There wasn't much light. As he had done before, Dr Seer moved me into position and stood beside me.

Now, this next step is not about recognizing what you feel and what's going on inside you.

"It's not? Why the mirror, then?"

You are being very attentive – that's excellent! We use the 'Look in the mirror!' perspective to attain self-knowledge. But I'm interested in something else right now: self-love. This exercise is about the attitude you apply when looking at yourself in the mirror. Look with kindness!

And as I looked at him dumbfounded, he added:

Don't worry, I don't expect you to force yourself to pull some kind of saintly expression. But a smile wouldn't hurt. Here is what I would like you to do: I want you to pay yourself compliments. To tell yourself what is likable and admirable about yourself. What it is that you like about yourself.

"Blimey, Doc... I don't know if I can do that. Besides, I can't really think of anything."

We both looked at my reflection. He gave me a wink of encouragement.

I can well imagine. After all, you're only just beginning to learn how to look at yourself with kindness.

"There's not really anything that I find particularly great about me, to be honest."

Hold on there, my friend! You're not getting off that easily! And, incidentally, self-pity doesn't really go hand-in-hand with self-love.

"Well, OK. I'm just not used to this kind of thing... what you're asking of me isn't easy."

I know, I believe you. Wait, I'll turn up the light, so you can more easily see your positive qualities!

He flicked a light switch at the end of the corridor as he spoke, and appeared beside me again in a matter of seconds. I have to say that the bright lights didn't necessarily make the experience any more pleasant for me, though.

Is there really nothing that you are even a little bit proud of?

I suddenly found myself thinking about that moment a few weeks ago – or was it even months? – when I found myself standing in front of this mirror for the very first time. How insecure and sad I had felt back then, how chaotic things had seemed at the time, and how little I had believed in myself. My feeling was so fundamentally different now – even if I was still having difficulty with this exercise.

"Yes, Doc! I... I *have* changed – for the better, I mean – ever since I've been coming to see you. I've got way more self-confidence than I did at the beginning. I've learned a lot."

You see! And you have yourself to thank for it! It is you who has set out on this path! And you have committed yourself to it very admirably indeed... But please, continue. Pay yourself compliments! What have you gained of late? How have you grown?

"Well, I've learned a fair amount of new perspectives... how to see things from the outside, from above, with the eyes of a tiger. I've learned how to make decisions, how to deal with explosive volatile bosses and get a pay rise... how to look a pretty lady in the eyes... how to travel into my inner sun and discover what real relaxation is for me... how to free myself from negative emotions... I've forgiven my father, to a certain extent... and freed myself from the painful experience connected with my last relationship..."

Patiently, Dr Seer listened to me speak.

"... and most importantly, I've come closer to myself. Yes, I reckon that's the way to put it... I believe in myself more. I feel it, too. I've no idea why I had such strange thoughts earlier – thinking that I was a hopeless case, what with my lack of self-confidence."

These notions appeared, and therefore they were clearly important. They only wanted to be seen. With kindness.

"Yes."

He turned away from my reflection, and towards me.

Let me tell you something: The strongest messages you can give yourself are 'I AM' messages. They create a huge space within which positive qualities that you recognize in yourself and that you want to reinforce can resonate. Any sentence beginning with 'I am' and ending in a word that evokes positive associations, be it sincerely spoken or thought, has a strong impact on your self-confidence – and how you steer your life in the direction you want. Did you know that?

"No, not as such."

It's something you've experienced unconsciously many times. 'I am' messages can have a strengthening or weakening effect. You alone decide how you want to look at yourself! Now, please formulate three positive 'I am' sentences. Take your time.

He stepped back and stood a little way behind me, so that I could still see him in the mirror but felt I was on my own. I concentrated, tried to smile at myself in the mirror, and took a deep breath.

"I am... brave. I am... confident. I... am... lovable."

Dr Seer quietly moved back to stand at my side.

Well done!

He handed me a sheet of paper on which were written sentences in an even hand – produced in an instant from who knows where.

Please read these sentences. Read them to yourself. And feel them.

Gently, he disappeared into the background. I looked at the list and I noticed that my heart was pounding. My hands shook slightly. After clearing my throat, I began to read aloud:

"Even though my life is often not as I wish it to be, I am worthy.

I believe in myself and my abilities.

I always value myself.

I take care of myself.

I love myself – unconditionally."

As if in slow motion, my hand holding the note slowly fell to my side. I stood, connected with my reflection. I was immediately overcome with a strong sense of wellbeing, so much so that I had to downright grin at myself. And the man in the mirror actually smiled back. So I stayed there for a while.

I am proud of you!

Softly, the Doc came to join me and handed me a glass of water.

Drink – I'm sure you're thirsty.

I gratefully took the glass and gave him back the piece of paper. I drank the glass of water in one go.

"Thank you, Doc."

How do you feel?

"Wonderful. I... I'm happy. Yes, that's the best way to describe it. I just feel kind of happy."

Dr Seer winked at me.

And there is plenty more where that came from. If you look at yourself with kindness, see the positive within you and trust yourself, then your potential will develop more and more. You will carry on down your path, and life will be your best friend! It is important that you give yourself time. Some things just need time until they fall into place the way you want them to.

"Yes."

Please try to integrate this way of seeing into your life and, in particular, how you live it on a daily basis. Whenever you find yourself facing a situation in which you tend to make yourself small, devalue or even blame yourself, look at yourself with kindness! Enter into your deepest inner self-confidence! You don't have to be perfect: you are on your journey, and you will learn as you go.

"I'll do that. Thank you. I understand."

I can see that you understand, and that pleases me greatly. Now follow me!

Dr Seer led me along the lit corridor to the way out. When we arrived at the front door, he gave me the piece of paper back.

Please take this with you, and read it whenever you feel like it.

"Oh, thank you! Tell me, Doc – did you write this note especially for me?"

Smiling, he shook my hand.

Who else would I write it for? It's all about YOU.

"Yes. But it would help lots of other people too, I'm sure."

That it will. You'll see! Goodbye. And good night!

"Good night, Doc!"

16 Look into the distance!

Dealing with emotional crises

It was becoming increasingly clear that looking at myself with kindness was the key to greater contentment – perhaps even true happiness – in life. I practised applying this golden perspective many times in the days following my meeting with Dr Seer. Our last session made me realize that I had been selling myself short for decades – at work, in my relationships, in terms of my skills, and in terms of the range of options I believed were open to me. *"If we believe something consciously or unconsciously and give it our attention and energy, then we create reality"*, the Doc had said. This phrase kept repeating itself in my mind. Did I in fact have much more influence on my life than I dared to assume? A joyful feeling arose within me, and gave me new strength – and yes, even a new sense of self-confidence.

It was Saturday afternoon, and I was glad that Dr Seer had offered me the chance to visit him today. I didn't feel like doing any of the things I'd typically spend my weekend doing, like shopping, or sitting around in a crowded café. OK, so I'd just stopped by my favourite café – but only in the hope of bumping into the attractive woman, who I found myself thinking about more and more of late. Emily was her name, as I had found out in passing one time. Had I seen her today, I would even have spoken to her. But she wasn't there, so I had a quick espresso and headed out again, with plenty of time to stroll over to the Doc's house via a detour through the park. Just as I reached the park, however, a torrential rainstorm broke, seemingly out of nowhere. And with that, in a matter of seconds, the quality of my day took a turn for the worse.

To my great annoyance, a strong gust of wind blew my umbrella inside out, and as I wrestled with it, the thing fell apart in my hands. I gave up and discarded it in the next bin. I battled on through the developing storm, getting soaked to the skin. I pulled my jacket up over my head, and tried not to lose my temper. In my mind I heard Dr Seer's voice, telling me to take a step back and not give in to negative emotions. In all honesty, I couldn't do it. And as if that wasn't enough, about halfway along the road I suddenly spotted my ex-girlfriend with her new partner! They were headed straight towards me. It was definitely still the same guy – the one she had left me for. They were cuddled together under a colourful umbrella, and were obviously enjoying the unpredictable autumn weather. They were laughing, and seemed to be deeply in love. Thankfully they didn't see me, because I managed to slip behind a tree just in time. I hadn't seen Sarah in nearly four years, and now here she was. She looked exactly the same – if anything, I found her even more beautiful.

And the sad truth is that it took all of about ten milliseconds for my new-found self-confidence to evaporate. My stomach clenched, and I started trembling. What with all the excitement, I'd completely forgotten about my jacket, which had slipped back down, exposing my head and shoulders. I was now completely soaked through. My hair was plastered to my head, and water ran down my nose. I stood there feeling like a drowned rat, gazing back at love's young dream.

An arrow had pierced me right through the heart, and the pain was incredible. I tried to collect myself, and to take deep breaths, but it didn't work. My knees were trembling. 'I'm such a wimp!' I thought to myself. '*I am*' – the most powerful message you can give yourself, according to the Doc. 'I'm – yes, I'm a wimp! A total loser!' Who said I'd broken free from the pain of lost love? I'd done nothing of the sort!

The sky was completely overcast, filled with dark, ominous-looking clouds. Lightning flashed and thunder growled... just the right setting for my current mood. Somewhat dazed and feeling trapped in my emotional pain, I pulled myself together and started to walk in the direction of Dr Seer's house. At that point, the only thing keeping me going was the thought that I was on my way to see him.

I arrived at his house wet through. Just as I was about to ring the bell, he opened the door. Wordlessly, he held out a thick, white towel, which I draped over my head and shoulders. I stood at the front door, unsure of what to do next.

Good afternoon, Mr Allman.

He gently ushered me through the door and into the house. He had clearly already picked up on my mood. Presumably he knew how I was feeling even before my arrival. He smiled at me, and placed his hand on my shoulder.

You look like a ghost!

"Sounds about right. It's pretty much how I feel."

I rubbed at my nose with the corner of the towel. I cleared my throat in an attempt to get rid of the lump I felt there, but to no avail. Dr Seer watched me with kindness in his eyes.

It's not been an easy day today, is it?

"You can say that again!"

It was pitch dark because of the storm, so he flicked the light on and guided me further down the passageway in the usual direction towards our room, where the light was on. The white candle on the table was already lit.

I have laid out something dry for you to put on.

He pointed to "my" red armchair, over the arm of which lay a dark blue tracksuit made of some sort of soft material.

Change your clothes while I go and make you a cup of tea.

All this care and attention made me feel uncomfortable again.

"That's really not necessary, Doc. I can manage..."

The Doc smiled in his typical fashion.

I have no doubt that you can manage. But if you accept my help, things might be a little easier.

"I suppose so. Well then... OK. You're right, of course. Thank you."

His infinite patience is something I find hard to put into words. How did Dr Seer manage to always be so kind, balanced, and present, and to always demonstrate such great wisdom? He understood just about everything, and seemed to tolerate every emotion, every human weakness, and could handle the most banal problem or complex issue. It felt like he knew everything, could answer every question, and had limitless energy when it came to helping me with issues I'm struggling with.

I towelled my hair dry, got out of my wet clothes, hung them over the radiator and put on the blue tracksuit. To my surprise, it fit like a glove and felt very comfortable. As I sank into my chair, the Doc returned with a steaming cup of tea, which he placed on the metal table in front of me.

Drink that, it will do you good.

I took the cup and inhaled the scent of the tea. Dr Seer had now taken his place in his chair, and was watching me with a calm expression.

What happened? Tell me about it.

"Oh… today's just not my day, I guess. Basically, it's been a totally crappy day…"

Not an easy day, as I suspected. And the storm isn't the only thing that has spoiled your mood, am I right?

I'd never tasted tea quite like this before. I took a sip, and sighed deeply.

"Doc, I've just seen Sarah. You know, my ex-girlfriend. And she was with… with her boyfriend, or husband, or whatever."

I see.

"Why does stuff like this have to happen to me? Especially now, just when things were starting to look up."

A few seconds passed.

Seeing Sarah again really affected you, didn't it.

"I'll say! It was awful! I feel really crap, to be honest."

I felt myself growing angry. And I was torn between wanting to talk it out on the one hand, and stonewall him with a kind of stubborn indifference on the other – admittedly as an expression of the incredible pain I was in.

"I won't be able to think about anything else for days now, I just know it. I know how I tick! Situations like this always knock me for six. There's absolutely nothing anyone can do. It'll probably take weeks... or even months..."

Dr Seer watched me in silence. I found it a little unsettling.

"Doc, I know you always have my best interests at heart, but please: not another new perspective. Not today, OK? It won't help. I'm simply in pain, and it hurts like hell. I'm unlucky in love, that's all. It's just the way it is."

I felt miserable, and couldn't look Dr Seer in the eye. It was as though I'd lost all courage. I stared at my feet. The situation in the park kept flashing through my mind. Sarah's face, and how radiant she looked, walking along beside that guy... What did he have that I didn't? Why had life forced me to be alone for so long? Didn't I deserve to be happy?
Dr Seer interrupted my thoughts by standing up and walking to the back of the room.

Please make sure you're sitting comfortably. And take deep breaths.

He lingered at the back of the room for a moment, looking out of the window.

I think it's good that you allow your emotional processes to take place. It's not easy, especially where love is concerned.

"Hm. I don't think I have choice in the matter."

The lump in my throat had become unbearable, and I had to fight the feeling that I was about to run out of air. I tried to pull myself together.

206

"I thought I'd gotten past the pain. But I was wrong – I'm nowhere near over it."

Without saying a word, he walked back over to his chair and sat down again.

I understand you.

He needn't have said so, as there was so much understanding and compassion in his eyes that it almost moved me to tears. And I felt the desire to open up, and to engage in the conversation. We looked at each other for a while.

Take your time. We've all the time in the world, as always. As you know.

"Yes."

What's happening inside you right now? What are you thinking and feeling? Let's take a detailed look!

"OK, so... what can I say... on the whole, I've felt better and better over the last few weeks, as you know. I was feeling stronger, more optimistic. And... well, that experience in the park just now has somehow ruined everything; it's like my self-confidence has been shattered. Rarely have I felt so small! It was like I was going to pass out, or something. Not particularly manly, right? But I can tell you, can't I."

Of course.

"Why did this encounter knock me so completely sideways, Doc? I saw Sarah with her new bloke, and it hurt so much that I wanted nothing more than to sink into the ground! It felt exactly the same when I saw her four years ago. I feel just as crappy now as I did then. It seems that my feelings haven't changed that much after all. Maybe I'm actually still in love with this woman... I don't know. I don't know anything right now..."

Dr Seer listened to me, nodding his head as I spoke. I felt my throat close up again, as if it was being squeezed shut.

What else is there? What are you feeling at this very moment?

"I... I feel afraid, to tell you the truth."

What are you afraid of?

"I'm afraid that I'll fall into a black hole... I feel totally thrown. You see, when I accidentally bumped into Sarah about a year after we broke up, I fell into a really depressive phase. I couldn't think about anything else for weeks afterwards. I barely slept, and drank way too much. Oh, and I smoked like a chimney..."

Your thoughts and feelings at the time completely revolved around this experience for weeks and weeks.

"I couldn't break the cycle! Sarah was all I could think about. I kept wondering what I could have done better, what might have encouraged her to stay. I blamed myself incessantly. All the pain came back, and it was even more intense than at the time of our separation! I felt completely alone and abandoned – so much so that I became convinced that I was never going to be happy ever again. That I'd never find a woman who loved me, anyway. I lost all interest in things around me, and lacked the energy to do anything at all. Everything suddenly seemed meaningless. And all because I'd seen my ex-girlfriend again. Just like I did today..."

And now you're worried that it might turn out the same way this time, too?

"... yes, and I'm worried that what happened today will ruin everything that you've helped me to change about myself. I don't want it to set me right back to square one."

How did you find your way out of this phase at the time?

"Actually, I didn't. At some point, daily life just kind of reasserted itself again."

I looked out of the window. It was still absolutely pouring down outside. It looked as though it would keep going all day today.

How do you feel right now?

"Pretty tense."

A little awkwardly, I picked up my cup and took a sip.

"Doc, do you think I'm still in love with Sarah? And that that's why it still hurts so damned much when I see her – even now, five years after we parted ways?"

He looked at me with a searching expression.

Does what you are feeling right now feel like love?

This question stopped me in my tracks. I tried, as best I could, to connect with my feelings.

"I... don't really know. I feel weak. But that's not love, is it? It feels more like fear. And... well, if love and fear are polar opposites, as you once told me, then it shouldn't be possible to feel both at the same time, right?"

The Doc listened attentively to what I was saying, but didn't answer my question. Instead, he stood up, went over to the window and opened it a little. At that very moment, a strong gust of wind blew into the room and extinguished the flame of the white candle. As if he had anticipated the candle going out, he immediately reappeared at the table, relit the candle and settled back in his chair with a straight face. Something had changed, somehow – though I couldn't for the life of me say what it was. I noticed the shift because I was suddenly able to breathe more deeply and found myself feeling calmer inside. In a firm voice, Dr Seer began to explain:

Let's take a closer look. The feeling of love and the longing for love should not be confused. Whenever old feelings flare up that relate to something we've actually already worked through, it doesn't mean that our processing efforts were useless or unsuccessful. It's more of a reminder as well as an impulse encouraging us to make a new start in this particular area of our lives – provided we are willing to accept the impulse.

"Hm."

Try looking at it like this: Today's encounter may have shown you, in no uncertain terms, just how much you yearn for a fulfilling relationship."

"But why is it still so painful? Why does it feel just as bad as it did before? We worked through all this before, when we talked about looking into my past and all that stuff."

It's not about becoming immune to all emotions. You don't have to detach yourself from the impulse to react emotionally, as it's a completely natural part of being human. Our feelings and emotions are an essential aspect of our experiences! They are also there to guide us. The aim is to learn new ways of dealing with painful emotions that stop us moving forward. We can view these emotions as signals that reveal truths about our inner state – and by recognizing what it is that needs to be identified, we can resolve any associated pain. Ultimately, this approach allows us to feel more clearly the true emotions hidden in our hearts and the desires we carry in our souls.
By working through the pain you felt from your previous relationship, you have created emotional space within yourself. As a result, upon being directly confronted with the situation all over again, any remaining hurt can now show itself immediately. The memory of the pain, or any residual hurt, no longer tunnels its way into your subconscious, but is instead experienced there and then. These emotions are not a sign that you haven't processed things, however: they signal that your feelings are undergoing a process of transformation. This process may be unpleasant, at first, but it can ultimately lead to important personal growth. It can help you to experience a new quality within yourself – an innate desire for love.

"Hm. I hadn't really considered that aspect. To me, it felt more like a defeat... like I'd failed, because my emotions had completely overwhelmed me."

Encouragingly, he gave me a wink.

Here's the key to it all: You don't have to let the pain you are feeling right now drag you down for weeks on end and rob you of all your energy any-

more. There are much quicker ways to process your experiences. You can apply different strategies, and take a mindful approach that allows you to draw valuable conclusions. You are already in possession of the required level of awareness to do so.

I felt myself relax a little. The mental pictures of the encounter in the park still kept whizzing through my head, over and over. But the panicky feeling that made me think I was headed for an emotional breakdown gradually subsided. Dr Seer read my thoughts, as usual.

Please bear in mind that you have done so much work on yourself that you are now in a position to decide for yourself. You alone must choose whether to connect this current experience to the old sensation of pain and sadness, and to once again enter a "depressive phase", as you called it.
You can fixate on the alleged problem, keep propagating your own personal drama, and go round and round in circles, mentally and emotionally. All the while anxiously anticipating the worst, of course.
Or you can choose to take personal responsibility, and decide to free yourself from all the drama by adopting a different perspective.

He smiled at me.

And this will allow you to find immediate relief, generate new strength and open yourself to new experiences. Would you like to try it?

"Is there a golden perspective that will help me with this as well, Doc?"

He went to the window, which was still slightly open, and closed it.

What do you think?

"It sure sounds like it."

Come with me! This aspect of THE GOLDEN VIEW is going to take us higher!

He gestured for me to follow him. Purposefully, Dr Seer headed down the corridor of mirrors and then turned right into a passageway that I had never noticed before, let alone explored. I trotted after him. The situation struck me as a little odd, as I had no idea where he was taking me.

"Doc, I'm not wearing any shoes!"

You don't need shoes for this! You can change your perspective in your socks!

We turned down yet another corridor that led to a white door. When Dr Seer opened it, we found ourselves stood right in front of a spiral staircase leading upwards. The light seemed much brighter, here. 'What a labyrinth this place is', I thought to myself. I couldn't really picture the floor plan of the house any more.

Don't worry, we're nearly there. Please, after you!

He let me go first. I started climbing the narrow staircase, following the spiralling steps up and up. I wasn't in the best physical shape, but I kept telling myself that there was bound to be a good reason for all this effort. We climbed at least a hundred steps.
I could hardly believe my eyes when we reached the top. I found myself on a beautiful, vast roof terrace paved with lightly coloured stone. To my amazement, the rain had stopped. The sun had come out, and it was surprisingly warm. The ground was dry already.

"Wow! This is not what I expected!"

You see! If we expect nothing, we are able to be pleasantly surprised. Why? Because it means we are open. Open your eyes, and open yourself to new experiences!

As he spoke, Dr Seer made an expansive gesture that seemed to embrace all that lay before us. The view from up here was incredibly impressive.

What might be the name of the golden perspective that I'm going to show you here today?

"Well, looking around me here, I'd have to say something like 'Look to the horizon', perhaps?"

Chuckling, he nodded.

Very good, my friend! You're very close. This perspective is called: 'Look into the distance!'.

"Sounds good!"

Follow me!

Full of enthusiasm, he led me into the middle of the spacious terrace.

Please take a deep breath, and let the air and the unobstructed view work their magic. I brought you here to familiarise you with the perspective that will help you to break free of acute emotional drama.
This view symbolically represents the very strategy we need to adopt when we find ourselves going round and round in circles where a particular problem is concerned – when we find ourselves stuck, mentally and emotionally, or are completely fixated on something and can't break free. Lift your gaze, and look into the distance! Spread your arms wide, expand your chest, take a deep breath, and as you breathe out, allow the heaviness in your heart to fall away.

I breathed in the cool air, squinting in the light of the afternoon sun, which lay low in the sky. With eyes half closed, I looked out over the city and the green landscape in the distance. I imagined that I was standing in some sort of observation tower from which I could see the whole world.

Free yourself of today's drama in the park! Look into the distance! And recognize that the emotion you're feeling at the moment is but a small part of the huge emotional spectrum you have at your disposal!
Please remember that the aim is not to suppress your current emotion, but to accept it as part of an overall process that is enriching and that is helping you to see your way more clearly.

I looked into the distance and took in what Dr Seer was saying. He was stood about two meters away from me, and spoke with a flowing voice that was a little louder than usual, given how windy it was up here.

With each passing minute, I felt better and better. My tension fell away. I thought back to the encounter in the park, and how much it had thrown me off balance. It had hurt like hell. But did I really want to imbue this experience with so much importance that it had the power to pull me down so far and make me feel so small?

When the moment was right, the Doc carried on.

You alone decide whether to link what you are currently experiencing with the pain and sadness you felt in the past, or whether to deal with it differently this time by observing yourself and your emotions, and by detaching yourself from the perceived problem a little.

"Yes, I understand."

Broaden your thoughts, and open yourself up to life! Fill yourself with hope, and trust that life will help you. Be open to new possibilities and impulses, and allow your experiences to guide you to your true feelings and desires.

I let my gaze drift off into the distance. A flock of birds appeared in the sky, perhaps already heading south. 'They'll be back next year,' I thought. 'And many things will be different then'. 'Look into the distance' – did this also apply to time?

Time heals all wounds, of course. But you don't have to wait for time to pass. Once you free yourself a little from your prevailing emotion and widen your perspective, symbolically speaking, then you're already undergoing the healing process.

Dr Seer stepped closer, and for a while we simply stood there in silence, gazing towards the horizon. A kind of longing that I had never felt before gently arose in me. Yes, it had to be longing. But for what?

Gently, he placed his hand on my shoulder.

Life is on your side, my friend.

I couldn't answer him, because I felt so moved and caught up in the moment. The wind had picked up, and I felt like I was being carried – by the air, by Dr Seer's words, and by the new sense of confidence and hope that arose within me. In clear, distinct and yet whispered tones, I heard him speak again.

Whenever we feel longing, our hope is awakened. It is the longing for love. And the hope of finding it.

I closed my eyes and felt the wind on my face. For a moment, I imagined I was standing at the bow of a sailing boat in the middle of the ocean. Did life still hold some promise for me? Would even I someday be able to say of myself: I'm happy. Even happy in love?

"Thank you, Doc."

You're welcome. Whenever you experience something that affects you so much emotionally that it robs you of your power, look into the distance! You don't need a rooftop terrace. All you need is you.

I opened my eyes. Dr Seer winked at me.

And by the way: Wisdom comes from what we do.

Quietly, he walked back to the stairs, leaving me alone. I knew I should linger here a while longer.

And as I gazed once more into the distance, I realized the following truth:

> 'Life becomes full of possibilities
> when we open ourselves
> and find the courage
> to turn our past experiences,
> however painful they happened to be,
> into valuable ones...'

17 Look upon what's to come with joy!

Influencing the future positively

A few days had passed and I was in a much better place, emotionally. I hadn't fallen into a hole after all; looking into the distance had indeed saved me from that fate. At the end of the day, I had Dr Seer to thank for all the progress I had made. But it was practising the golden perspectives I'd learned that was the crucial factor. How had the Doc put it? 'Wisdom comes from what we do.'

Today I had some good news to report. I'd finally overcome my shyness and found the courage to speak to Emily, the woman in the café – this time without immediately running off after proffering an embarrassed 'Good morning'. Granted, I didn't exactly find it easy to carry on making small talk with her. Despite the developments of recent weeks, and my growing consciousness, as the Doc called it, I still felt quite overwhelmed. But nonetheless, I managed to get her phone number, and had even arranged to meet her next Friday. I went to see Dr Seer hoping he could help me prepare for the date. Having come this far, the last thing I wanted was to fail miserably. The truth was, I still didn't feel particularly comfortable with the idea of flirting.

The front door was open when I arrived. Dr Seer, however, was nowhere to be seen. It was an odd situation, and I wasn't sure if I should go on in or wait outside. I was so familiar with the entrance area and could find my way to our room without any problems... so what to do?
I rang the bell a few times, and called his name. When he didn't appear or even respond, I stepped inside and stood in the corridor. It was around noon, and milky-white rays of light streamed in through the high windows.

"Doc?"

There was no trace of Dr Seer. What could this mean? It made me feel a little uneasy, entering the house uninvited. Hesitantly, I proceeded down the corridor, following the route we normally took. The door to our room stood ajar. I knocked, and gently pushed it open.

Come on in, my friend!

His voice simply added to my confusion, as I couldn't see the Doc anywhere.

"Where... where are you?"

Was I mistaken? As I spontaneously turned, he suddenly appeared right behind me. I don't think I've ever been so startled in my life. How on earth did I not hear him cross the hall? How could his voice have come from *within* the room if he had been following behind me? Had the prospect of my forthcoming date left me so bewildered that I'd started imagining things? Perhaps the idea of meeting up with an attractive woman again after what felt like a hundred years of solitude, and feeling sad, was messing with my senses? Or was it this peculiar house, in which so much seemed somehow different? Was everything I experienced here with Dr Seer nothing more than a dream? No doubt about it, he was certainly very 'unique'. And, all things considered, my meetings with him probably ranked among the strangest and most valuable experiences in my life so far – excluding the shock I received in the last few seconds, that is.

"My goodness, you startled me!"

Cool as a cucumber, Dr Seer just grinned at me.

That was not my intention.

I tried to pull myself together. In a way, the situation was almost comical – but my knees had turned to jelly. I gasped for air.

"What then?"

What do you think? Come on, let's sit down.

Smiling, he waited until I had regained my bearings and had dropped into my chair. Then he sat down.

Why did I let you enter the house alone, Mr Allman?

"I haven't the slightest idea. Maybe you had something more important to do than to come and greet me?"

Do you really believe that?

"Well, I... I haven't a clue."

I was still quite confused.

If we always do things the same way, we never permit ourselves to have new experiences.

"That's the reason you didn't open the door for me?"

Was the door shut?

"Um, no, it was open."

You see: It was open for you. You merely had to use your own initiative.

"Yes... well, that's what I did."

And now for the important part: How did you feel?

"Well, to be honest, I wasn't entirely at ease."

Why not?

"Because I wasn't sure if it was OK for me to just enter on my own like that."

He studied me searchingly.

Did anything occur to suggest that it might not be OK to just walk in?

I found his questions increasingly unsettling, albeit without any real reason.

"I don't know. When I think about it... no, nothing happened."

And yet you hesitated.

"Yes. Pretty stupid, huh?"

Not stupid at all. But restrictive towards yourself. You allowed your feelings to limit your experience of the situation. You could, for example, have felt joy, or curiosity. You've already experienced the enlivening effects of curiosity and open-mindedness.

His expression was almost mischievous.

Who knows... perhaps my sudden appearance wouldn't have been quite so terrifying with that kind of mind set. What do you think?

Spontaneously, we both burst out laughing. I liked his dry sense of humour.

My intention was to create an opportunity for you to enter a new and unknown situation in which you had to rely entirely on your feelings.

The laughter relaxed me, so that I was better able to ease into the playfulness of the situation.

"And I failed right away."

Again, we had to laugh.

Not at all! It's not like you stayed outside and just left.

Dr Seer winked at me.

"But where *were* you, Doc? Your voice came from inside the room, I'm sure of it!"

I am everywhere, Mr Allman.

He was clearly in a jokey mood today. And it was safe to assume that, as always, he was pursuing a particular goal with our conversation.

Did you close the front door behind you?

"Um, I don't think so... should I have?"

There were no fixed rules about how you should or shouldn't behave.

"I didn't want to do anything wrong. But what you say is true. It was probably a bit timid of me to behave like that. I wasn't sure what to do. And yet I know that I *can't* really do anything wrong when I'm here. And I know that I'm welcome... should I go shut the door?"

Would you like to?

"Yes. It shouldn't really be left open, should it?"

Decide what feels best for you.

He still had a smile on his face.

Sometimes in life we have to close certain doors in order to open others.

After a moment's thought, I stood up. The whole thing was kind of funny. And instructive, at the same time. The Doc had the uncanny knack of turning everything into a lesson.

"You'll still be here, right?"

If you trust it to be so, then it will be so.

When I returned he was still sitting in his chair, from which he watched benevolently as I took my seat.

"That feels better!"

Very good! When you accept responsibility and trust that you have control over what happens to you, then you'll always feel better!

He straightened up in his chair and raised his voice. I understood that he was about to impart an important lesson.

You can use the feelings that you create within yourself to influence any situation you enter into – especially ones that are new to you. If you go into things filled with joy and trusting that every experience and encounter has the potential to enrich you in some way, then you open yourself up to new possibilities. You have a tremendous amount of influence on what you experience, remember?

"Yes, that came up a few times before... But is it really possible to *create a feeling in oneself?*"

Let me pose a counter-question: What happens to your feelings when you go to the cinema and watch a romantic film? A love story, say. When you watch the couple in the film and see them making intimate eye contact with each other, watch them kissing and sharing tender moments with each other... how does it make you feel?

"Errm..."

I found the question embarrassing. Or rather, the topic, as it felt like an allusion to my lack of flirting ability. Completely undeterred, Dr Seer proceeded to ask questions in his skilfully analytical way.

So what happens to your feelings as you sit there in the cinema and watch the love scenes unfolding on the big screen?

"Hm. I... I guess my feelings kind of follow what's happening in the film. I mean, it's not like I turn into a gibbering emotional wreck in the cinema or anything. But I do find romantic films quite moving, of course."

Of course you do. And why do people choose to go and see love stories at all? Why not watch an action movie, for example?

"Probably to be able to indulge in a bit of romance every now and again, wouldn't you say? Since not everyone experiences romance in their every-day life. Although women are more likely to watch those kinds of films than men are."

That means, at least subconsciously, that you want to experience and produce these sorts of feelings in yourself. You feel along with the characters in the movie. Something happens to your own feelings when you watch the love scenes. Correct?

"Yes, that's true."

You see! And in the end, whether or not you liked the movie depends primarily on the extent to which it touched you emotionally. In other words, when you chose to see the film you unconsciously declared yourself ready to be moved, to produce these feelings in yourself! This proves that it is in fact possible to induce feelings in yourself.

Dr Seer rose from his chair energetically.

And if you were to now to consciously apply this to the movie that is your life, supported by openness and trust, then you will experience more and more of what you desire. You can use your mental attitude, positive approach and imagination to influence the course and outcome of future events, even in advance.

"Interesting, I've never looked at it that way before!"

He walked towards the back of the room. Standing pretty much in the middle, he spread his arms wide and began to recount the following:

Please remember that consciousness plus energy creates reality! And you know what? Consciousness expresses itself in your clear intention and your vivid imagination. And the carriers of this energy are primarily your feelings. With your power of imagination you project your desires onto the canvas of your life. And your feelings empower the mental images and thus carry them out into the world. Your real-life experiences are based on what you have projected onto your personal canvas. You experience that which you think and believe and imbue with your feelings.
This context provides the key to positively influencing upcoming events and manifesting your deepest and most heartfelt desires in life. For example, if you want a fulfilling relationship, then you must create your own love story in your mind, and really feel it. Feel in love! On the other hand, whenever

an event is coming up that causes you to worry or feel uncomfortable in any way, then imagine yourself in the best version of that particular situation and reverse the poles of your feelings about it. Trust, and feel joy!

Of course, as with all the golden perspectives, it's not about eradicating or bypassing any negative feelings that already exist. It's important, as always, to explore them first, to perceive and to accept them. Only in doing so can we release them and find more self-confidence.

Dr Seer's little speech led me to believe he already knew exactly what I wanted to discuss with him today. Either that, or it was an extremely happy coincidence that his examples just happened to hit the nail right on the head.

I straightened myself in my chair.

"OK, Doc, so we were actually on topic. I did in fact want to discuss something specific with you today."

With a sweeping gesture he spread his arms wide again, and enthusiastically declared:

You're ready to open up to love again, I can see it!

Hats off to him for his commitment, but his boundless enthusiasm made me feel a little uncomfortable. As I mentioned earlier, this particular topic left me feeling a bit overwhelmed.

"Well, I... I managed to get that woman's phone number. You know, the lady from the café. And... I... errr, I have a date with her, this coming Friday. At the café. Her name is Emily, by the way."

Beaming, the Doc came back to where I was sitting. I, meanwhile, had begun to fiddle with a button on my jacket, twisting it back and forth.

Why so nervous? Love is a wonderful thing.

"I'm nowhere near yet. All we did was chat for a few minutes, upon which she said that we could perhaps do it again sometime. Then she gave me her number. I called her the next day, and we agreed to meet again. So we arranged this, um, this date."

There you go! That's great!

"Yes, it is. I... I'm happy about it, really I am. Only now I don't know what to do. You know how inexperienced I am when it comes to these things. I don't know how it all works anymore, the whole 'taking someone out for a drink' thing. I don't think seeing with the eyes of a role model is enough to help in this case, either. I'm afraid I'll mess everything up before we've even started."

Full of understanding, Dr Seer let me ramble on and on, watching as I fumbled with the button until it finally came off in my hand. What an idiot I was!

Excellent. Let's use your date as learning material for today's lesson!

"And that is...?"

Why, how to positively influence upcoming situations by adopting an attitude of trust, and nurturing the intention of having a good experience, of course. We generate a positive feeling within ourselves using the power of our imagination. The method for this is called 'Look upon what's to come with joy'!

"Hm. Maybe we'd do better to carry on with those flirting classes instead."

He smiled and nodded at me.

The one doesn't rule out the other, you know.

After a brief moment of silence, he leaned in towards me a little and lowered his voice:

I had to challenge you a little there, my dear Mr Allman. Don't worry, we'll get to the bottom of exactly what's going on inside you. And then I'll show you what you can do now to have a positive influence on your upcoming date.

Without doubt, it always takes two to tango where love is concerned. And whilst you can't manipulate others to move in the direction you'd like them to, you can however ensure that you feel more secure and open – thereby playing your part to help the situation develop the way your heart wants it to.

I grew calmer. Dr Seer had always been able to help me up to now. And as I realized in that very moment, I had already learned a few helpful perspectives that could be applied to this problem.

"Doc, I should start by looking at myself with kindness before I go on this date, right?"

Exactly! You should always apply that particular perspective and embed it deep inside yourself. It takes a while, but you'll soon see that if you continue to work with it, it will become a way of life. In fact, the way each individual views themselves is an essential factor in amorous relationships. Being able to trust, value and love yourself opens up an entirely new level of love, appreciation and trust towards another person.

He nodded at me, over and over again.

You want to get to know Emily more, right?

"Yes, I'm very interested to find out more about her. Whenever I see her I get this warm feeling in my heart. She has a wonderful presence. And she's really nice. I never thought I'd find myself going on a date with her."

What fears and concerns do you have about the date, my friend?

"Well, I worry that I'm too uptight, and will run out of things to say after five sentences. Or that I'll say something totally stupid, or something inappropriate. Or that she won't find me interesting, and will end up thinking 'what a freak'. It's a complete miracle that she even gave me her number."

Why?

"Well, because a woman like her could take her pick of loads of other guys who are more interesting, attractive and intellectual than me... who are wealthy, athletic, and whatever else."

Dr Seer looked at me in silence, and I soon sensed what it was he wanted to tell me.

"I know, I know! I shouldn't put myself down like that. I don't think I do it nearly as much as I used to. I now have a much better idea of who I am, and of things that might even be likeable about myself. But..."

No word of a lie: for the first time since meeting him, Dr Seer cut me off!

No buts! Leave it up to Emily to decide whether or not she feels drawn to you and sees your special and lovable sides. If you are able to trust yourself and open yourself up, then you already control how you feel deep in your heart.

And by looking ahead to your meeting with joy, you actually influence it in a positive way before it's even happened. You achieve an inner state that makes it possible for you to reveal yourself, thereby setting the conditions for a beautiful encounter. This, in turn, will make it easier for Emily to open up, too. And then you can create something beautiful between the two of you.

Think back to the beginning of our conversation earlier today: You have the choice of whether you go into an unfamiliar situation filled with fear and self-limitation, or with joy and confidence. And depending on your inner attitude and your underlying feeling, you have considerable control over how you will experience the situation.

This applies for all future events – whether they are situations you actively participate in, such as a date with someone, or taking an exam, or situations in which you play a more passive role, such as undergoing surgery. The secret is this: We are already able to influence all future experiences, goals and achievements by directing our thoughts, imagination and feelings in the NOW. And the way to do this is by visualizing the best possible version of the event and evoking positive feelings about it!

"Sounds good. But isn't it a bit selfish to try and make everything go in my favour?"

He gave me a searching look.

Is confidence selfish? Is it selfish to feel joy and happiness?

"Hm. If I don't disadvantage anyone else, then it can't be, right?"

Look at it like this – you're not manipulating anyone by doing so. This method applies only to that which you experience and attract into your life. You put yourself in a positive state. And this inevitably has a positive impact on all those involved. It's not about adopting an intellectual strategy, but about creating your own mental and emotional state of openness, trust and joy. Depth and genuine joy in your own heart cannot harm other people. It's not possible.

"I think I understand."

Dr Seer seemed happy, and flashed me a big grin.

Now back to love.

He leaned over the arm of his chair, reached behind it and brought forth a lush, red rose. He handed it to me with a wink.

"Oh! Where did that come from?"

See this rose as a symbol. Women love flowers, right? Especially roses, which have such strong associations...

I clung to the rose awkwardly. The Doc certainly seemed to know what he was talking about when it came to the subject of love. He must be very popular with women.

Well, Mr Allman, are you ready to look with joy upon your date with Emily, and to let go of your doubting, limiting thoughts?

"Yes. I'm ready. What do I have to do?"

It's not difficult. And you've just grasped the basic principle of this golden perspective. Please find a comfortable position, and allow yourself to relax. We'll envision the most positive version of your date. I want you to really see it and feel it, so give yourself plenty of time.

"OK."

Without further ado, I placed the rose in my half-full glass of water, sank deeper into my chair, as I usually did with these sorts of exercises, and began to slow my breathing. My eyes closed of their own accord as Dr Seer began to give instructions.

Please begin by imagining that it's about half an hour before your date. It's early Friday evening. You've just freshened up, and are about to head to the rendezvous in your favourite café. What sort of feeling do you want to have, ideally? How would you like to feel just before you go on your date?

I controlled my breathing as best I could, and tried to visualize the scene he had just described. As if I'd just flicked a switch, nervousness spread through me. I tried to pay it as little attention as possible.

"I... want to feel secure. And good. Relaxed."

Alright. Then feel it! Visualize yourself just before the rendezvous, and embody these positive feelings. Take deep breaths, and allow yourself to feel your excitement, sense of security and state of relaxation.

Amazingly, it wasn't nearly as difficult to ease my way into these feelings – now linked to the image in my mind – as I first thought it would be. I noticed that I was actually really looking forward to the date. And this enabled me to let go of some of my doubts. After waiting a while, Dr Seer continued.

Imagine yourself walking into the café and looking for a quiet table where you won't be disturbed. Smile as you do so. You sit down and wait for Emily to arrive. A few minutes later she comes in and smiles at you. You are both looking forward to seeing each other.

I could now see everything right before my eyes. How lovely it was to imagine her coming to the café just to meet me. Picturing how happy she would be to see me felt refreshingly good. I breathed in and out, taking deep, slow breaths. The Doc gave me a moment, and then continued.

Can you see and feel the situation?

"Yes."

Now go a little further in your imagination. Allow the images free rein, while always holding on to the sense of what your heart is longing for! Imagine how good it feels to be sitting with Emily at that cosy table, drinking a coffee or a cup of tea, and talking to each other.
Naturally, you can't mentally plan out every single topic you'd talk about in advance. You also can't predict Emily's behaviour. What matters is that you create a positive overall picture, and that you have a good feeling about the meeting. Focus on yourself in this imagined scenario!

I found the exercise quite easy to do, particularly as I was so familiar with the location itself, the café. I made a real effort to remain focussed on myself, and tried to create a feeling of self-assuredness. I pictured myself acting with confidence and openness, laughing and telling Emily about my life, and listening with interest to all she had to say. It was fun! But was it realistic?

As usual, Dr Seer followed my thoughts.

The aim is not to paint a realistic picture of the event, but to create an image that evokes a good feeling inside you. Your personal experiences are just that: personal. There is no objective authority that judges whether your own experiences are realistic or not!

I whispered "yes", and understood. This lifelike visualization had a pleasant effect on me. My worries retreated. I felt a sense of anticipation – I was actually looking forward to the date with Emily, and couldn't wait to experience it 'for real'.

Embed this image and the joy you feel deep inside. And then, please open your eyes, slowly.

I was thrilled.

"Wow! Now I can't wait!"

Dr Seer looked at me, and grinned.

"How come I haven't discovered this method before? Imagining things in a positive light isn't all that hard, after all. I mean, you can imagine just about anything! And the good feeling automatically follows."

Well, how do you feel about the date now?

"More open to it, somehow. And more relaxed. I've actually come to realize that nothing bad can happen. I'm looking forward to it!"

That's a wonderful starting point. It feels very different to all that uncertainty and 'not wanting to do anything wrong', doesn't it.

"Totally! I'm even curious about meeting Emily, now."

I burst out laughing again. Dr Seer beamed with pleasure, too. I think he was a little proud of me at times, his hard-working student.

When you apply this perspective, you can choose whether to positively visualize a particular section of the future event, or the event in its entirety. For example, if you have an exam coming up, you could imagine yourself successfully passing it, and how relieved you'd feel once it's over.

He gave me a promising wink.

Luckily for us, your upcoming date is nothing like an exam. The most we'll be testing is whether or not you are truly ready to open your heart. And, as I see it, the odds are looking pretty good.

"Wow... all the things you see! But tell me, why does the visualization idea work at all?"

Visualizing a future situation in its most positive version delivers an impulse to the present. This impulse causes one to feel courage, hope and confidence. If joy is also generated on the inside, the result is the creation of a good mood, or vibration. And that alone is a tangible benefit – as you have just experienced. This inner state of being then literally attracts positive things into our lives, thereby raising the likelihood that your innermost desires might actually come to pass. You'll experience this yourself. This phenomenon is also referred to as 'the law of attraction', and 'the resonance principle'.

"I've heard of that before. But I didn't really know what it was, let alone how to apply it."

Laughing, the Doc placed his hand on my shoulder.

Now you know: By looking to the future with joy! Incidentally, this works just as well for aspirations. Visualize what you wish for as precisely as possible, and feel it with deep joy. Paint a picture in your mind; use your internal movie screen to depict your wishes. Or write it out, whichever you prefer. There are no limits to your dreams, and this perspective does not differentiate between 'realistic' and 'not realistic'. The actualization always begins with the visualization – linked with your positive feelings!

"I'll do that every time, from now on!"

Wonderful! Integrate this way of seeing into your life and you will attract valuable and beautiful experiences. And I'll give you another tip: when defining and visualizing your desires, make sure to feel gratitude! Feelings of gratitude combined with feelings of joy are the strongest sources of energy for manifesting our desires. Gratitude is a tremendous force. With it you give yourself the certainty that you will realize what you desire. You will strengthen your faith in life and your inner serenity. Try it! Picture your wishes and say 'thank you' in your heart.

We stepped out into the corridor, and walked slowly towards the door. Dr Seer stopped in front of the wall of mirrors.

You forgot something!

With a wink, he handed me back the rose again. I hadn't noticed that he had taken it out of my makeshift vase.

Take this with you. As a symbol.

"Of what?"

As we reached the front door, he let me go first and signalled that I should open the door myself.

Whatever you like! Of the fulfilment of your wishes! Of a wonderful encounter. Of the opening of a new door in your life!

We shook hands.

"What would I have done if I hadn't found you?"

You would have continued on your path, and continued searching. And you would have found me! Besides, there is nothing more important for me than welcoming you. Goodbye, Mr Allman!

With the rose in my hand I stepped out into the world. 'Maybe I'll just hand it to someone I meet coming the other way', I thought. I'd never done anything like that before. And perhaps that is the very reason why I would probably do it now. An indescribable sensation accompanied me throughout that afternoon. For the first time in years I felt free and truly open to new, positive experiences – experiences I had not dared to dream of before.

18 SEMO - See more than meets the eye!

Understanding the emotional dynamics of interactions

I was deep in thought as I made my way to see Dr Seer today. I thought of Emily, and our meeting a few days ago; about how I would love to see her again, but also about how puzzling her behaviour was to me. Or was I generating all this confusion myself, because I was feeling things I hadn't felt for years? Had I fallen in love?

As I tried to cross the road in front of Dr Seer's house, an unexpected occurrence suddenly interrupted my train of thought. A cyclist shot past me at lightning speed and knocked me to the ground. But that's not all. Just as I was getting my bearings and starting to check whether all my limbs were still where they should be, someone began yelling at me. "Hey, open your eyes and look where you're going! You bloody well cut me off, you complete idiot!"

It's a well-known fact that it only takes a matter of seconds for the body to release adrenaline when necessary – and I reacted almost instantly. I was furious. "Idiot yourself!" I screamed back at the fool on his bike, as twenty swear words popped into my head, begging to be shouted out. At the same time, my mind was filled with thoughts of all the bad things I wished upon him.

Amazingly, I was more or less unharmed, except for my right thumb joint, which was swelling up nicely. Somewhat dazed, and cursing to myself, I staggered to the Doc's house. Why were there such nasty people in the world? And why did something like that have to happen to me? I had lost all interest in talking. I was done for the day.

The path is sometimes difficult – all the better that you are here now! Welcome, Mr Allman!

Dr Seer was already standing at the front door, holding out his hand to me.

Who has upset you so?

Annoyed, I reached out to shake his hand with my left hand, and pointed to my now very swollen right thumb.

"How am I supposed to know who that idiot was! A cyclist just mowed me down – and then, to cap it all, he screamed abuse at me!"

That must have been an unhappy individual.

"I honestly couldn't care less what his problem was. Absolutely disgusting behaviour. What a bastard!"

First things first: why don't you come on in. We'll take a look at the situation together.

"All I need is something cold to put on this thumb, and a glass of water. Then I'll be fine."

I can get you those things. Follow me!

Just as he had when I arrived in the middle of the thunderstorm that time, Dr Seer pushed me gently but firmly down the corridor to our room.

Sit down. I'll fetch everything we need.

Then he was gone. Grumbling to myself, I plonked down in my chair and stared ahead blankly. It seemed like the Doc was inspired and energised today, which I found somehow irritating. Positively elated, he returned with a pitcher of water and a huge ice pack. Without any warning he placed the latter on my right hand, making me howl from the shock of the piercing cold.

"HEY, that's bloody freezing!"

Exactly! Then it's doing its job.

"Well, it looks like *you're* on top form today, at least..."

I heard the sarcastic tone in my voice, and was annoyed by my lack of self-control. Dr Seer, as usual, noted every nuance of my mood.

You're feeling aggressive now because you felt like you were being attacked earlier.

"I've no idea."

Undeterred, he continued.

Whenever we feel attacked, then in truth we already feel hurt. In moments like that, we no longer embody our inner self-confidence. We feel like we are not respected, being treated unfairly or not being seen. We feel unvalued. And we allow ourselves to feel offended.

I was clearly not in the mood for this kind of analysis.

"So?"

And this creates emotional stress. If we do not consciously perceive this pressure, examine it and try to resolve it, then it robs us of more energy and self-confidence. It takes us further away from ourselves. To rid ourselves of the pressure, we start to pass it and the injury we have suffered on to other people. We behave aggressively ourselves.

This time, his immediate psychological dissection of the situation was most likely a deliberate strategy to lessen my anger. And what he explained admittedly did not sound uninteresting.

You know what? I'm now going to tell you one of the most important secrets of human interaction. Anyone who assimilates this knowledge, and is able to combine it with a keen sense of awareness and solid self-confidence, can arrive at a place where he or she is no longer vulnerable. This person no longer resonates with aggression, and therefore has hardly any need for defensive behaviour. They are 'untouchable', so to speak, because they no longer take the aggression of the other person personally. The secret lies in understanding the following truth: An aggressive person is a wounded person.

I was struggling to keep up with Dr Seer's words, but he had once again succeeded in putting me under his spell – or under the spell of the truths he was so relentlessly relaying.

"Sheesh, Doc, you always have something new up your sleeve, don't you!"

This seemed to make him happy.

Let's look at what we have here. Your sarcastic remark earlier, about my good mood, was passive-aggressive behaviour on your part. That behaviour didn't affect me, because I choose not to take it personally.

"I'm sorry. That was dumb of me."

Don't worry about it. But the interesting question is, why did you behave that way? And the answer is simple. First, because you allowed yourself to be hurt! And second, because you haven't dealt with that hurt consciously. What hurt you the most was not the physical shock, or your sprained thumb, but the way this man treated you. That he insulted you, and belittled your worth.

"Yes, that's true."

Without thinking, you entered a place where all you felt was hurt. And a split-second later you unconsciously converted this injury into aggression.

"Hm."

The ideal would be to not let yourself get hurt in the first place, right? But if it happens, perhaps because your aggressor touches a raw nerve, a weakness within us, then we still have the option to rid ourselves of the injury rather than pass it on. You already know the process. If we try to step out of the acute emotion we're feeling and look at what's really going, then we can resolve the injury and even heal it. We act with self-awareness and so experience immediate relief.

He stared at me intently.

And another thing. Passing on injury in the form of your own aggression can't have any healing effect, because everything we do to others, we do to ourselves. A person who treats another aggressively devalues himself in that very same moment. We'll come back to this later.

The Doc took one of the water glasses from the table and handed it to me.

First drink this and take a deep breath. I know it's stressful for you. But we may as well use this experience to aid your personal development!

The Doc gave me a few minutes, during which I drank a big gulp of water and adjusted the ice pack on my hand. I tried to calm myself, settle in to the moment. I did my best to go along with his suggestion as I was so appreciative of the tireless support he had given me since our first encounter. I wanted to show him how much I respected him – something that had briefly fallen away when I threw out that upset comment earlier in the session.

He spoke again.

You know that I'd never judge you, Mr Allman. I simply wish to challenge you to always go beyond your immediate reaction, because you have reached the necessary level of awareness to do so. What's more, your experience today brings an opportunity to significantly expand your level of awareness. Let's seize this opportunity!

Something inside me told me that this was very important. His words, as always, made perfect sense. It felt like something more – like a missing puzzle piece was slowly emerging from within me.

Try to let this connection sink in. You were emotionally injured earlier. And the source of your injury most likely also felt injured. Now, please consider the following law of nature: First and foremost, a person's behaviour always has to do with themselves. The cause of their behaviour lies IN THEM! Maybe the cyclist had slept badly, or maybe he's filled with anger because he hasn't achieved what he set out to achieve in life. Maybe he's just lost his job, and doesn't know how he's going to pay the rent. Or perhaps his marriage has just fallen apart, and his emotions are pulling him into a very dark place. Maybe he never acquired a genuine sense of self-confidence. And perhaps he has never looked at himself with kindness!

My anger flared up again for a brief moment. I couldn't help it if the guy had had a 'shitty childhood' or whatever other problems. It's not like my life has been all that easy, either!

"Yeah, well, that might be so, but what he did there was bang out of order. And completely inexcusable!"

It's not about wanting to excuse his behaviour: it's about not taking it personally, hard as that is to do. No question, this is far from easy in your case, not least of all because you suffered a shock and your physical safety was at stake. It could have turned out very tragically indeed. You were lucky. Nevertheless, stay centred and don't allow your power to be taken away. Don't take it personally!

"OK, fair enough, I'm sure he didn't intend to hurt me personally. But what do I get from it all? He mowed me down, regardless. I could get upset about it all over again... I should have given him what for. But he took off straight away, unfortunately."

For a while, the Doc said nothing. And suddenly things began to churn around inside me.

"Now hang on – please don't tell me I should even consider looking at this guy with kindness!"

Dr Seer smiled.

You don't have to. Not yet. But you can look into him, figuratively speaking. I congratulate you, because you are about to learn one of the most important golden perspectives for all human interaction. It is called 'See more than meets the eye!' – or 'SEMO', in short.
This method requires us to remain firmly anchored within ourselves to protect ourselves emotionally and, in particular, to ensure we don't surrender our personal power in conflict situations. When you have internalized this particular way of looking at things, conflict situations don't even have to arise. Too many conflicts develop because we relate the negative feelings generated by others to ourselves and feel attacked as a result. Go beyond what meets the eye and recognize that the reason for this man's behaviour lies within him!

I listened to Dr Seer's words, and felt what can only be described as a kind of 'click' inside me, as everything fell into place. I understood. My grudge

238

against the cyclist faded as I grasped the idea that *he* was the root cause of his behaviour towards me, not me. The fact that I had been involved was nothing more than coincidence – it could just as easily have happened to anyone else.

"That's why you said earlier that the cyclist must be an unhappy person, right?"

Dr Seer nodded approvingly.

Correct.

"Hm. But... I've no way of checking the facts with random events like these."

But you don't have to. When you apply this perspective, it's enough to imagine what his problem might theoretically be. But even that isn't absolutely necessary. If you adopt this perspective as a matter of principle, all the time, then you are permanently aware and safe in the knowledge that, fundamentally, you no longer have to take other people's behaviour personally. SEMO thus helps you to understand that, in the majority of cases, people don't mean to hurt you personally. It was not his intention to cause you pain. Please keep in mind that this particular perspective of THE GOLDEN VIEW is not primarily concerned with excusing aggressive behaviour, but with not taking this behaviour personally.

"And what about those people I can't avoid – the ones I'm always coming into contact with, and where conflict seems to follow? What about family? Or friends, who can be really quite unfriendly every now and then? Take Andy, for example: he gets so annoyed sometimes, it drives me mad!"

This perspective is just as important when it comes to dealing with people we encounter regularly, such as work colleagues or people we are very close to, such as partners or family members, as it is for dealing with strangers. SEMO enables you to turn even the most difficult situation around and ultimately to respond to the person. Once you no longer feel like you're being attacked, you don't have to be on the defensive – instead, you can pacify the situation, thus significantly helping to improve relations between those involved. This then allows you to understand what's motivating the other person's behaviour by initiating a conversation with them and asking why they behaved as they did. The right tone will come naturally to you, because you're interested in clarifying and resolving the issue, not launching some sort of counter attack.

I was impressed. I had to let it all sink in first. As I contemplated what the Doc had explained, a loud sigh escaped my lips. Smiling as he stood up, Dr Seer went to the window and opened it. He stood there for a moment.

Let it work in you!

I sat back, and noticed that my body was finally relaxing.

"Doc, how come I'm only now learning to SEMO, as it were?"

He gave me a friendly nod.

Because any earlier would have been too soon. It requires a high degree of willingness to go beyond your own emotions and consciously deal with yourself and your own experiences. The ability to not take anything personally is a very sophisticated skill.

"I see."

He gave my thoughts time to freewheel.

"But what about those people who are violent towards others? Do we have to assume that these are all injured people, then?"

Stepping softly away from the window, Dr Seer returned to his chair. His facial expression suggested he was about to tell me another secret.

Some people have not yet regained their self-confidence, and live unconsciously. Most of them carry deep injuries, it's true. They feel small and unloved. Often they themselves have experienced physical or psychological violence and have never known what it is like to feel self-worth, to feel love and to carry it in their hearts.

240

Let's look more closely. A person who lives consciously and who trusts themselves will not treat others disparagingly. You always pass on to others what you carry inside.
Those who make others feel small in fact feel small themselves, deep inside. Those who devalue other people have no real self-esteem of their own. Those who show others little respect have little respect for themselves. And only those who love themselves can show love and appreciation to others. These are natural laws, so to speak.
Actions that are full of violence and aggression are not justifiable. But by looking into the aggressor and still remaining self-confident, we can break out of the spiral that sees experienced aggression triggering anger within us. This also applies to the passive observation of aggressive actions. We can meet aggression with a higher consciousness and inner level of peace, and hence avoid being subsumed by the negative energy it brings. We maintain our positive energy and thereby spread something good, something which counteracts the violence.

"Wow – incredible. If everyone knew and applied this perspective, then there'd be fewer conflicts and less violence in the world, right?"

Certainly. Every individual would act with greater consciousness and develop self-confidence and self-love. This, incidentally, is also the higher purpose of THE GOLDEN VIEW.

Wordlessly, we looked at each other. It felt like I had reached a new level today.

"So is THE GOLDEN VIEW the key to a better world, Doc?"

His green eyes flashed, and the atmosphere in the room shifted. It was one of those timeless moments.

It is one of the keys, yes.

Silence filled the room, and I felt gratitude wash through me. Dr Seer stood up and walked to the door.

I'd like you to rest a little now. You have experienced and learned a lot today, and it will take time to assimilate it all. You may take a nap, if you wish. Would you like a blanket?

"OK. And yes, thank you, a blanket would be good. It's a bit chilly."

All of a sudden I felt very tired. Dr Seer left the room and returned a few moments later with a fluffy silver-grey blanket.

We're not quite done for today. I can see you still have something on your mind. But rest a little, for now. I'll wake you later.

I didn't know what exactly he meant, but everything felt right. Sat in my chair, I snuggled down into the thick blanket, and suddenly felt so exhausted that I couldn't keep my eyes open. Dr Seer dimmed the light and slipped out of the room. I fell asleep.
In my dream different situations and images mingled. One scene was very clear, however, and has stayed with me to this day. I dreamed that the cyclist apologized to me and said that he was sorry. His wife had left him because she had fallen in love with someone else, and he felt completely lost. I felt genuine empathy for him. The highlight of my dream was that he then showed me a picture of her. And to my great surprise, the woman in the photo was Emily!

✻✻✻✻✻✻✻✻✻✻✻✻✻✻✻

You slept for quite a while, my friend!

Dimly, I recognized Dr Seer standing in front of me, cup of tea and plate with a slice of cake in hand, smiling at me. I struggled to open my eyes.

"Oh, Doc... what time is it?"

You have slept for exactly three hours. It's 7 pm.

"Oh my goodness."

Did you have something else planned?

"No, no, it's not that... why did I sleep so long? Have I held you up in any way?"

He handed me the teacup and placed the plate with the cake on the table.

Everything is exactly as it should be. You needed the rest. And now fortify yourself!

I smoothed my hair as best I could and tried to wake up fully. I felt as though I'd slept right through the night. The cake looked delicious – so much so that I devoured half of it in a single bite. The tea was some kind of herbal tea, a little bitter for my liking, but in combination with the cake, pleasingly aromatic. As I helped myself, I noticed that, to my great surprise, I could move my right hand completely normally. My thumb was no longer swollen.

"Doc, where's the ice pack? And my hand... take a look, it's back to normal."

Dr Seer smiled.

Your nap was a restorative one, in several respects.

I chuckled. "I don't know, eh... the things I experience here!"

You experience the things that you are ready to experience. Once we are on the correct path, everything that happens to us can be regarded as a signpost. The SEMO perspective teaches you not to take the behaviour of other people personally. And if you still take something personally, then look at it and deliberately ask yourself: How much of the negativity in fact derives from me? What can I learn from the situation, in order to heal myself? Do you understand where I'm coming from?

"Yes, I think so."

This is a very crucial point: If we are conscious of our feelings and personal issues and work on ourselves, then we can recognize in our own reactions

243

why something touches us personally. And in this case, it is important to look very closely indeed, as the outside world serves as a mirror for what we still have to learn. Please take another look, this time with a little distance. What exactly was it that so upset you so much during that encounter with the cyclist earlier today?

"The fact that he knocked me over. That he didn't see me, and treated me with such contempt."

Can you combine these feelings into one?

"Hm. I guess he made me feel... well, small."

I observed that I was now able to recount the experience quite calmly, almost neutrally – it no longer provoked a reaction in me. And that felt good.

"Or, to put it another way, I *allowed* myself to feel small. You'd probably say that I felt small because I entered into the feeling of inferiority, am I right?"

Dr Seer nodded eagerly to me.

Very good, Mr Allman! So it somehow affected your feeling of self-worth. You could say that you allowed your self-worth to be weakened – or, figuratively speaking, that the experience touched an old wound that was still in the process of healing itself.

"Sounds plausible. I've not seen it that way before."

It's linked to looking at yourself with kindness. You're still internalizing that one, aren't you.

"Yes, you're right."

It was liberating to see how far I'd come, and how much I'd learned. I felt very differently about myself than I did a few months ago. A world of difference lay between my first mirror experience and today. How hard I'd found it back then, trying to realize what was going on inside me. And now this insight came so quickly, within five minutes, and without costing me much energy – on the contrary!

I took the remaining piece of cake from the plate and finished it off.

"Tell me Doc, wasn't there something else you wanted to discuss with me? I think you mentioned something about it before I fell asleep..."

You have been paying attention. Tell me, what do you think it might be?

"I've no idea. What more could there possibly be today?"

Dr Seer's eyes twinkled. I had no idea what he was getting at.

How was the date with Emily?

The question immediately provoked a very different emotional response within me. Emily's face shot into my consciousness and I felt myself grow hot. I only remembered the strange dream I had during my afternoon siesta at a later point. But the feeling that had accompanied me on my way to the Doc this afternoon was back again, and I found it somehow irritating.

"Oh, Dr Seer, it was... it was nice... very nice even, but... oh, I don't know."

What don't you know?

"Well, the short version of the tale is that I don't think anything is likely to happen between us. With her and me, I mean."

That's a very swift prognosis, my friend. Shall we not take a more detailed look at it all?

I was suddenly overcome by that old, familiar sense of uncertainty.

"I'm not so sure."

Why not tell me how the meeting went. It can only help to relieve you.

"Oh, alright then. It was really nice, actually... and because I had looked ahead to our date with joy, I felt relaxed throughout. I had the impression that Emily also enjoyed the evening."

That sounds pretty promising.

"Yes, I... I keep thinking about her. She's a wonderful woman. She has these beautiful eyes... oh, Doc, you should see her eyes! We must have talked for three hours, nonstop. We ordered wine, and she laughed a lot, and told me about her children... by which I don't mean her own children, of course, but the kindergarten children. She's a kindergarten teacher, you see. I think she's a wonderful person. So loving, and at the same time so eloquent. She's also quite sporty, and regularly goes jogging. She told me that she paints, and... oh, and that she has a dog."

You certainly sound very enthusiastic about her.

"Do I?"

Allow me to make a bold conjecture. Could it be that you have fallen in love?

Without warning, all the blood rushed to my head and I turned a bright shade of red, which I found extremely embarrassing. I felt like an awkward teenager.

"I think I may have done, yes."

Dr Seer beamed at me, as if ready to congratulate me on my upcoming wedding.

That's wonderful! I'm happy for you! Love is a beautiful thing, and you are now ready to open yourself up to it.

"But I don't think Emily feels the same way. I'm pretty sure of it, actually."

Well, in the first instance, it's your own feelings that count. And then we can look at Emily's behaviour. We can form hypotheses about her internal landscape later – but with the correct attitude. You have already learned the perspective this requires today.

"You mean I should 'look into' Emily?"

Yes, in the correct way: by not taking anything personally.

"It's hard when you're in love and hoping for more though, isn't it. Don't we all take things personally in this kind of situation?"

The Doc lit a candle, and smiled.

Without question, love is one of the most difficult areas as far as not taking things personally is concerned, you're absolutely right. But once you have SEMO internalized, it allows you to live out love on a whole new level. Particularly if it's still early days, and the relationship is only just beginning to unfold – as long as it's still unclear whether a partnership will truly flourish, the parties involved are very much inclined to take every word, gesture and action, and especially any failure to act on the other person's part, extremely personally. You see, the problem is that every behavioural nuance is evaluated as an indication of whether or not someone likes you.
And that is often the cardinal error that couples make during the stage of getting to know each other. You relate everything to yourself, no matter how the other behaves, and are disappointed when you don't see clear signals of interest coming your way. You yourself have determined what these signals should look like. And in actual fact, all the other person has done at this initial stage is provide information about herself – not signs of rejection.

"Well, you certainly seem to know your stuff."

These are very straightforward laws, once you've established the principle within yourself. But let's look at it in yet more detail! From what you've told me about how the date unfolded, it doesn't necessarily sound as though Emily is uninterested. What did you notice that makes you think she has no further interest in you?

"Well, to start by talking about how it ended, when we parted company she didn't reply when I said that I'd like to see her again. We left the café, and embraced, briefly. And when I suggested that we could meet again next Friday, she said she wouldn't be able to make it, unfortunately. And then she said we should just give each other a call. Which is a pretty clear signal, wouldn't you say?"

Dr Seer scrutinized me.

Clear in what sense, exactly?

"Clear that she doesn't want to see me again."

Why?

"Because otherwise she would have suggested an alternative date."

He chuckled in his inimitable manner.

"You're laughing at me now, Doc?"

My friend, it's a good thing that THE GOLDEN VIEW is helping you to better understand interpersonal encounters. In particular, those between men and women.

"I believe so, too. But it's pretty obvious, isn't it – when I 'look into' Emily, it's as good as crystal clear that she kept things vague because she doesn't in fact want to see me again."

Please pay close attention to how you apply the SEMO perspective. Whilst you are 'SEMOing' by really looking into Emily, you're still relating her behaviour to yourself from the outset. In so doing, you are ignoring the most crucial component of this golden perspective – you have already taken it personally. And as a result, you think Emily's offer to speak on the phone was merely made out of courtesy, am I right?

"Yes."

Isn't it also possible that she meant it as a genuine offer? If you look into Emily again without taking things personally, what reasons could there be for her not accepting your proposal to meet on Friday, and for not suggesting an alternative date to get together?

"Hm... let me think. I guess it could be because she doesn't in fact have any time on Friday. And that she didn't have her diary with her and so didn't know when she would next be available. Although she's not really the time-management type... maybe she's got a man waiting at home, and so can't get away."

Do you have reason to believe that she is in a relationship?

"She mentioned her ex-partner twice, sort of casually, and it sounded as if the separation was quite recent. But it may be that the two still live together and are not properly separated yet."

The Doc listened attentively to me as I spoke. He radiated infinite patience. And I realized that I now felt very glad that he was analysing this topic in such detail with me.

Dear Mr Allman, always assume the best! This woman means a lot to you and you want to get closer to her. Why would she lie to you? And if it is true that she is still in the process of separating from her ex, then it is entirely understandable and indeed responsible of Emily to not drag you into it.

"Yes, you're right. I think I've really fallen in love with Emily, and I guess that makes me feel totally insecure. You know, when she told me that she jogs on a regular basis, and is a vegetarian, that she paints, and even meditates from time to time – well, I find all that really fascinating. I thought, 'Wow, what an interesting woman'. And on the way home after our rendezvous, my mind started going into overdrive, telling me things like 'you complete idiot, how could you even believe for an instant that such a special woman might find *you* interesting'. I think I've gone jogging maybe twice in the last five years, for at most thirty minutes. And besides which, I haven't a clue about meditation."

Dr Seer nodded at me.

Please take a deep breath. You know, you're not as far removed from medi-tation as you think you are, incidentally. But we'll get to it another time.

I noticed how tense I was, and would in fact have started breathing more deeply of my own accord, so familiar was this method to me now. So I focused on my breath, and felt the tension ease within me. In a calm voice, the Doc continued.

Now examine closely what you have just said about yourself. You unconsciously perceived Emily's descriptions of her own lifestyle, if that's the way to put it, as a kind of attack. You took it personally, and allowed it to touch a nerve. You once again felt small because you yourself wouldn't describe yourself as athletic, or as someone who meditates. But it has nothing to do with you! She was talking about herself and about the things that are important to her. It was a statement about herself – not a statement about how Emily sees you, or an indicator that you would only be of interest to her if you also jogged and meditated.

Slowly I began to realize what the Doc, with infinite patience, was bringing to my attention. Not taking things personally was clearly key, of that there could be no doubt. Even when it came to love! I let out a deep sigh and immediately felt better.

"I think I'm slowly getting it, Doc. Fascinating, how wrong our thinking can be sometimes!"

He moved the candle to the very centre of the table.

Not wrong, but self-limiting, remember?

"Yes. Why is it that we so often assume the worst? Especially with things like this – such as when we fall in love?"

What do you think?

"Hm. Out of fear, perhaps. Because we are afraid of getting hurt."

That's right. And what is the antithesis of fear?

It was pretty clear that Dr Seer liked to test me every now and then. And this, in turn, gave me the chance to prove what I'd learned – something I was proud of, and happy to show.

"Love. That is, if you carry love and self-trust within yourself."

You have truly understood.

Silently, we gazed at one another. At that moment I sensed the deep connection that had formed between us. Perhaps this connection had been there from the outset, since our very first meeting, and it was simply that I could see it better now. He had become my mentor, teacher and confidant – as well as a really good friend. In a calm voice he continued.

Look gently and without pressure upon your desire for this relationship. Love needs time to grow, and partnerships must be given the chance to develop. For this it is important not to draw hasty conclusions – although that doesn't mean you should ignore any potential signals.
The context is as follows: If you don't take anything personally, then you are much freer to involve yourself with Emily. And at the same time you are more centred in yourself because you're not constantly resorting to fearful interpretations. This also allows you to better feel and respond to your intuition. Time will tell whether something develops between the two of you or not. You feel free, and are better able to reveal yourself to the other. Love arises when you are willing to show yourself. And that's what you want.

"Yes."

Dr Seer stood up, walked over to me and placed a friendly hand on my shoulder.

Love always opens you up to being vulnerable, without question. But it is also one of the greatest gifts in life. And this gift can only come to you if you open up and accept the supposed risk of being hurt.

251

I felt confidence rising within me, accompanied by the same joyful feeling that I had enjoyed just before my date with Emily. Could it be the 'butterflies in the stomach' people are always talking about?

"What would you do if you were in my shoes now, Doc?"

Have you called Emily yet?

"No, I didn't feel confident enough."

Then I'd start by doing that. Be direct, and ask Emily straight up if she would like to see you again. Just like that. Without any pressure.

"OK, I will."

Let yourself be guided by your heart and not by the fear of rejection, and you'll do everything right. Trust yourself. When the feelings of love and affection for another human being are so strong, then it often feels like you have no time to lose. Everything has to happen incredibly quickly, in part also to silence your own insecurities. Give it the time it needs! Proceed gently, with yourself, with Emily, and with this encounter. Show her your true feelings, but without conveying any expectations. In so doing, you present her with a gift. She herself will decide whether she wants to accept it or not.

He led me to the front door, and we shook hands.

"Thank you, Doc. That's how I'll do it, I promise."

You have nothing to lose. And you will gain something wonderful, my friend. Goodbye!

The cool, clear night was filled with stars. And a warm feeling in my stomach accompanied me back home. It was as if there had been a leap in time.

I felt deep gratitude in my heart for all that I had understood today.

19 Focus!

Using your own resources productively

On my way to see Dr Seer, I once again felt annoyed with myself. I had learned so much, and experienced so many new things – after our last session I had felt convinced that I now understood all the essentials. And yet, within a week, I once again found myself overrun by the events of daily life. Like a rubber band, these had snapped me back into my bad mood, reawakening my frustration about life and its 'day-to-day madness'.

It was late in the evening because, as usual, I hadn't left the office on time. I almost wished I could hide my mood from Dr Seer. I was embarrassed and frustrated about once again having sunk so low. But I had no choice: it was too late to cancel our meeting, so meeting him was unavoidable. I stood outside his door, hoping that the extent of his patience with me would indeed prove to be infinite.

Scowling, I rang the bell. The Doc appeared immediately.

"Good evening."

Good evening, my dear chap! You look rather stressed.

He looked at me searchingly.

Sometimes the daily grind catches up with us more quickly than we'd like, doesn't it?

"You've hit the nail on the head. I don't just look stressed – I *am* stressed! Totally stressed out, in fact. And I feel really uncomfortable about turning up so late, and being so worn out before our session has even begun."

There's no need to feel that way, none whatsoever. Come on in! This is a place in which you can relax – you know that.

With a welcoming gesture, he led me into the house, as usual.

Please go ahead and make yourself comfortable. I'll be right with you.

I fell into my chair. Three minutes later, Dr Seer returned with a big cup of steaming hot chocolate. Smiling, he placed it on the table, indicating that I should help myself.

That will do you good. It calms the nerves. So, tell me: what's going on?

"Nothing particularly dramatic has happened. Just a thousand different things, all at once."

A thousand sounds like an awful lot.

"Oh come on, don't go pulling my leg! Obviously I didn't mean it literally."

I'm glad to hear it.

"Doc! You know exactly what I mean."

Yes, Mr Allman. Of course I do. I just wanted to loosen you up a little. Often a touch of humour can help to shake off a negative mood. Allow me to repeat my question, in all seriousness – what's wrong?

In fact, his sense of humour did help me loosen up a bit. In my head, however, there was nothing but a confused muddle. I raised the warm cup to my lips, and took a sip.

"Well, this time of year is always crazy at work. But this year it's a complete nightmare. There's no way we can do all the things that have to get done. We're in the final stages of a project, and have the accounting to do, the Christmas celebrations to plan, bonus payouts and final appraisals to complete – and we also have to draw up our plans for next year. Meetings are being scheduled for both annual and project kickoffs, and we've a load of budget and resource planning to prepare. On top of which, we have to submit our holiday requests for next year. I mean... how should I know what my holiday plans are that far in advance? I've no idea where I want to go, and with whom. To cap it all, the company is closed over Christmas and New Year's – effectively a sort of compulsory vacation that everyone has to take. So we've only a few weeks left, and everything is in total chaos."

That's a big workload, and does indeed sound like a very chaotic situation.

"You can say that again!"

I took another sip of hot chocolate. Patiently, Dr Seer watched me.

I'm no business expert, but I believe THE GOLDEN VIEW has a suitable perspective that can help.

"Wow – no idea about the issues involved, but a solution at hand... this I have to hear, Doc! But then you've always been able to help me so far, I guess."

A smile twitched at the corners of his mouth as Dr Seer noted how het up I was. He himself did not seem in the slightest bit fazed.

Alright, let's get straight to the point: the particular perspective required for this situation is called 'Focus!'.

"Very funny. That's what I've been trying to do the whole time, but it doesn't work! It's all just too much!"

Let's take a closer look. Please describe for me how you would go about tackling all the tasks you mentioned. How was your day today at work?

"Hm. Well, I have everything I need to hand, that is to say, open on my desk – either in paper or electronic form. There are always at least ten documents open simultaneously on my computer, and I switch between them to access whatever information I need or to dig out whatever others want from me. Stress central. Oh, and then I'm also constantly being interrupted by phone calls and colleagues who just pop in to ask a question, or to flag something up that I should take into account during the planning process. I once took part in a training workshop called 'Working effectively', but either I've forgotten how to do it or the method just wasn't that effective. I suppose I'm either unable to deal with the mess, or

I'm just not capable of multitasking. But it's a well-known fact that men can't multitask, in any case, so it's pretty hopeless."

Alright. Now, before we get to the 'Focus!' technique, I'd like to clarify the following two points.

First, effective working is essential. Ultimately, it gets us where we're trying to go. What we need in your case, however, is a way to work efficiently, so we require an approach that achieves the objective and does so in minimum time.

Second, the assumption that we can save time through so-called 'multitasking' is a myth of the modern meritocracy. Processing several streams in parallel ultimately saves no time at all. Switching from one stream to another consumes energy. Even though running multiple activities or thoughts at the same time may seem like it delivers results, it is not so. What happens instead is that we constantly and rapidly switch back and forth, which ultimately gets things done even more slowly than if you were to deal with the activities one after another.

I almost choked on my drink. "Oh! Really?"

Absolutely! And now we'll start applying 'Focus!' one step at a time. First, I'd like you to do the following: Sort through and prioritize all the tasks that you have to complete according to two criteria: time, and degree of importance.
Then list all the tasks for which you require information from other people, and all those you can do alone.
Here is a blank sheet of paper. I'll leave you alone for a few minutes, and then we'll take a calm look over everything together, and decide on the next step. As I mentioned before, committing one's thoughts to paper may in and of itself already help to clarify things for you.

Dr Seer handed me a sheet of paper and a selection of colourful pencils, all of which he had suddenly conjured up from somewhere. I set about my task, and tried to calm the chaos in my head – initially trying to prioritize my own workloads and then trying to draw up the list of things I couldn't do without others. After a few minutes the Doc came back into the room and stood next to me.

How's it going? Everything alright?

"I'm making progress. At least it doesn't look as chaotic on paper as it did in my head."

Excellent! Could you describe your findings for me?

"OK, so I found rating the importance quite tricky. Holiday planning is definitely not quite as important as other tasks on the list – besides which I'm not particularly fussed about it anyway. But the annual financial paperwork needs to be completed, and is a prerequisite for being able to plan the outlook for next year."

There you are: that's an insightful realization already.

"Yes. I've also established that approximately half of the tasks require information and input from colleagues – the rest I can complete independently."

Dr Seer sat down in his chair. As always, it was very obvious that he was very concerned to find a lasting solution to my problem.

Excellent. Now we can continue to apply the 'Focus!' principle. Let's consider how you could efficiently implement what you have just theoretically recognized – and how you could do so without getting bogged down in 'multi-tasking' endeavours.

"I suppose I have to find a way to do one thing after the other. And I'd need to avoid any interruptions from phones ringing and people dropping in unexpectedly."

Spot on! So how might that work, in practice?

"Oh come on, Doc – can't you just tell me? You're bound to have the perfect solution in mind already."

He gave me a challenging look, as if wanting to motivate me and spur me on to perform better.

Dear Mr Allman. You are the master of your situation! You're able to find the solution yourself.

"Alright, I see where you're coming from. Let me think. Right, well: the things that I can do alone I could do at home. We're allowed to work from home a couple of days a month, so I could schedule two afternoons next week where I could work – undisturbed – at home. I could use the time to write the completion report for the project. I already have all the info I need, and it's an urgent and important task that has to get done a.s.a.p. The same applies for some of the other tasks, too."

Sounds like a very good plan!

"Next, I could email those members of staff from whom I'm still waiting on information and ask them to send me what I need in writing and by a certain date. That way I'd reduce the amount of disruption caused by phone calls and people coming in and out of my office."

Fantastic!

"And as a general principle, I'd make sure I work through the list of priorities in order, one task at time."

Dr Seer seemed satisfied.

Sounds good! You have managed to clearly prioritize your activities. You have created space in which to concentrate on the tasks in hand. This means you will be able to focus and get done what you need to do in a pretty relaxed emotional state. After all, you don't want to be utterly exhausted by the end of the year now, do you? So how does it all feel, now?

"Good! I feel kind of relieved, actually. A few things have just clicked into place – even though the actual steps I needed to take in order to increase my ability to focus weren't all that difficult. But, to be perfectly honest, I wouldn't have thought of them on my own. It seems so stupid now, my belief that I should try and do everything all at once."

Please don't ever forget to look at yourself with kindness. You'll never achieve your goal without a positive attitude towards yourself. It's a valuable thing, when such small, pivotal adjustments prove helpful to you. And after all, it was you and you alone who came up with them in the end.

"But only thanks to an all-important push on your part, I have to say! I'm pretty impressed, you know. It turns out that THE GOLDEN VIEW does in fact work just as well for professional problems – despite the fact, as you say, that you're no business expert."

I'm glad. Actually, the content or subject area is often only of secondary importance. By applying the right technique, you can get straight to the heart, or the essence, of any problem. Which brings me to another little piece of advice. You can use 'Focus!' to shed light on an infinite number of issues, even everyday matters, and approach them accordingly.

It seemed that nothing got past Dr Seer 'unseen'. And it was good to witness that he was also a brilliant counsellor for matters of such a practical nature.

Allow me to provide a simple example: grocery shopping. There are a number of ways to go about it:

Option A: You know exactly what you want to buy, go straight to each item in the shop, put everything in your shopping trolley, pay for it all, and you're done. You're back at home in no time at all.

Option B: You don't know exactly what you want. The fridge is empty. You go to the supermarket and wander through the aisles, picking things up and adding them to your trolley, continue browsing the shelves but feel unsatisfied, and like you've forgotten something. So you go back to the entrance and start over again.
Maybe you change your mind and take something out of the trolley. Eventually you end up at the checkout, and if you're lucky you'll have

bought things you actually need and items you're happy to have selected. If nothing else, the fridge will be fuller than it was before.

Option C: You're feeling creative, and want to cook something new. So you decide to go to the supermarket and let yourself be inspired. Filled with curiosity, you browse the deli section, and perhaps the vegetable display, and ask for a few suggestions. At some point you settle on an idea, and know what you feel like eating. Then you go and buy the ingredients you need, plus a little cheese for afterwards, and maybe something for dessert.

Now tell me: Which shopper was the most focused?

"The one from option A, clearly."

And who do you think had the most fun shopping?

"I guess it would have been the shopper in option C, given the way you told it."

Was shopper C not focused?

"Hm. Yes, they were. But on something else."

Precisely. But on what?

"On trying something new."

Very good. That too can be a focal point. And what about shopper B?

"B was... more indifferent, I suppose."

Correct. Shopper B was not focused. There are always numerous ways to approach something. But the golden rule is always: Know what you want! What is really important to you? What do you want to achieve? This awareness gives you focus and lays the foundation for implementing and achieving goals.

"It's so obvious! And so I can use this method to tackle absolutely anything?"

Dr Seer nodded enthusiastically.

Yes, that's right. Let's review both examples.
Where your workload was concerned, the focus was on prioritizing the tasks at hand and structuring the processing method so that you could complete them efficiently. Focussing in this way enables you to clear the clutter and save time and energy. That's what you wanted.
The same applies when you go shopping. Here too you should first decide what you want, or what your ultimate aim is. For example, your aim might be to procure the things you need in the shortest possible time. In this case you would focus your grocery shopping by preparing a shopping list that you either have in your head or written down somewhere. You then use this list to target only the shelves and aisles you need when you enter the store.
I would ask you to internalize the following principle of the 'Focus!' perspective: Before anything else, it is essential that you first identify and define what it is that you want to achieve, and, in the second step, how you plan to achieve it.

He gave me an encouraging wink.

And if we were to expand our focus to include the major themes of life, we should also look at a few other useful pointers.

"So was I wrong? Can the 'Focus!' not be applied to everything after all?"

Patience, my dear Mr Allman. Or do you want to make your all-important life decisions as quickly as you decide on your shopping?

"No, of course not. But right now I don't exactly have any life decisions to make. And we've already solved my main problem today – which I'm thrilled about!"

Alright. And I think you're now ready to lay the foundation for the upcoming life decisions you'll face.

"Doc, your comments are making me a bit nervous. Are you saying there's something large and difficult coming up that I don't know about? Should I be worried?"

Not at all. Think of it positively. I see that you can unfold your potential even further.

"OK then, if that's how you see it..."

For a moment, Dr Seer was silent, and I knew that he had an important point to make. Life decisions were not something he mentioned lightly. After a while he spoke again.

What is your focus in life?

The question completely threw me. I had to take a deep breath.

"What do you mean?"

What path are you on? Is it a path you really want to be on? And where is it leading you?

"Oh wow, here we go – here come the really big life questions. But what do they have to do with focus?"

Everything! Answering these questions will show you how focused you are in the living of your life.

"Hm. Isn't it enough to be focused in certain situations? Do I really need a 'big focus' that overarches everything else – you know, like a life focus or something?"

Dear Mr Allman, I sense a degree of resistance in you, which I can understand only too well. You feel like you have to question the direction your life is headed in. Have faith! And remember: Focussing on something means giving it your attention. And where attention goes, energy follows. Wherever this energy flows, something new can arise. Is it not wise to know where you want to focus your attention in your life? To be clear about what you really want? Especially where those "big life questions" are concerned, as you say.

"Yes, of course. Makes sense."

Let's begin by looking at what gets you going. What are your drivers? This will help to reveal your path. Let me put the following questions to you:

What's important to you?

What motivates you – or rather, what inspires you?

What gets you out of bed in the morning?

What have you always wanted to do?

Please take a moment to answer these questions.

Dr Seer got up and went over to the window. It was as if he wanted to give me more space, so I could find my own answers to his questions. My thoughts circled through my mind. I found the questions quite peculiar... I'd certainly never asked myself anything like them before.

"Could I have a piece of paper, please? I think I'll need to write this down."

Of course.

Dr Seer handed me a few sheets of blank paper.

Take your time!

I made a few vague notes while he gazed out the window, his ability to remain silent seemingly boundless. I didn't find the exercise particularly easy, but something inside told me that I should definitely complete the activity as requested. After a few minutes, I approached the Doc.

"OK, so I've come up with a few answers. But I don't know if they answer the questions properly."

Don't worry about that. Now, please share your answers!

"Alright then, here goes. So, to start with, a really good day would be one on which I don't have to go into the office. I'd open my eyes and think, 'Wow, the sun is shining and I can do whatever I want!'. I'd get up in the peace and quiet, make myself a cup of coffee, and think about what I might like to do with my day. I could go to a photography exhibition, for example. That kind of thing really inspires me. Or better yet, I could pick up my camera and just head out the door, taking pictures of any interesting objects I encounter along the way. Another thing I like to do on days off is to hang out with Andy, over coffee or with a beer and a sandwich, and to philosophize about movies and books... in summer, I'd sit outside, in the garden of the café, for example... Sometimes I wish I could write, too..."

Dr Seer had now returned to his chair, and seemed to feel encouraged by my remarks.

Fabulous! Your description reveals a number of answers to questions about what inspires you and what is important to you.

"Really? I thought it seemed rather wishy-washy. Aren't these the sorts of things that everyone wants to do on their day off?"

Without doubt there are plenty of people who'd like to have that kind of experience. In essence, people are very similar. Everyone wants to be happy. Let's direct the focus back on you, though. Allow me now to identify the essential elements deriving from your description: Freedom – serenity – spontaneity – creativity – connection.

I found these words somehow stirring. Whilst I didn't find my description of my ideal day particularly meaningful at first, I now realized that it had a certain significance, and contained some valuable information. A sudden sense of longing flashed through me.

"It's true, all those things are important to me!"

Dr Seer was visibly pleased.

It moves you!

"You can say that again! Listening to your summary could almost lead one to think that I'm quite profound."

You are profound, my friend! Beautiful things in particular touch us deeply. The words resonate within you, so you are touched emotionally. And this shows that the concepts of 'freedom – serenity – spontaneity – creativity – connection' are motivational forces in and of themselves for you. What's more, it shows that they provide energy that sustains you on your journey and moves you forward. These terms constitute personal values for you.

"Incredible. Totally mind-blowing!"

This brings us to the last item on the agenda for today. With the help of your imagination, we're now going to find out what you are attracted to, and what constitutes a positive impulse for you.

"How can we find that out?"

I would now like to invite you along on a little trip into your future. Taking this journey will enable you to pick up an image of the vision slumbering in your mind, that is, in your imagination.

"I'm ready and willing, Doc. How exciting!"

He smiled at me with a promising twinkle in his eye.

You should be.

He walked over to the window again and opened it wide. It was now pitch dark outside, and a gentle breeze blew in through the open window.

We need air for our virtual journey! Please take a deep breath, and fill your lungs!

I leaned back in my chair and tried to relax. I was tired from what had been a long day. That being said, today's conversation with Dr Seer had given me renewed energy. As usual, he knew exactly what I was thinking.

In these kinds of exercises, which don't involve the intellect, feeling a bit tired can actually prove quite helpful. It allows you to open yourself to other levels of consciousness with greater ease.

He closed the window, returned to his chair, and lit the candle on the table.

"OK, I'm ready."

Wonderful. So let's begin our journey, and take a virtual flight into your future. Please make sure you're sitting comfortably. Take a few deep breaths in and out. Close your eyes, or, if you prefer, focus your gaze on a point on the floor in front of you. Remember that there is no right or wrong in these exercises. Pictures might appear to you, in colour or black and white, or you might find that certain thoughts or feelings arise – all of which is totally normal, and nothing to worry about. Allow yourself to journey into your vast inner world, and focus on my words.

Although I had already learned a number of mental exercises through THE GOLDEN VIEW – like learning to travel through my body as a miniatureised version of myself, or to mentally visit my tropical island – right now, I felt as if something entirely new was about to reveal itself to me.

After a moment of silence, Dr Seer began to speak in a quiet, melodious voice:

Imagine that you are an eagle.

You are sitting on a fence post and looking into the distance.

You feel the warm wind on your feathers, and you feel comfortable.

I closed my eyes and allowed myself to be guided by his words, which although clear, increasingly felt as though coming from further and further away. He occasionally left long pauses in between his sentences, so that my mind was carried away with him as he spoke...

You take off and set out to explore the area, rising high into the air.

You feel the wind under your wings.

You glide over a vast landscape.

Below you are green meadows and fields.

You glide through the air and enjoy the sensation of flying.

In the distance, up ahead, you now see a small spot.

It's you.

You see yourself as a person in the future – as you will be in one to two years' time.

You are curious, and fly a little lower in order to take a closer look at your future self.

You examine yourself.

Look closely!

What do you look like?

What are you wearing?

What is your facial expression like? Are you smiling?

What do your eyes look like?

How do you feel?

What are you doing there – in your future?

How does it feel?

You fly a little further, and begin to circle around yourself.

Are there any people in your vicinity?

Who are these people?

What relationship do these people have to you?

How do you behave around them?

How do you communicate with each other?

Now widen your circle still more.

Where are you?

What kind of landscape are you in?

What does it look like?

What colour is the landscape?

What are your living arrangements there?

How does it feel to live there?

My sense of time seemed to melt away. I flew through the air, and saw everything clearly laid out before me. After a while the Doc's voice seemed to grow louder, as if he had come a little closer.

Circle through the air and take in the scene a few more times. You feel happy about everything you have seen, and now rise higher into the sky once more. You fly further across the green countryside, and eventually head back to your fence post, where you alight and rest from your trip.

I must have drifted far, far away. With eyes still closed, I noticed that I was only now slowly beginning to feel my body again. I tried to continue following Dr Seer's instructions.

Breathe deeply in and out a few times. And when you're ready, bring your attention back to our room. But take your time.

Slowly, I opened my eyes. I felt a little dazed by the trip I had just been on and all the images I had just seen. It had all seemed so real – so colourful and beautiful. I had a leaden taste in my mouth, almost as if I had slept for a long time. To clear my head, I took a long swig from my cup.

Dr Seer watched me with a smile, and gave me the time I needed.

How was it?

"It was incredibly impressive, Doc."

What impressions have you brought back from your trip to the future?

"I saw a lot of pictures in my mind's eye. It was strange: at first I could see the green countryside, but later, when I landed next to my future self, I saw that I was on a giant sailing ship. Did I do something wrong?"

Not at all. You've done absolutely nothing wrong. Please describe the scene to me. What did your future show you?

"Well, I was sat on the deck of a huge, magnificent three-master, feeling happy. A pleasant breeze was blowing and you could hear the cries of the seagulls and the sound of the sea. I looked out over the wide, deep blue sea, and then down at my lap, upon which there lay an open book with a black leather cover. The pages of the book were empty, which confused me a bit at first. Then I saw that I was holding a pencil in my hand as if I wanted to write or draw something. And my camera lay right next to me, within easy reach. Goodness me – what a wonderful experience."

Were there other people around you?

"Errm... it's kind of embarrassing. Please don't laugh, OK?"

His impish smile suggested that he already knew what was coming.

"You see, um, well... oh blimey, how to put it... well, Emily was there. She was lying next to me, wearing a brightly coloured bikini and soaking up the sun. There you go... I guess we could chalk that one up under 'typical male fantasizing'."

Do not be judgmental about your vision! It's beautiful! And very meaningful in terms of revealing your desires.

"Mm, that was lovely!"

Talking of Emily: What's the status quo on that front?

"Oh yes! I forgot to give you the update. I rang her."

Well done! And?

I knew that, in reality, there was no need for me to say anything at all: Dr Seer knew everything anyway. He had an incredible understanding of people. And, believe it or not, to cap it all he was also clairvoyant – of that there was no longer any doubt.

"Well, I called her, and we agreed to meet for another date. But we've both got so much going on that the earliest opportunity is in almost two weeks. We wanted to make sure we'd have enough time for a proper get-together, you see. And we can only manage that in two weeks' time."

A big grin spread across the Doc's face.

You see?

"Yes, Doc. You were right. I guess I jumped to premature conclusions. I was wrong to think that she wasn't interested in me, just because she didn't agree to my proposed second date straight away. Everything was easy in the end, and I got the impression she's really looking forward to it."

And are you?

"In truth, I can hardly wait to see Emily. But let's wait and see. You never know, eh..."

'Seeing' is where the wondrous secret lies.

Dr Seer definitely seemed to know more than he was letting on, and I was curious to find out what it was. Instead, an entirely different question popped into my mind, and came out a little clumsily.

"And so what do we do now?"

The Doc nodded at me.

What is your question?

"Well, in my imagination everything looks fabulous and I feel inspired. It all fits together. The things that inspire me, that matter to me, and the picture I have of my future – dreamed up, if that's the way to put it, during my eagle-flight."

What valuable insight!

"Yes! Only the problem is: it doesn't match my current life. Does that mean I have to give everything up and go on a journey? Because I can't see that happening, no way. It's just not feasible. I'm a bit confused about it all, now."

Don't worry! You're not expected to go running to the nearest travel agent. You have now experienced those things that touch you at a deeper level, that awaken you, and move you. You've also discovered what attracts you; your vision has revealed itself to you. All of these elements give you positive energy. This is a gift, and one that you have given yourself today.

Take the 'big focus' idea home with you, be aware of it and be mindful of the associated needs and impulses. Everything else will happen by itself. You will draw new experiences and opportunities into your life, and you will automatically know what to do at the right time. What you have done today is to lay the foundation stone, or sow the initial seed, within your consciousness.

"Wow. I don't know what to say to that..."

You don't have to say anything.

It was hard to put into words what I felt in that very moment. It was as if I had reached out and touched my own truth, and called it by its name.

We walked slowly back down the corridor. For the first time, I noticed that there was a clock hanging high up on the right-hand wall. It was set in a brass frame. I peered at it, trying to make out the time. It felt to me as

271

though Dr Seer and I had spent days together – but to my great surprise I discovered that today's meeting had lasted only two hours.

"Oh! I've only been here two hours. It seemed like much longer."

Dr Seer winked at me and glanced at the clock.

When you are focused, you gain a lot of time. And much more besides.

"I'm not sure that I quite get how all this stuff works, but whatever it is, it feels very good. Thanks a million, Doc."

You do understand it. You'll see!

Outside it was now pitch dark. I headed home in an almost trance-like state, overwhelmed by the insights and images that I had experienced within myself today. What had started as the search for a solution to a practical, everyday problem had resulted in a vision.

Where would it all lead?

20 Look back from the future!

Discerning what really matters on your life's journey

I kept asking myself what that last session with the Doc was about, and where my experiences would take me. I didn't have to wait long for a response, and when it came, it was so incredible that I almost fell off my chair during our usual Friday morning team meeting. It seemed that my changed behaviour had begun to influence my surroundings – including my working environment. For one, my boss' explosive temper had completely disappeared, and he actually praised me for working so efficiently. And then came the unbelievable part: having announced that the forecasts for next year were not as rosy as expected, my boss explained that the management team had decided to offer employees the option of taking a sabbatical, in order to avoid potential layoffs. Anyone taking a sabbatical could do so safe in the knowledge that their old job would be waiting for them when they returned. And would you believe it? The very next thing I heard my boss say was 'Who knows – maybe one of you has always wanted to sail around the world, or something like that'. Had I misheard him? Could this just be some sort of weird coincidence? It was only last week that I had taken that imaginary journey at Dr Seer's house – that magical flight that led me to the sailing boat. And having envisioned myself aboard the boat, I was now being presented with the opportunity of experiencing the exact same thing – for real, this time. As the Doc said at the time: 'You will draw new experiences and opportunities into your life, and you will automatically know what to do at the right time.' One such opportunity had apparently just opened up. It may sound contradictory, but I had no idea what to do. I had so longed for change. But now, with it right under my nose, it unnerved me. I felt completely overwhelmed.

Our next meeting took place on the weekend, so I arrived around noon at Dr Seer's house. He stood in the doorway with a mischievous smile on his face, as if he already knew everything I was about to report.

"Doc, you won't believe what's happened!"

273

Oh, I think I will. I told you that you'd attract new opportunities to yourself, didn't I. Welcome, Mr Allman!

Chuckling, he shook my hand.

The question is whether or not YOU can believe it.

We both burst out laughing. What with all the excitement, I guess my joy somehow just bubbled over. We made our way to our room, where he let me begin the conversation.

"How can it possibly be that the very opportunities you announced last week should suddenly drop into my lap? That's one heck of a coincidence."

You can view it as a coincidence. Or you can pat yourself on the back and congratulate yourself for instantly manifesting your vision.

"Hm. Do you really think there's a connection? Is it possible for wishes to come true so fast? I have to tell you absolutely everything that happened – and I have a decision to make, a big one."

Dr Seer looked at me pointedly.

Is it really about making a decision at this stage? Perhaps, in the first instance, it's about recognizing what really matters. By identifying what's important to you, the answer will clarify itself. But please, tell me all about it!

"So, my boss – who, incidentally, has been incredibly nice of late and hasn't had a single outburst, at least not with me – announced yesterday that he is offering staff the chance to take a whole year off. He called it a 'sabbatical', with the option of returning to work once it's over. Meaning you get your old job back at the end of the leave period. The sabbatical is unpaid, so you don't take home any income except for social benefits. But the details aren't even important right now. The upshot is that, theoretically, I could soon be on a sailing boat, drifting over the ocean. It could even happen by the beginning of the new year."

Fabulous!

"Hm."

You see it differently?

"I don't know. It all seems too good to be true, really."

My joy upon realizing that my dream was now so closely within reach felt noticeably overshadowed by something. Gently, the Doc helped me get to the bottom of these feelings.

Does it not seem realistic to you?

"It does, it does. That's not it. But I've got so many thoughts rushing through my head. Everything's suddenly moving so fast. Too fast for me, anyway."

I understand. 'Be careful what you wish for', as the saying goes, right?

Dr Seer seemed to be enjoying our current subject. But to me it all felt pretty exhausting.

"Speaking of 'fast' – it strikes me that not everyone will be able to take the bosses up on their offer – else they would have to close the business. The selection process will undoubtedly operate on a 'first come, first served' basis. So I should make sure I let them know as soon as possible, if I'm really interested in doing it."

So the question we need to address today is whether you sign up for this sabbatical year or not.

"Yes, exactly. I bet that from where you're standing it probably seems like a no-brainer: My vision of wanting to travel round the world by sail boat was crystal clear – so what am I waiting for, right?! Off we go! But it's not that simple, as far as I'm concerned."

Dr Seer nodded at me.

What thoughts are going through your head?

"Oh, far too many to list... besides which, I've got a few other voices sounding off in there, too!"

So you have your own reactions and thoughts regarding the sabbatical idea, and in addition you have opinions provided by other people?

"Precisely. You see, in my excitement I immediately called Andy to talk it through with him, and in the evening some colleagues and I went to a bar and discussed the whole thing in detail over a beer."

You had to process the news, of course. And you chose to do so by talking to other people about it – which I can totally understand. So tell me: What are all the things buzzing around in your head right now?

"Well, on one hand I'm thinking 'Yeah, go for it! I've been more or less waiting for just such an opportunity to come along – so say yes immediately! But then all these concerns start popping up: Can I trust the company to hold my job for me, or will it be gone by the time I get back? Is this just a cunning way to fire us? This was my colleagues' main concern. Of those I spoke to, none were interested in taking up the offer. They're totally sceptical of the whole idea."

I understand.

"The next voice that pops into my head then immediately criticises me for being so suspicious – even though that mistrust was generated more by the others than myself. I mean, I'll have a contract, after all. And then there's the question of financial security: I won't earn anything during the year out, and I would have to use up part of my savings to cover it, especially if I decide to go travelling for that length of time. Andy thought the whole idea was utterly ridiculous. And yet I'd been so certain that he, of all people – as the free spirit par excellence – would find the plan absolutely brilliant. As you may have noticed, I'm wracked with insecurities one moment, and yet totally thrilled and ready to go for it the next! Free at last, money no object! But then... does it have to be a full year's sabbatical? Can't I start on a smaller scale, to see how it goes before committing to twelve whole months? Oh man, it's driving me crazy. Back and forth, round and round... I'm tying myself up in knots."

I felt as though my head would burst from all the conflicting thoughts zipping through my mind. This made me all the more grateful to be able to sort through everything with Dr Seer.

These thoughts are only natural, you know.

"Hm."

Tell me, is there no-one with a positive take on the idea?

"Oh yes! I totally forgot! The only person who thought it a great idea was Emily. We spoke on the phone again, because she rang me to postpone our meeting by an hour. We chatted for a bit, and I mentioned the sabbatical idea. And, like I said, she thought it sounded fantastic!"

Now isn't that interesting! In your imagination she was with you on that sailboat, wasn't she.

Dr Seer could barely suppress an auspicious grin. Although it didn't do much to help sort my jumbled thoughts.

"What should I do now?"

Grinning, he raised his hand to his brow as if he were a ship's captain looking out over the ocean. I presumed he wanted to signal that there was a new golden perspective coming. After a moment, he spoke again.

There is a perspective of THE GOLDEN VIEW called: 'Look back from the future!'. **This is the one you need.**

"Oh! So you can help me make a decision about the sabbatical?"

Does that surprise you?

"Well, no, of course not. That's terrific!"

It's good that you feel so much joyful energy, despite the chaos in your head. Please note your current mood. It's an important clue.

"OK."

Dr Seer straightened himself up, and began to explain:

Looking back from the future entails an imaginary trip into the future. You will travel to a point in time far ahead of where you are now.

"Oh really?"

From there, you look back on the present moment and other significant periods in your life. The objective is to use this new perspective to clearly identify what really matters in your current dilemma – that is to say, what is most valuable in your life.

I listened to his words, full of expectation.

Let us first consider the central themes affecting everyone in life. During adulthood, it's about deciding on an apprenticeship or a degree: What makes me happy, what are my talents, what options do I have? This then leads us to career choices: What, where and for whom do I want to work? Or should I start my own business? All the while, love and partnership is usually in the foreground – closely followed by the desire to start a family, in many cases.

"Yes, these are the things that everyone between the ages of 20 and 50 is busy dealing with."

What you're saying is very important. Everyone is facing these same issues, some more consciously than others. They are all questions that are linked to certain time periods. Some issues can be dealt with flexibly within a relatively long space of time – such as the decision to do a training course, or switch jobs. You could retrain at 35, or change your profession at 50, if you want. You could even find a new partner after many years – these choices remain open to you for a long time. Some factors, however, have natural boundaries – time limits beyond which it is much more difficult to realize choices.
It is also important to recognize that there are opportunities and encounters that cross our paths only at certain points in time – and quite possibly only

once, unless we are lucky enough to be given a second chance. It is therefore important to be awake, and live with our eyes open, in order to consciously deal with the issues and opportunities that present themselves to us in life.

I suddenly felt uneasy again. I could only hope that I'd gone through my life so far with my eyes fully open. I suddenly felt like I'd rather not know.

"Doc, I understand what you're saying. But why do we need to look back from the future? Can't we just tackle my problem today, in the here and now? It seems very clear to me what stage of life I'm in and what the opportunity is that I'm being offered."

You ask an intelligent question! As always, by applying one of the perspectives of THE GOLDEN VIEW, we gain important information that we would not otherwise obtain. Let's take another more detailed look at your current situation.
You've a lot of thoughts spinning around in your head. Then there are out-side influences, and your emotions are tied to the whole lot. It's wonderful that we were able to use 'Focus!' to establish which passions are carrying you and what your dreams and visions are pulling you towards. Still, in the present moment we must recognize as real any additional external and internal influences that are affecting you – everything that is directly flowing to you right now. And then you want to free yourself of these influences in order to recognize your own truth. Looking at the situation from above would also be quite helpful, as you could view the scene from the meta-level in order to sort out what is going on and introduce more clarity.

Dr Seer watched my reaction closely, and undoubtedly noticed that he was pushing my powers of concentration to the limit.

Do you follow me?

"Yes, yes, certainly."

Alright. Now, what you will find when you 'Look back from the future!' is that the precision it brings will be decisive in moving you forward. The influences we just mentioned – that is, everything related to the current situation – become insignificant when viewed from the future. Or at least their significance becomes very much reduced. Some issues naturally resolve themselves over the course of the years, and in the end it comes down to something completely different. Namely, to having perceived and used opportunities that presented themselves to you along the way. To have lived what was really important to you. And you will be able to see that with crystal clarity using this perspective of THE GOLDEN VIEW.

"OK."

I suddenly felt the mild urge to flee. This topic seemed to be assuming ever greater proportions, and, as he was wont to do, Dr Seer made use of it to impart a significant lesson.

With a firm voice, he continued:

So how do we implement 'Look back from the future!'? It's simple. Begin by selecting a date in the future. You then look back on your life from this point in time. Please forgive me for being so blunt, but I cannot emphasize enough the importance of the decisions that you make in life. You see, at this stage, it's also about recognizing and feeling the fatality of all the unlived possibilities that may pass you by.

"Oh Doc, I can feel my throat closing up. How terrible that sounds – the fatality of unlived possibilities."

In some ways it is terrible. People allow their fears and negative beliefs to limit them. They let an unbelievable number of possibilities pass them by, and thereby cut themselves off from the opportunity to live a free, happy and fulfilled life.
But don't worry, we can convert this oppressive feeling of yours into a helpful insight. When we look at life from a future perspective, potentially missed opportunities reveal themselves very clearly. This way of seeing things also reminds you that life is not forever. It's an illusion to think that you have unlimited time to realize your dreams. I don't want to panic you – I simply want you to understand how precious your life is. And to think carefully about what you make of it.

"I don't want to miss any chances, ever!"

Nor shall you. Therefore, let's now look at your life using the appropriate perspective. Nothing 'fatal' has happened yet. You still have freedom of choice.

His words gave me considerable relief, and I was able to relax for a while. I took a deep breath before Dr Seer announced the first step.

What we're going to do now is select the point in time from which you will look back on your life. The impressive thing about this perspective of THE GOLDEN VIEW is that the further you go into the future, the clearer the picture becomes. The significance of situational contexts diminishes as a result, and the potential fatality of unlived possibilities is revealed very clearly. But let's put it positively: What we want to do now is identify which opportunities are opening up for you, how important they are for your life, and whether or not you want to seize them.
Let's choose a relatively high age from which to look back. When do you think you'll no longer need to work? At what point will you retire?

"Um. When I get my pension, I suppose. Who knows? It's possible there won't even be any pensions when I reach retirement age. Let's say 70?"

Alright, 70 it is. And what age do you think you'll reach?

"How old will I get? I don't know. What a question."

This isn't about making a realistic prediction, but about how it feels for you.

"Maybe around 85? If things go well."

Alright. Then I suggest we take the age of 77 for the purposes of our exercise. It's an age at which you will probably have reached the end of your working life, and at which you are likely to still have a few more years of life ahead of you.

I found this whole subject very challenging. I had often contemplated how old I might become. Who hasn't? But having to name an exact number and pin things down in the here and now was somehow strange. I suspect that this is precisely what the Doc had in mind, as a way of making me aware of the scope of my personal responsibility. I let out a deep sigh. Dr Seer waited a moment.

"OK, let's do it."

Great. Right then, please close your eyes and breathe deeply in and out. We're going to revisit the movies in our minds. Imagine that you're sitting in a big, comfortable, red cinema seat. Lean back and relax. Your work is done. You are now 77 years old, and a big chunk of your life lies behind you. Today's cinema showing is from the second half of your life to date. A retrospective, you might say. The film starts with a musical flourish, and the first images appear on the screen. You look back from the future to the moment when you were offered the chance to take a sabbatical, and let the film run its course...

I thought I could hear actual music. Had the Doc put on a CD? The first few images began to appear in my mind's eye. I felt as though I was actually sat in a cinema, watching myself up there on the big screen as the main character, acting a little confused and agitated.

What do you see?

"Well, I see myself. I'm confused, and agitated."

And then? What happens next?

"Doc, it's a shame, you're not in the picture. I see myself going to work. It's a day like any other, with nothing out of the ordinary happening. I carry on as before. Hm... I looked a bit confused and agitated at first, as if something unexpected had happened, but everything seems to have settled into a routine now."

Good. Now please fast-forward a little. Let Christmas go by on the screen, and see yourself starting into the New Year. Please remember to

keep seeing things through the eyes of that elderly gentleman looking back on his life.

"OK. Yes, I see it... it seems like nothing has changed. I return to work in the office. The festive season is over, and my Christmas break has ended. Funny. I guess I haven't taken a sabbatical, then."

Puzzled, I opened my eyes.

"Hm, then I guess things will probably stay the same? I could always just take a 14-day sailing trip next year, I suppose."

Yes, you could. Please close your eyes again and watch a bit more of the film.

"OK. So the New Year comes along. New projects kick off at work, and everyday life runs its course. I book the sailing trip for early summer, and find myself looking forward to it."

Alright.

"Yes, so far, so good. I don't look unhappy or anything. I'm apparently still glad that I didn't accept that new job a few months ago. It would've brought me nothing but stress, and a bit of extra cash. Everything seems OK."

Great. Let's continue with the film.

"Hm. The year takes its normal, predictable course. Nothing worth mentioning happens in the first few months. I presume I spend them looking forward to the summer holidays but I can't clearly see what's on my mind. In early summer I go on the sailing trip and enjoy two weeks of sun and sea. Yes, it's a lovely time."

How does the year continue?

"In the summer and autumn everything proceeds as usual, followed by the nerve-wracking phase that heralds winter. This period is insanely stressful every year, and by the time it's over the year is almost at its end. And now it's just before Christmas again. Even though I didn't take the sabbatical year, I still had a great holiday and was even able to put some money aside for a rainy day. Oh – sorry Doc, would you give me a moment? I need a short break. I don't feel so good, all of a sudden!"

Out of nowhere, I felt a strange sense of unease well up inside me. It was as though something was pinning me down, forcing me to stand still without moving.

What's changed?

"Nothing, really. But that's just it! If what I'm seeing here was a real movie, one that I'd paid good money to go and see, I'd have stood up and walked out by this point. How boring and uninteresting it is! The same old treadmill. And to think that I let the chance to escape it all pass me by when it was held right under my nose. All the joyful energy, as you called it, is completely gone!"

An extremely important clue! Please look at it closely. Things should become very clear.

"I think it's already pretty clear. Goodness, no! No way – that's not what I want at all!"

Alright. Now return to the film, and look at the years that follow. How do the next five years go? Do you get offered a similar option again at a later point?

"Who can say? What happens if I don't? Maybe it's a one-off opportunity, one that never comes around again! Maybe I just missed out on something special. And am now stuck with marching to the same beat of the same drum, year in and year out, forever. Well... maybe for the next 20 years. Twenty years without ever getting to go out and experience something new. I'm absolutely appalled!"

What you are feeling is very significant. What does it look like once your working life is behind you? Is there then scope to experience something new?

"You mean, once I'm retired? And I look back from the future to myself at 70 years old? And I'm finally free to act upon what feels important to me in my heart?"

Yes, exactly.

It was hard to keep my eyes shut, but somehow I managed.

"Doc, who knows what might happen! I'm supposed to start living when I'm 70? No, no way! I can't see it. And I feel a kind of reluctance to go there right now."

That's fine, and this is all valuable information for us. Please describe for me what you're thinking and feeling right now.

"I'm wondering whether I'll still be in a fit state to get out there and do all the things I want to achieve at 70. Will I really have the money then? And should I really wait another 25 years to see if this 'maybe' pans out? This is crazy! It depresses me just thinking about it. What am I waiting for, anyway? Am I waiting until I'm old enough to finally figure out all the things I *could have* experienced, only to realize that it's too late to go back and make them happen? Oh no! I'm past that point now. I've developed so much already, and now it's time to put all that inner growth into practice and live it! I don't want to have any regrets when I'm old!"

Although my eyes were still tightly shut, it was as though the scales had suddenly fallen from them. I saw how precious my life was, and how urgent it was that I begin to treat it that way, and start to transform it into the kind of life I want to lead. I couldn't aspire to 'live consciously' whilst clinging to the secure treadmill of my usual routine – these two approaches were incompatible with one another. Once again I felt something click into place inside me – in a big way, this time!
I sensed that Dr Seer was delighted by my obvious Eureka-moment.

This is hugely insightful!

"Perhaps I even find such happiness during the sabbatical year that I don't bother returning to my day job – and if I do, at least I might come back reenergized, full of inspiration and new impressions. I could start over and do everything differently – I could be more creative, more free. If I *don't* go, everything will stay as it is and my dreams will never have the opportunity to come true. I want to experience something completely different, and not just once I reach my seventies. This could turn out to be *the* year of my life!"

As if wanting to applaud me, the Doc softly clapped his hands together.

Indeed it could be!

"How could I explain to my children, if I ever have any, that I didn't seize my big chance because of money worries, or because I was afraid, or others were sceptical? What kind of role model would I be? And at the moment I have absolutely no responsibilities beyond myself. There's simply no reason to pass over opportunities."

Dear Mr Allman. You are now seeing things very clearly, and speaking wise words indeed. Let me explain something important about responsibility: You are always primarily responsible for yourself. Take care of yourself first, and then you can take care of others. Find your inner balance, and that balance will also have a positive impact on others. An unhappy person cannot bring happiness to anyone else. Remember this well, should you one day start a family. Don't look outside for arguments or even excuses for your actions. Never close your eyes to your own truth and reality. It will always come to light. And this shouldn't happen purely at the point when you have your back to the wall. Missed opportunities can cause a lot of pain, both to yourself and to your fellow man.

"I get that. And yet I still have a stupid question."

There's no such thing as a stupid question, Mr Allman. Certainly not where you and I are concerned. But then you know that already.

"You're right. I guess I'm just wondering whether that means I should now start rushing around all over the place, trying to experience anything and everything. Good grief... should I up and sell all my things, and set off with a backpack? Should I throw myself into every adventure that comes along so as not to miss anything? Buy myself a copy of "100 things to do before you die" and start working my way through it?

Dr Seer clapped his hands again, a gesture that most likely served some other purpose. Did he perhaps want to wake me up, or shake me out of my reverie?

What an excellent question! And the answer is: no. Don't worry. The solution is not to indiscriminately try out everything and anything and throw yourself into a wild kind of lifestyle, but about striving to live according to what is important and true for you. It's about following your vision!

"And how do I know what exactly is important and true for me?"

You just know. You see it already.

"Yes, I suppose."

What else do you see when you look back from the future?

I had opened my eyes again. And in that moment, everything appeared clearly in my mind's eye. The movie screen earlier had probably just helped me apply this perspective correctly.

"You know Doc, things have changed a lot since I've been coming to see you. I've come a long way. I see things differently now, and am much better at dealing with myself. I think I now move through the world seeing things with different eyes. And today I've realized that, for the next step, I must now trust myself to make radical changes in my everyday life. I notice how tired I am all the time, and I keep wondering how much longer I can cope with the ongoing stress – whether I'll eventually end up burning out, or suffering a heart attack. It's not worth it! What am I doing all this for, anyway? Sure, I have to earn money. But I could also choose to live a very simple and modest life. I don't need much. I spend most of my time doing things that are far removed from life's existential essence and the creative powers of creation."

Smiling, Dr Seer nodded to me.

"Besides which this world we live in is pure madness, with its focus on success, power and money. I believe that focusing on the wrong things in life is absolutely fatal. That's how I see it, at least. Or rather, that's how I've now come to see it. Thank goodness."

You have summarised it beautifully! I admire your courageousness, of course – but please try to look kindly upon yourself and others. Next time we'll examine more closely how you can look at other people with kindness. For now: Don't judge! It's asking a lot to just let go of everything and suddenly forego all security. Some never manage to do it, nor do some ever want to. There is no universal formula or right and wrong way of living. It's just as likely that a person may discover that they want to stay right where they are – and that this is then the best choice for them.

Suddenly adopting a more serious expression, Dr Seer sat bolt upright in his chair and addressed me in a slightly louder voice.

It's important that you also understand the following point: Everyone lives and learns at their own pace. Everyone is different and reacts differently. Everyone has his or her own unique themes and visions in life. Everyone can decide – consciously or unconsciously – which priorities to set and how they want to live. Therefore there is no single, clearly defined ideal path. By the same token, there are no universal errors that apply to everyone – your mistakes will not necessarily be the same as someone else's.
Of course there are obstacles that people often unconsciously place in their own way. Many never face their fears and inner pain, and so repress their feelings – and thereby their own truth. This shrouds their true desires and visions under a veil that often only lifts when it's almost too late – when they find themselves in a personal crisis, or suffering illness or unforeseen loss. It doesn't have to come to this if you consciously engage with yourself. This you have known for quite some time now. But now back to your current situation. If you feel ready to do so, then distance yourself from external influences and the expectations of others. Explore your own values, and utilise your opportunities!

"I want to, I really do! But why do other people want to impose their opinions on me at all, and why does it influence me so much?"

Other people's expectations and opinions often serve as an expression of their fears and beliefs. When interacting with you and expressing themselves, they unconsciously use you as a screen upon which to project their own feelings. In turn, your unconscious response is to want to meet the expectations of others fairly, and to avoid criticism and setbacks. Ultimately, this is because of your desire to be accepted and loved. That's the reason you take to heart what people around you say.

"So what you're saying is that those giving me advice and expressing their opinions are basically speaking about themselves... and so their concern is not really to help me with my decision?"

Dr Seer winked at me.

Indeed! And this is a very common occurrence. Of course, most people don't do so consciously, and so generally speaking they don't have bad intentions. Don't forget about seeing more than meets the eye: A person's behaviour is primarily determined by their own inner state. The advice a person gives you largely depends on their own situation. This too is a question of consciousness, of awareness. The more consciously a person is able to deal with themselves and others, the better they can free themselves from their own emotions and concerns when advising others.

"OK, that seems logical. So those who are truly conscious are probably very few in number, right? Hm. I've become more conscious over the last months, haven't I. So that must mean I'm not so easily influenced by others, right?"

You'll get there. You have worked on yourself a lot, but a little more is required to dissolve your fears and negative beliefs completely. The utterances of other people still activate the remnants of deep fears and limiting beliefs that lie hidden within you.

"What are these fears and beliefs you speak of? Is it along the lines of the whole 'making myself feel inferior' thing that we've already worked on a few times?"

As if from nowhere, a strong sense of unease rose up inside me. Had I still not overcome this feeling from long ago? I felt an uncomfortable pressure on my chest and tried to breathe more deeply. The Doc noticed what was going on, and proceeded in a gentle manner.

Dear Mr Allman, it doesn't mean that everything was in vain, you know. Your self-image has already changed, and you have grown much stronger. If it were otherwise, you would not now be able to give yourself these valuable impulses for your life! It's possible that you still carry a few negative beliefs concerning your future. And all that means is that now is the time to recognize them, and eventually dissolve them.
Let's now look together at any limiting beliefs still remaining within you concerning the current sabbatical year dilemma. What objections come to mind when you think about making the trip.

"Well, for a start I won't earn any money."

Why would this matter while you are on the trip?

"Because I'd have to rely on my savings."

What's the consequence of using up your savings?

"I'd lose my security."

What happens if you lose your security?

"In the worst case, I end up on the street."

Dr Seer wouldn't let up.

Why would you end up on the street if you had no more savings in the bank?

"Because I don't know if I could get another decent job if I couldn't return to my old one."

Hm. So if you don't get your old job back – an eventuality that shouldn't actually arise thanks to the contract, as far as I understand it – and you have used up your savings, you worry that you won't be able to find a new job.

"It sounds kind of funny when you summarize it like that, but – yes, that's about the long and the short of it."

OK. Why do you think you wouldn't find a new job?

"Oh, I don't know. I'm not really the career type. I'm nothing special. No-one will be waiting for me to show up, I can tell you."

I see. Why not?

"In terms of professional skills I'm just not particularly good. There are thousands of great candidates out there – you know, real experts and high-flyers. Why on earth would they want me?"

Dr Seer could get very serious when I drifted off into self-deprecation. It had been a while since it last happened with such intensity, and I now picked up on it myself. He gave me a penetrating stare.

Mr Allman, may I remind you how highly motivated you were when you finally decided you wanted a pay rise? At that point in time you argued that you were a 'top employee' who definitely deserved a better salary. And by using the 'eye of the tiger' perspective you managed to achieve what you wanted.
With that in mind, now consider what you're feeling at the moment: look closely at the mechanisms at work within you. In terms of your future career, you are devaluing yourself massively!
You're not looking kindly upon yourself. What we're seeing here is a negative belief, the deep-seated fear associated with it, and a lack of self-esteem. On a deeper level you are still questioning your professional competence. This is the cause of your insecurity, and what is inhibiting your ability to make a free choice.

"I actually thought I was pretty good at the whole 'looking at myself with kindness' thing. But what you say is true. Although I looked at the salary increase as being absolutely justified, I obviously still didn't really

291

acknowledge the extent of my professional competence. I wouldn't have thought that this was still an issue lying dormant in my subconscious. I guess what this means is that I don't trust myself to go on this trip because I don't have enough confidence in myself regarding my career and the degree of financial security linked to it. Is that it, Doc?"

It seems you have a considerable degree of self-doubt where this aspect is concerned, yes.

"Hm."

Let us now look back for a moment, so that we may arrive at the core of your doubt. Do you recognize this feeling from the past? Have you ever experienced unemployment, or have you ever lost a job because your performance was not good enough? Was your existence ever threatened by such a situation?

"No, not really. The jobs I've had were not necessarily all that fulfilling, but I've never been without employment of one kind or another. That is to say, I was once, but only for a few weeks. It didn't threaten my existence, though."

You see. And yet the fear is there. This is associated with a belief that you may have even taken on in earlier years.

"Yes, you're right. My mother was very frugal – she was always worrying about not having enough. And after my father left us, our lack of money became a constant issue. I guess that left its mark on me. I felt so utterly helpless at the time."

Thus we can see that this existential anxiety is based on real experiences that you had as a child. You've picked up this worry from your mother. However, as an adult you have not yet had a real experience that would "legitimately" sustain the fear: the fear is instead based on a limiting belief. People carry all sorts of beliefs like this inside them. Thoughts such as: 'without financial security I'll end up on the street'; 'I'm not good enough'; 'only accomplishment brings reward'; 'I'm not worth it'; or even 'I don't deserve to be happy and cared for'.

Almost everyone accrues and embeds these kinds of convictions in them-selves over the course of their lifetime, especially as a result of experiences gathered at a young age. We already looked at this when we learned about looking at ourselves with kindness.

The more consciously you engage with yourself, and the more you integrate THE GOLDEN VIEW, the more clearly you can identify and resolve your limiting beliefs. So much so that you will eventually no longer be affected by them. Once again: the choice is yours.

"Does that mean I can consciously decide to no longer feel inferior at work, and thus to not miss out on any further opportunities? Because I deserve it?"

Dr Seer seemed satisfied. And suddenly I felt relieved.

That is exactly what it means! If you make the decision deep in your heart, and anchor it emotionally, then it will work.

"My eyes have suddenly been opened, Doc! Yes, of course: why ever not? Even without the option of taking a sabbatical, I'd still have to leave! I can't let old professional fears influence my big opportunities in life! We're talking about my whole life's happiness, here!"

Wonderful! Be generous to yourself! Anxiety is a very human trait. And the security of the double floor, a sabbatical year with the option of return, is absolutely fine. A superb solution that will undoubtedly lead to new opportunities. Who knows if you'll want to return to your old job at all after going on your big trip?

"Yes, I've asked myself the same question. Right now I feel so free! It's clear that I need to move on, and head out into the world. There is so much more out there than my daily routine here. So much to discover! The way I feel right now, I'd have no fear of completely letting everything go."

Beaming, the Doc clapped his hands in appreciation. I broke out in a big smile.

My compliments, Mr Allman! You've come a long way, much further than some manage in their entire lives. Not holding on to supposed security is very important. For at the end of his life a man can take nothing, absolutely nothing, of material value with him. By that point at the very latest you have no choice but to let go of everything anyway. How wonderful that you are already capable of doing it now. It will open up endless possibilities in your life, and provide a lot of freedom on your path to self-realization. You are clearly now ready to live this.

"I totally get it now. But tell me Doc, does this mean that anyone on the path to self-realization should stop doing anything that is purely for the sake of earning money? I'm not talking about my plan to not work for a year, of course – that's all about self-realization, isn't it. I guess I'm thinking about afterwards. Could I then take a job purely on the grounds that it would make me a lot of money, or would I then automatically be working against my journey of self-realization because the primary focus would be on the money?"

I'm pleased that you ask this question, because it's undoubtedly something that preoccupies many people who are on the path to self-discovery. On the whole, there is of course no reason why you should not undertake something for the money. The fullness of life can and should be lived, including materially. There is no reason not to also pursue the goal of being financially well off, or even very well off, and to be able to satisfy material desires. Having a secure existence is actually a prerequisite for anyone on the path to self-realization. Material prosperity can help to ease and beautify our lives.

At the same time, you should take pains to ensure that the realization of your desires and the fulfilment of the true needs of your soul don't get neglected. It's like a balance sheet with costs that have to be paid. When you invest all your time in a job that is not in line with what your soul wants to realize, then the account will be overdrawn – even if the job earns you exorbitant amounts of money. Going on that luxury Caribbean holiday once a year will not ultimately make you happy, and nor will the expensive car or the huge apartment you live in.

Very many people succumb to the fallacy of believing that they can be truly happy only when they are rich. So they chase after money, but discover that filling up a bank account doesn't bring them happiness – on the contrary. Even those who suddenly come into a lot of money don't suddenly acquire the inner contentment that people imagine comes with large financial gains. Why do you think that is?

"Hm. Maybe because they still continue to repress their fears, and don't take a closer look at what's going on inside themselves? They don't get to know themselves any better just because they're suddenly rich. Instead, they continue to cover up what's going on in their souls, just as they did before, right? So in spite of being rich they still don't know what they actually desire."

Very well recognized! Money cannot buy consciousness. And consciousness is essential for true happiness.

"Yes, you taught me that when you taught me the 'Stop right there!' perspective – 'to find happiness we must become conscious!' Now I understand it even better! But does that mean the reverse is also true? Are unhappy people unconscious?"

No, not at all. Feeling unhappy could simply be an initial signal that you want to change something, and so it can mobilize awareness. Highly conscious people can also experience phases of unhappiness. Even so-called 'enlightened' individuals are not immune to such feelings. The difference is that such people are better equipped to get to grips with their emotions and change the situation much faster.

If you consciously engage with yourself and have enough time to recognize and live your own unique authenticity, according to what your soul wants, then theoretically you can also pursue a profession that is primarily about money. However, you will come to see and experience that consciousness brings with it the steadily increasing desire to link self-realization with your professional path. Some discover this sooner, some later. But even this does not contradict the idea of making money. If your occupation brings you joy, or even satisfies an inner calling, then there's no problem with it also providing you with enough money. On the whole, it's about pursuing both financial security and the realization of your journey with vigilance and trust. Only then will everything come together.

"Thanks Doc, what a great explanation."

This little excursus was based on your excellent question.

"Thank you for always empowering me so much, Doc! I now find myself wondering why on earth I was so confused at the beginning. It all seemed so complicated at the time."

The human cognitive process begins with what is often a simple, but seemingly unsolvable, question. This is then followed by what is usually a complex process that involves many thoughts, feelings and options. This is the phase in which things appear complicated. Finally, insights crystallize, and are revealed in terms that are once again clear and simple.

"What a great philosopher you are! And it's absolutely true. Suddenly everything seems easy. I'll do it. Most definitely. First thing tomorrow morning I'll sign up for the sabbatical year."

Bravo! Congratulations on your newly won freedom!

Dr Seer gave me his hand. And I felt new energy rise up within me – a huge feeling of anticipation that was hard to put into words.

"You know what?"

I think I do. What do you mean specifically?

"Wouldn't it be awesome if Emily came with me on my journey? In her bright, colourful bikini... that would be a dream! Ha – my imagination's running away with me now."

Dr Seer placed a friendly hand on my shoulder, and clearly could not resist a smile.

You know what power your dreams have! And love is what it's all about. This possibility, too, should not remain unlived. You'll see. And yes, you're very well prepared for your date with Emily. Be open!

"Yes, I am. Gosh, it would be way too good to be true. I have to say that I'm amazed at my own courage as it is – but somehow my plan feels absolutely right."

I'm proud of you!

"To be honest, right now I'm even a little proud of myself."

You should be!

Laughing, we left our room and walked down the corridor of mirrors. Everywhere I looked I was confronted with my grinning reflection, multiplied along the wall.

"Wow, I can't believe what looking back from the future has done for me. I'm so glad you're here, helping me to know and live what is true. What would I do without you, Doc?"

You're following your path either way, Mr Allman. And I can support you and accompany you. I'm happy for you. You are awake now.

We shook hands once again.

"Yes, I feel absolutely awake! And full of this joyous energy again – it's incredible."

And you know what? The more awake you are, the faster and better you'll recognize other opportunities that life offers you. These opportunities will come and make themselves known to you!

"That sounds good! I thank you, Doc! From the bottom of my heart!"

It's my heartfelt pleasure, my friend!

Part III

HEART-OPENING & SELF-REALIZATION

21 See with the heart!

Love as a way of life

I was happy! For the first time in my life it felt like everything fit together just as I wanted it to. I had spoken to my boss and applied for the sabbatical year. A whole year of freedom in which to realize what had hitherto only been dreams. I felt completely liberated at the thought! But that wasn't all: I had met with Emily again, and was head over heels in love. And she was too! Could it really be that love had found its way into my life? And, on top of it all, that the doors leading to the realization of all my dreams were now fully open?

When I arrived at Dr Seer's house I felt like I was walking on air.

You're beaming, my friend!

I could say the same of him. Grinning broadly, he stretched out his hand.

"Yes, I feel fantastic, Doc!"

One look at you and the diagnosis is clear: You're in love, aren't you. What's more, you're sensing your heart! I'm glad to see that you're now ready!

"What do you mean?"

I almost felt a bit cocky.

"Ready to go on that trip around the globe? To get married? Or to just get out there and embrace the whole world! To finally be who I really am?"

Dr Seer stopped in front of the wall of mirrors in the corridor.

All that and much more! Come, follow me. Today we'll go to another room.

This time Dr Seer didn't turn down the passage on the right as usual, but instead headed to the left. It was the corridor we had gone down once before, when we went up to the roof terrace. Without further explanation, he went through one of the doors at the back.

Please follow me!

A huge room opened out in front of me, at least three times as large as the two rooms we'd used for our many meetings over the past weeks and months. Once again I noticed that I had absolutely no concept of the lay-out of the house. From the outside it didn't look particularly big or tall, but once inside there seemed to be countless rooms and floors. In one sense, this house was a physical representation of the way in which perception always depends on the point of view of the observer. Each perspective determines its own respective reality. The room itself was completely white, like the last one, and seemed much brighter even though it had the same number of windows. It also had a higher ceiling, at least five or six metres high, which made it feel more like a modestly sized hall. In the middle stood two armchairs covered in a white silk fabric, with a white marble table between them. The walls were bare apart from a mirror on the far wall that was at least three by three metres in size, edged with a broad, golden frame.

Welcome to the inner core!

Dr Seer's voice echoed in the lofty space. I was impressed by the atmosphere in the room, which was somehow pure and clear. The thought occurred to me that perhaps this was the first time anyone had ever been inside it.

"Is that what this room is called?"

Dr Seer nodded to me.

It's called, 'The Inner Core'. You have arrived at your own inner core.

Reverently, I entered the space and walked across the seemingly endless hall. The Doc gave me time to gather myself. I stopped in front of the mirror with the golden frame and gazed into it for a while. Doing so felt completely different to the time when we practised looking in the mirror. I

301

now felt more comfortable, because a friendly face looked back at me. I felt anticipation and confidence – and courage. I was aware of a softness that gave me strength. I looked at myself and saw that I had changed. Apparently the fact that I hadn't smoked for a while now had also had a positive impact. What's more, for the last few weeks I had frequently gone outside for a 'conscious walk' in the fresh air, even though winter was approaching. I was much more in touch with my body. My complexion was fresher, and overall I thought I was looking a lot healthier than before. Dr Seer came over to where I was standing and looked over my shoulder at my reflection, as he was wont to do.

Do you know what it is that you are seeing here?

"What do you mean?"

What feelings do you see?

"I see several. Positive, good feelings."

Carefully, he stepped back a little, while keeping his gaze on me. He took an audible breath, waited a few seconds, and then spoke in a deep, sonorous voice:

I see love.

His words filled the entire room, and absurd as it might sound, it felt as though they echoed within *me*, too. I stood before the mirror and noticed a strange warmth sweep over me. I closed my eyes and tried to focus on perceiving what was happening to me. My breathing was calm and deep. Suddenly, I heard the Doc's voice, somehow sublime, as if coming from far away and from everywhere all at once – and yet also as if rising out of my own self.

You have opened your heart.

When I opened my eyes again, I noticed in the mirror that Dr Seer had taken a seat in one of the white armchairs. Beckoning me over, he asked me to join him.

Come, take a seat!

As if dazed and yet fully conscious at the same time, I went and sat down beside him in the other white armchair. Everything seemed so pristine and precious here that I felt compelled to be very careful with my movements.

Please, feel completely at ease. Make yourself comfortable!

I leaned back and sighed deeply. The Doc watched me in his inimitable, reassuring way. After a few minutes he began to speak.

Love. Love, my friend, is a feeling that we carry in our hearts – a feeling that gives meaning to our existence. It provides us with the spiritual and emotional energy to live. It is a feeling we can sense for ourselves when we are ready. It is one of self-confidence and self-worth. Love is the antithesis of fear. You have experienced all this in recent weeks and months. You have understood it – and felt it.

I listened attentively to what he was saying. It was as though I was being addressed by an oracle or something, although this strange perception was probably due to my own somewhat altered state.

Love for another person and love in partnership manifests itself in the interpersonal flow of trust, esteem, respect, dedication and passion. Ideally, it is like a gift that we give to each other again and again. It helps us to evolve and grow on a personal level. Being in love releases a wonderful energy that gives us lightness and depth of feeling at one and the same time. It is the beauty of life that you can feel in yourself. You're experiencing it right now, aren't you?

"Yes, it's wonderful."

With a concentrated expression he held his gaze on me.

Love is the overarching emotion that encompasses all positive feelings in life: trust, devotion, faith, compassion, appreciation, understanding, forgiveness, gratitude, joy. All positive feelings derive from love. In the spiritual sense, these feelings have a high vibration. They cause us to draw positive encounters and pleasant and beautiful interpersonal experiences into our lives. Do you remember? Joy is what makes our longings and desires a reality.

"Yes."

What we shall look more closely at today is how anchoring love deep in our hearts enables it to become more than just a state of mind – it becomes a way of life.

I recalled that Dr Seer had once spoken of looking at things with love.

"Is there a golden perspective for it?"

What do you think?

"It sounds like there should be. Called 'the look of love', or something like that."

You're very close! And clearly well-versed in THE GOLDEN VIEW. This fills me with great joy. But before we consider how love looks at things, we'll first stick with how love feels. I'd like you to anchor and expand this feeling within you.

Knowingly, he winked at me.

I'm pretty certain you have something to tell me, do you not?

My heart instantly began beating faster. With an awkward motion I tried to sit up straight in my chair. This subject was so important to me that I almost began to stutter.

"Doc, I... yes, I met with Emily again. And... well, I thought of you and of what you advised me. That I should show my feelings. It was incredible... beautiful, even. We met at the café again, and we talked for hours. It was quite different to our first meeting. More familiar, and somehow closer. I felt more free, and much safer. I managed to detach myself a little from the need to evaluate every word she spoke, which meant I was able to simply listen to her. And she kept looking at me so warmly and openheartedly that I almost melted into a puddle at her feet! She's an amazing woman!"

Dr Seer was pleased with me.

Your happiness is obvious!

I sensed how important it was for me to tell him everything, right down to the last detail. At the same time I was so swept up in the intensity of my feelings for Emily that it hardly seemed possible to recount everything in full.

"By the way, Emily explained to me that the reason she reacted the way she did after our first date was because she was still going through the final stages of separation from her ex-boyfriend. That's all over now, and she said that she now feels total relief. Doc, you won't believe it, but after a few hours I touched her hand, just like you said. And she responded! She said that she feels like we might be soul mates. Is there such a thing? And she stressed that she feels utterly safe with me, as though we've known each other forever."

I had to sigh deeply.

"Emily wanted to go for a walk, and she asked me if I would like to go for a late stroll with her. So then, just before midnight, we went outside and walked in the park, hand in hand, in silence. It was pretty chilly outside, but utterly beautiful. To be honest, I've never been all that romantically inclined. Whenever Andy gave me passages to read from his romance novels, I often felt wooden. I've never known this kind of romance and passion before. Well, I have to say that I find Andy's style a bit extreme sometimes, what with the emotional highs he sometimes hits when he's drunk on love."

But I believe I now have an idea of what romance means for me personally."

You have to experience it yourself to really feel it.

"Yes. On our night-time walk I told Emily that I'm in love with her. And you know what she did? She kissed me! We kissed! Doc, it may sound weird but I've never felt so much in a kiss before. It was as if the whole world was dissolving around us."

After telling Dr Seer all about my experience with Emily, my feelings now seemed even stronger. Something in me felt reborn. It's incredible to think how long it has been since I last felt this feeling of being in love. I had probably never even experienced the real thing. It gave me strength and a special kind of optimism that is difficult to put into words. Through it, everything seemed lighter. What had I missed, over all these years!

Dr Seer followed my thoughts as usual.

You experience love when you are willing to experience it. You first had to work on yourself and follow your path in order to be able to open to it.

"That's so true."

I was very grateful to Dr Seer. What immense good fortune to have his guidance and support. Each of our conversations had made me ever more conscious of that fact.

I wish you and Emily a wonderful, loving relationship.

"Oh Doc, I can hardly believe that something as wonderful as this should happen to me. It feels so good! Do you honestly think I can manage it?"

Dr Seer smiled.

You're already doing it now. You just need to let it in. You've come a long way. You have learned so much about yourself, about life and about love. Now you need to live it.

Involuntary, tears rose in my eyes.

"I'm totally ready for it, Doc."

Dr Seer nodded at me. After a while, he once again began to speak.

Are you aware that the fact that your heart is now open is not just because you're in love? You have centred yourself in your own self-trust and self-love. You have experienced your fears and pains, examined them, and allowed them to become experiences from which you have grown. When we look directly into our fears and dissolve them, then we move ever more into our love, into our trust, into our own personal power. The power of our hearts.

Thus you are now ready to let love become a way of life, as I said earlier. Would you like to learn this perspective of THE GOLDEN VIEW?

A strange silence filled the room, making it somehow difficult to speak. At the same time I felt as though I was about to make a big announcement, one that would affect my life from top to bottom. Meaningfully, and as if in slow motion, I nodded in response to Dr Seer's question.

This perspective is called 'See with the heart!'. When you see with your heart, you pour love into the world! In every interaction with another person you not only create something positive, you create an opening. And thanks to the principle of resonance, this inevitably comes back to you. You will reap what you sow...

I intuitively understood what it was all about. And yet I wanted to know more.

"So how exactly does this perspective work? Is it kind of like looking at the world with kindness?"

Yes, precisely!

"So that means trying to see the good in others instead of all the things I don't like. Forgiving those around me if they hurt me... and trusting them?"

Motioning from his heart to mine with a sweeping gesture, Dr Seer demonstrated his appreciation of my definition.

You won't be needing me much longer, I can tell!

"Oh, Doc, don't say that!"

We both laughed. After this light-hearted moment, the Doc again took up the thread of what he had been saying – clearly this was a lesson that was very important to him.

Let's take a closer look. Seeing with the heart isn't about reciting ethical principles to yourself and trying to be a good person. It's not about the rational intent to act in a morally correct manner.
This perspective brings about a lot more, and in doing so affects our entire being. It greatly influences your own behaviour, and will determine how other people react to you. It gives a whole new quality to your life and leads you to a new level of self-realization and manifestation of your potential.
Seeing with the heart doesn't originate from the intellect, but from the self-confidence and feeling of love that we engender in ourselves. And the beauty of it is that this, in turn, also encourages you to trust that you are able to greatly influence your own life.

"Why is that?"

Because we are all energetically connected to each other. How you see the world is how you see yourself. Most people have yet to realize this. Each judgment we make about other people is a statement about how we see ourselves, deep down inside. Do you remember? Everything comes back to us. Anyone who trusts themselves, and endeavours to work on and grow from their so-called failures, will not devalue another human being. Self-reflection and personal growth allow us to accept that others make mistakes and are currently on their own unique paths.
Everyone gets temporarily trapped in negative emotions from time to time, leading people to behave aggressively or rudely to each other. You grasped this when you learned 'See more than meets the eye!'
And with every interaction, every encounter, every imminent conflict you are involved in – starting afresh every single day – you have the choice. It's up to you to decide: Will you allow yourself and others to enjoy positive experiences, and will you steer your life in a happy and peaceful direction, or will you keep living out old patterns of injury, aggression and reciprocal devaluation? The key to it all is that, once you decide to see with your heart and to live and truly feel it, then you will naturally follow this path.

Going forward, your feelings will deepen, and widen. This is your consciousness, the consciousness you have attained. Development of consciousness and opening of the heart go hand in hand.
To live in unconditional love is to be connected with a conscious way of dealing with yourself and other people. Also with animals and plants, and thus all living beings. Yes, even with nature in its entirety, and the environment as a whole. Do you understand?

"Yes, I think so. Tell me, is that why people say that 'enlightened' figures in history like yogis and monks radiate so much love and mercy? Is it because they are so conscious?"

Yes! Exactly!

I found what Dr Seer was telling me today fascinating. A broad web of understanding opened up before me – one that I wanted to grasp right down to the smallest detail. For I sensed with utter conviction that seeing with the heart was a valuable secret that paved the way to a wonderful life.

"But... is it even possible for us mere mortals to always look upon the world and other people with love, and benevolence – to forgive and to pardon? We're only human, after all, and not saints."

I'm grateful to you for raising this question, as it motivates us to finally clear up a misunderstanding. In life, it's never about being perfect. It's about kindness. It's about growth, and thereby gaining awareness and self-realization. When you look and act from the heart, then you need not suppress or erase your needs and inadequacies in any way.
Looking at the world with kindness, as you so aptly put it, is inevitably connected with looking at yourself with kindness. Can you see the connection?
Be aware of the special and unique features you possess, acknowledge your errors, recognize your feelings and forgive yourself for the things that you would now resolve differently than you did in the past. You have already grasped this. Likewise, see other people as valuable, and forgive them for their mistakes and moods. Try to truly absorb the fact that we are all constantly evolving.

It all sounded promising, and I felt so energized that I wanted to understand more about the concepts the Doc was explaining – maybe even challenge him a little.

"But in our fast-paced western way of life, won't this approach eventually cause people to be left behind, and resigned to the 'loser' pile?"

Dr Seer seemed always to welcome critical questions, presumably because they gave him a definitive impetus for further important explanations.

When you have internalized the essence of love, because you feel the truth that it contains, then it will lead you to your own unique original power. This force in turn empowers you to consciously decide what and how much you want to give to other people. This power also gives you the sensitivity to feel if someone wants to take advantage of your kindness. You can recognize whether your counterpart is also looking and acting, at least to some extent, from the heart or not at all. Your awareness and intuition then enables you to freely decide how to deal with their behaviour. Figuratively speaking, this means you can decide to give them a gift or to simply withdraw. The decisive factor is to not become dependent on other people's judgements of you or on what they give back to you.
Consequently, if your primary way of dealing with others is to be soft and pliable in order to please them, then you are not acting out of your own truth, but out of the need for recognition. Whenever this need is large and powerful, it comes from fear and not from love. In this case, for example, that fear is the fear of being alone.
So what is the answer to your question?

Now he challenged me in return. I found myself very much enjoying our conversation today – sparring with the Doc was so stimulating.

"Hm. Well, I suppose the answer is: When you see with the heart, then it becomes impossible for others to use you because you're aware of what you're willing to give. And because, in this state of mind, you can *freely decide* what you wish to give. Is that right?"

Grinning, Dr Seer nodded at me. He was clearly proud of me, his diligent student. Inside, I beamed.

I told you that you'll soon no longer need me!

Then he leaned forward a little, and whispered:

When you deal consciously with yourself and others, you LIVE love. And this love brings forth alertness. Put bluntly, this means you will no longer be manipulated by others. You are no longer dependent on their judgments. Emotionally, you no longer depend on conditional recognition, because you remain true to yourself and to your truth.
And never forget: If you act from the heart, in line with your own personal truth, then to a great extent it is you yourself who co-creates your inter-personal experiences and relationships. When you radiate respect and mindfulness, the very same comes back to you.

I felt everything the Doc was saying click into place within me like a complete jigsaw puzzle. It was indescribable. I was permeated with a new sense of clarity, which surprised me given that I had been so loved-up at the start of our conversation that I had felt unable to string a sentence together.

"Doc, this perspective is closely connected to 'seeing more than meets the eye', isn't it."

Very well spotted! These two perspectives of THE GOLDEN VIEW are indeed complementary. SEMO facilitates understanding of others, and seeing with the heart generates kindness and appreciation. Both are founded on respect. What's more, in a way you could argue that seeing with the heart is the fundamental basis of love.

"And the reason so many people don't see with their hearts is because they are acting out of fear and not out of love?"

Dr Seer straightened up, and spoke with a more serious tone.

That's certainly one way of looking at it, yes. However, it's not only the emotion of fear that causes people to act the way they do. There is also a particular element of the human personality that has a tremendous impact on our actions: the ego. The ego is part of the human personality and sense of self, which is closely linked to the mind and so acts according to what a person wants.

Do you remember? The mind knows what you want, the soul knows what you need. The soul is connected in a spiritual sense with your heart and your own true feelings.

The ego takes on the task of self-assertion in a world that is not anchored in kindness – in a world where something can be taken away from you, where you will be devalued or made to feel inferior. Thus the fear of not being important or of not being loved is closely intertwined with the ego. If everyone, without exception, were to look and act from the heart, then no one would need an ego any more.

But our world has not yet developed that far. And each must go his or her own way to find their heart, and their self-realization – the realization of the abilities and desires that lie hidden within the soul. Until that is achieved, the role of the ego includes motivating you and providing an important impetus for the pursuit of your own goals.

Anyone who sees with the heart is in contact with their inner self, has a sense of their own worth and radiates self-confidence and strength. People like this rarely have to assert themselves via the ego.

Another piece of the puzzle fell into place. I was deeply impressed.

"I understand!"

The more we develop ourselves and look and act from the heart, the less our lives are dictated by the fear of worthlessness, that is to say, the component of the ego that renders us inferior, that restricts us and blocks our growth. We don't have to toss the mind overboard, because we need it in our complex world. We can use it, but then bring it into harmony with what our soul wants. And so we get to a stage where intellect and feeling, or head and gut, no longer have to work against each other. We sense the right thing to do, and are able to use our minds accordingly, as a tool to achieve the result we want.

I had to let it all sink in before I could ask the next question.

"So what you're saying is that seeing with the heart is in fact the key to unfolding our inner self, and interacting with others?"

That's it.

"It's the way *you* view the world, Doc, isn't it?"

That you can recognize this is proof of your development.

Silently, Dr Seer rose from his chair. As he often did whenever I was supposed to recognize or understand something, he strode over to the window and opened it. It had grown dark outside, and I hadn't even noticed. The light in our room remained curiously constant, although I couldn't detect a light source anywhere.

When I looked out of the open window, I was astonished to see that it was snowing. The first snow of the season! Clearly as delighted by the picturesque scene as I was, the Doc remained standing by the window as the flakes falling before him almost seemed to dance. At times Dr Seer had something otherworldly about him, something almost non-human. My heart began to beat faster, and I sensed a change in the room. What on earth was up with me today, that I kept experiencing such strange sensations?
As I once more looked over at the Doc, I suddenly had a kind of flashback. Had I experienced all of this before? Or dreamed it? If I wasn't mistaken – which I couldn't be, because I was completely conscious – I saw a bright flash of light shoot through the room. Maybe it was just my imagination.

Dr Seer stood unchanged in front of the snowy backdrop, and read my thoughts.

Your soul already knows all the things that you are learning through me and THE GOLDEN VIEW. You had simply forgotten it. Please close your eyes, take deep breaths and focus on your heart.

I closed my eyes. He continued speaking in a soft voice.

In the spiritual sense, the heart stands for all the pure and loving feelings we can sense, receive, give or send out. They are all the feelings a caring mother gives to her child – the kind of feelings that one has for a very close friend or even a beloved pet. They are also the feelings that cause you to soften inside at the thought of the person you are in love with.

I directed my attention to the feelings within. My pulse was still high, and yet I felt calm. I felt warm inside. I took a deep breath and felt both strength and softness inside me. I had to think of Emily and her beautiful face.

Then I thought of my mother. Out of nowhere, a scene from my childhood came to mind in which I was holding onto her skirt, eagerly anticipating the slice of bread with plum jam she was preparing for me. I must have been about three years old. In my mind I thanked her for the love she had shown me. She wasn't often able to show me this love directly, and yet I could now feel how much she had always loved me. A tear coursed slowly down my cheek.

Meanwhile, the Doc had closed the window and returned to sit opposite me. He whispered:

Feel LOVE.

He left me in this state for a while. A feeling of enormous gratitude came over me. It might sound corny, but I felt gratitude towards life.

After a few minutes I opened my eyes. Dr Seer reached for a carafe, and poured me a glass of water. I had not notice him slip away to fetch something to drink. Smiling, he handed me the glass of water.

Cheers!

"Thank you."

I needed a little time to gather myself.

"What... what happened just now?"

You went deep into your heart, my friend. With your consciousness.

I drank the water and set the empty glass back down.

"It was wonderful. I feel so... fulfilled."

Love fulfils our very being.

Dr Seer refilled my glass.

You were in contact with your mother just now, were you not?

"Yes. She suddenly appeared before my eyes..."

How long has it been since you saw her last?

"About six months. But now I feel a desperate urge to visit her."

Then do so!

"I feel so grateful, Doc. Even to my mother. I've never felt this way before."

Show her, Mr Allman. It is very important that we express our feelings, and show our love to the people we care about. Your mother has given you her best, even when she might not always have been able to be there for you in the way she would have wished. She deserves your love. It is very healing for us to truly connect with our mothers in peace and give them love and respect. After all, they gave us life.

"Yes."

After a few minutes I felt the desire to ask more questions.

"You say that 'seeing with the heart' is both a feeling and an attitude, and this I can understand. It enables me to appreciate others, to treat them with kindness, and to forgive them..."

Dr Seer helped me to continue my train of thought.

315

It also ensures you don't judge and condemn those around you. It enables you to open up to the possibilities that every encounter contains – even in conflict-ridden situations.

"That's precisely what I wanted to ask about. How do I see with my heart in a conflict situation?"

Approvingly, he smiled at me.

That is an important question! Let's examine it more closely. Even in a conflict situation, you can show your counterpart kindness, and accept their emotions and points of view.
In order to see with the heart in a difficult situation, and thereby to invite a positive impulse into it, you must first open yourself. Perhaps the following image will help: It is only when you open the door that you can actually communicate with the person standing on the other side of it.

To open up does not mean that you have to disclose your entire inner life. Rather, you should clearly and unequivocally express your feelings and your needs related to the specific situation or the issue at stake.
Do not attack the other person, do not blame them, but formulate in words what you feel and what it is that you want. By doing so, you invite the other person to open up too. You could also try using SEMO to understand why the person might be acting, feeling and arguing the way that they are. Meet them with authenticity and honesty.

This applies to any conflict situation in general. Stay centred, and remain true to yourself! Refrain from participating in the negative energy of a conflict situation or the emotional drama of an attack. Don't invest any additional energy into the negativity, but instead adopt an approach that allows you to find a way out of the restrictive situation. SEMO and 'seeing with the heart' are two perspectives of THE GOLDEN VIEW that can help you to forge a path out of a negative spiral of human interaction and facilitate re-entry into peace.
We must start by looking at and within ourselves if we want to change something on the outside. This, too, is an immutable law of human existence.

With these words, Dr Seer rose from his chair again and gestured for me to do the same.

Come with me!

I followed him, unquestioningly. He went straight to the door, opening it softly before leading out into the hallway.

Today we're going even higher!

Before I knew it, we were back on the same rooftop we had visited once before. Only now it was completely covered in snow. The snow was still falling, and clad in a white, powdery veil, the world lay peacefully at our feet. Above us the clear night sky opened up into a vastness of stars.
Whilst I marvelled at the scenery, Dr Seer strode along the edge of the terrace, lighting several torches that lined the perimeter. The effect was impressive – the terrace was transformed into a kind of stage or arena, with a somewhat mystical feel to it.

I would now like you to make your own personal mark on this scene.

It was very cold up here, and our breath was clearly visible against the illuminated night air.

Send the world a message from your heart! What is the truth that you want to live? What is your message, the message you can give to people out of love? Draw it out, here and now, in the snow! It can be a symbol, or a word, or your footprint, whatever you like.

What extraordinary and creative tasks the Doc always had up his sleeve. This one felt particularly important. My heart began to beat faster. Before me lay a vast, white expanse of snow that was waiting for me to make my statement. I must admit I felt a little overwhelmed. Dr Seer noticed, of course. He passed me a long stick that he conveniently had to hand, and whispered:

Take your time! Feel your way into your heart and trust yourself.

With the stick in my hand, I focused and tried to breathe deeply. I closed my eyes and listened to Dr Seer as he continued in a quiet voice.

It is not only the great masters of this earth and the enlightened yogis and monks that have a message for the world. YOU have one, too! You carry it in your heart. You too are a hero who can change the world. Share your message!

With these words he left me, and retreated into the background.

A tingling shiver ran over me, and I suddenly had goose bumps all over my body. It felt like the whole world was looking at me and waiting to hear my truth. Determined and fulfilled I walked out into the middle of the white canvas beneath the dark blue night sky.

Using the stick as a stylus, I wrote in big letters in the snow:

HE WHO SETS OUT TO FIND HIMSELF
WILL GROW WITH EVERY STEP HE TAKES.
I FACED THE PAIN WITHIN MYSELF
AND FOUND THE PATH INTO MY HEART.
NOW, AS I LIVE LOVE AND TRUTH,
THE WORLD SHALL HAVE MY GOLDEN BEST.

signed, Allman.

22 Look out of the spiritual eye!

Connecting to higher energy

The laws of life are often unfathomable. Sometimes it takes forever to change something, or to reach the point where you're finally ready to tackle a personal problem. Some things work out right away – and others never seem to, even though you really want them to.

I'll probably never understand the whole complex secret of how everything I experience is interwoven. I gradually developed the notion that the inter-relationships of human existence were still a thousand times more complex and subtle than a single person would ever be able to grasp.

What I had now come to understand deep inside, and felt more and more certain of each day, was that my own consciousness is the key. If we are conscious of what we feel, think and desire, and look at all of that with awareness, and also understand that we have a tremendous impact on our lives through this awareness, then step by step we will be more fulfilled, stronger, and yes, even happier.

As well as that, it also became clear to me that it's not just about going through every day in a state of emotional happiness, but rather about the inner decision to remain trustful and connected with your own heart, to be aware of what you really need and which direction you want to go in. Of who you are. And then a very different kind of happiness sets in – a happiness supported by deep inner security, peace and gratitude. And the confidence that life, without exception, is always guiding us.

I had understood all of this through THE GOLDEN VIEW, and now that I was 'awake', as Dr Seer put it, it was clearly visible in my daily life.

These were the thoughts that came to mind as I waited for him, alone in the large, white room. The Doc had brought me here as soon as I arrived, but left me alone after a few minutes. He told me that a restful state was important for our meeting today, and that I should first calm and centre myself. He instructed me to take a deep breath, relax, and just allow my thoughts to float past.

I had no idea what Dr Seer had in mind for me today. But I felt good and had many things to tell him. And I felt the need to express my joy and share with him all that had happened to me. Because in a sense my life was currently building up to a climax – and I had no doubt that this was directly connected to Dr Seer's support over the past months.

So now I sat in the middle of the white room in one of the two white chairs. Before me on the table stood a large jug filled with water, and beside it a crystal glass. Countless flickering candles bathed the room in a festive glow. It was very quiet here 'inside the core', as the Doc referred to the room, and piles of snow lay banked up outside. It was just before Christmas.

I looked around and thought of Dr Seer's guidance in a bid to find stillness within. I noticed how grateful I was to him. I also felt grateful towards myself, too – for trusting myself to look at my life with total honesty, and to approach it anew. A picture on the wall drew my attention. It seemed vaguely familiar, but if I remembered correctly it had not been hanging there last time. It was a golden eye with a white star for a pupil. Where did I know this picture from?
I don't know how long I had been sitting alone in the room; maybe I had even nodded off at some point. By the time Dr Seer returned I felt quite relaxed. He entered the room gently, as if to avoid disturbing me. Smiling, he sat down in the chair opposite me.

How are you, my friend?

"Very good, Doc, thank you. Yes, everything's pretty good."

You have a lot to tell me, am I right? Please stay in your inner state of peace as you do so. It is important for today.

"Does that mean I should suppress my feelings of joy?"

Dr Seer smiled.

Not at all! On the contrary. When you are aware of yourself, then you will experience beautiful feelings more truthfully. Is it clear to you that we can be conscious in every moment of our lives? When you connect your awareness with your joy, then you move even closer to your soul and open up even more of the opportunities that life has in store for you. You walk the path of your heart. But by now you know all this. Tell me, what has happened in the last few days?

As if a button had been pushed, I had to smile widely.

"Oh, Doc, Emily and I... well, we're a couple! Can you believe it? She actually asked me if I'd like to be in a steady relationship with her, if that wasn't moving too fast for me. Oh, it's so beautiful! And no way is it too fast for me – on the contrary, I'd marry her today if I could. We spent the last three nights together. I think it's meant to be, the two of us."

It very much looks like it! This is wonderful. I'm very happy for you and Emily!

As I set about telling him more of my news, Dr Seer raised his hand in a gesture indicating that I should stop.

Please, breathe deeply and try to experience your joy consciously. I would like to bring you to an even higher level today.

I did as I was told.

You can use your breath to completely fill your body with energy, or, put another way, with light – can you imagine that? Breathing is consciousness.

In fact, my breathing did now feel different – somehow broader, and more expansive. Was it because my heart was opening, as the Doc had called it last time, or because I had finally experienced physical passion again? Could there be a connection?

Dr Seer smiled at me.

We'll look at the breath and what it can open up at a higher level later on. And without doubt, it can bring you feelings of true happiness! These, of course, are a little different to the feelings you were just thinking about.

Now I had to smile myself. It was quite impossible to hide anything from him, anything at all.

What other positive things have taken place in the last few days?

"Oh, the sabbatical year, Doc! My request has been approved! It's all arranged. I'll have a whole year off, starting from January."

Well, then, it seems there's nothing holding you back or standing in the way of your journey, then!

"You said it! And you know what? Emily's coming too! At least she's going to come along for the first six weeks. She still has some vacation time left over from last year, and will supplement it with some of her annual leave. For her it'll serve as a chance to recover and regroup from her separation, and all that. And then we want to see what happens. She loves travelling! And we're both completely open to whatever possibilities might turn up along the way. We've already started planning our trip. It's almost too good to be true!"

Dr Seer beamed at me. He was still focused on my conscious breathing. With another slight hand movement in which he lowered his arm and then raised it again, he indicated that I should keep controlling it. I kept breathing in and out deeply, and curiously now felt even more strengthened.

So you are going to journey to your South Sea Island together?

"Yes, that's the plan! I'm so looking forward to that moment when I find myself there again, back on my beach."

It will be a magical moment.

"We're just about to book flights for early January. We're already in touch with someone who has a sailing boat we can rent. He seems a lovely chap – we were put in contact through a friend of Emily's. He's going to come with us for a few days, so I can brush up on my sailing skills. And then we'll set off alone."

The Doc was thrilled.

"I told my boss about my plans, of course. And do you know how he reacted? He thought it very courageous of me, and wished me all the best. And he said he'll be happy to see me again in a year's time. I've never experienced such warmth and openness from him before. And what's more, a few of my colleagues – the ones who were so sceptical in the beginning – actually came up to me and told me that I've made an excellent choice. My colleague Carl said he wished he had as much courage as me! Funny how suddenly everyone takes you seriously when you stand by your dreams and show the world that you intend to realize them. I've got five more days of work to go, and then I'll be finally rid of the place. Crazy, I still can't believe it's actually happening."

Dr Seer smiled contentedly. My next piece of news just bubbled out of me.

"By the way, I had a good chat with Andy at the café last night. He's finished his romance novel and is over the moon. The publishing house he was hoping for has taken him on, and in three months' time his book will be on the market! Andy also congratulated me on my new-found love with Emily. He's happy for me – now that's what I call friendship. We laughed more than we have in a long time, and I had to promise him that, as my best friend and self-proclaimed expert on love, he would be best man at my wedding, should Emily and I decide to marry someday. He said it should be a fairy-tale wedding, with all the trimmings. What a character he is! It's a good thing that his novel is already finished, otherwise he'd probably have worked our story into it somehow."

Who knows, maybe one day you will find yourselves being worked into a story...

At that point in time I had no idea that this remark was actually a premonition, and was connected with other similar hints that the Doc had made along the way.

"So anyway, what I wanted to say about Andy was that he apologized to me for not being supportive of my idea about the sabbatical year. He said he had been thinking a lot about why he had been so against it, and he finally had to admit that his resistance stemmed from envy of some kind.

He himself had had this same dream for a long time. And on top of that, he didn't want to lose me, his best friend, for all those months. He said that it was selfish of him and that he was sorry."

You see! He, too, has become a little more conscious.

"Quite a change of heart for our 'self-loving super artist', isn't it? It's just as we discussed, Doc. His reaction to my plan actually had only to do with himself. Just as all my other so-called advisors actually argued their cases based only on their own emotions and fears. You have to be completely true to yourself. I see this so clearly now! You and you alone are the best counsellor when it comes to your own decisions in life."

You're now seeing it as it is because you have experienced it yourself. You have answered the call of your own vision and desire. That's why there is so much changing in your life right now.

"Indeed."

It suddenly occurred to me that, apart from Dr Seer and myself, no-one really knew what had happened to me in recent months.

"Incidentally, I still haven't told anyone about you. Not even Emily."

You don't have to yet, either. The right time will come.

For a while Dr Seer sat in silence, and just as in our last session, it suddenly felt as though something had changed in the room, as if a different energy could be detected. I noticed I had goose bumps. Perhaps these strange phenomena were somehow linked to this particular room? Or was it just my perception of it? Dr Seer soon gave me a clue.

You have not only become more conscious, but also more sensitive, Mr Allman. This allows you to feel the subtlest of changes in a situation more clearly.
Or do you still believe that everything that happens when two people communicate with each other inside an enclosed space, as we are doing

now, can be perceived just with the naked eye and our normal, everyday level of consciousness?

"No, since meeting you I no longer believe that, Doc."

He made a sweeping, circular gesture with his hand.

We all have a lot more energy available to us than most people realize. The universe, the world, everything that is living, consists of inexhaustible energy reserves. The more conscious we become, and the more we live from the heart, the more access to this power we acquire and the better we can perceive and use this energy.
Incidentally, there are people who can channel these higher energies in such a way that they are able to support the physical and emotional healing of other human beings. The ability to do so stems from their high level of consciousness – and the level of development of their souls.

I thought for a moment about what the Doc was saying. And once again things seemed to come full circle for me. When I had learned about seeing with the heart we had talked about the yogis and monks in the world. 'They radiate so much love because they are so conscious', the Doc had said to me. Was there another connection here to do with accessing these higher energies, an ability which, according to Dr Seer, even has powers to cure? Did that love lie precisely in this connection? Was it love that ultimately does the healing? And was not Dr Seer himself such a conscious person, who had supported my 'healing' through his high level of awareness and love?

"I bet that's something you're also capable of, isn't it, Doc? You're even psychic, if that's the way to put it. Is that a question of consciousness, too?"

He smiled and nodded at me before offering a rather indirect answer to the question:

Basically, every person has the potential within themselves to fully awaken. Everyone can find their heart and their truth. Those who live by the heart and in clear awareness radiate love and peace.

325

When a person follows this path, they will almost automatically train their higher sense and intuition. Intuition is the voice of the soul and the soul knows the truth, as you have experienced.

"What actually is the soul, exactly? And what is personality?"

Your personality is what you represent as a human being here today. It encompasses personal qualities, strengths, certain characteristics, behaviours and attitudes. The soul is your original self – that which reveals itself when you look deep inside yourself and are in touch with your inner being. Personal development, spiritual development and the evolution of your soul go hand in hand – although not necessarily at the same speed.

"Does that mean that my soul can evolve too?"

It will grow richer with every experience that you look at with awareness. It unfolds its full potential gradually. Thus your soul develops across your many lives.

"Are you saying that we live more than once?"

Your personality only lives once. Your soul lives many times. Reincarnation is not a religious assumption. It is a cosmic law.

We looked at each other in silence. My initial feeling that everything was much more complex than I would ever be able to grasp had just been confirmed. At the same time I had the impression that I had just received a further, special insight into the deep mysteries of life.
This time, without being prompted, I focused my attention back on my breath.

From now on, you should always check whether you're breathing deeply, Mr Allman – no matter where you are or what you're doing. For it is more than a method of relaxation. It is the bridge to a clear consciousness.

Once again my eye came to rest on the picture with the golden eye. Dr Seer observed me with a knowing expression.

That picture is hanging here today for a reason.

"Why does it seem familiar to me?"

You discovered it once before, when you looked out of my eyes. Do you remember?

"Out of your eyes? Ah, yes – that's it! When I learned how to see through other people's eyes! It was hanging on the wall across from me."

What do you think, why is it hanging here today?

"Hm, I don't know. I guess it generally fits well with THE GOLDEN VIEW."

That's right. But it has an even deeper meaning.

The Doc gave me some time to consider what he might mean.

It symbolizes the 'spiritual eye'. Can you make sense of that?

"I... don't really know."

The spiritual eye. It all sounded pretty mystical. I pictured a bizarre image: a huge, three-dimensional eye floating around the room, viewing me from above.

Dr Seer observed my thoughts and grinned.

The spiritual eye is much closer to you than you think. It is IN you, a part of you. Everyone has it. Some call it the third eye. And you know what? You have looked through this eye for a long time already. You just haven't been aware of it. And by the way, you've been meditating along the way, too.

Now I was knocked for six! I had this eye 'in me'? And when on earth was I supposed to have been meditating? In a calm voice, Doc guided me further to what was apparently going to be our subject for today.

For example, the time you became an eagle and flew to look at your future. That was a guided meditation.

"Oh. I always thought meditation was something else entirely. I've learned a few things from Emily, you see. She sits cross-legged on the floor, for example, which is enough to put me off right there and then. I'm not flexible enough for that. And she plays some sort of Indian background music the whole time. It's not something I know anything about, although I'm quite interested to learn more. Emily said she and I could do yoga together sometime. But I've no idea about all that stuff."

But you do!

He looked at me insistently. And it almost made me nervous. It was as if I was about to discover another truth.

"Doc, if... So if every person has this spiritual eye, where... um, where is it?"

A very good question! One I've been waiting for. It shows me that you are now ready.

"Ready for what?"

To consciously look out of your spiritual eye. And to utilize this perspective of THE GOLDEN VIEW.

Dr Seer pointed to his forehead, to the area between his eyebrows, and slowly moved his finger about half an inch higher.

The spiritual eye, my friend, sits here.

And in response to my somewhat stupefied stare, he added:

Even if you can't see it.

I had to grin. I hadn't felt this inept in my 'studies' for a long time. Dr Seer smiled too.

The perspective that you're going to learn today is called: 'Look out of the spiritual eye!'.

I was not at all surprised to hear that there was a golden perspective related to this topic as well – although I had to admit that I had no idea what on earth it might entail. As it turned out, my best guess was not so very far off:

"So... in looking out of my spiritual eye, am I in fact then meditating?"

Yes, absolutely! This perspective is indeed a form of meditation. Whenever you look out of the spiritual eye, you are in fact looking into the wide, inner world of your soul and heart. This enables you to open yourself to the world of higher levels of consciousness – the spiritual world in which you can find your truth. As well as answers, messages, and solutions.

"Umm... OK."

Try to picture it this way: Located on your forehead is a physical, non-visible point that can be seen as a gateway to the spiritual world. The spiritual world is a plane of existence that is not visible in the physical sense, but that is connected to the earthly world. Each person exists not only as a physical being, but also as a being in these higher levels or dimensions. You are much more than what your human body and personality represent here on Earth. Your full potential is stored in your expansive being, your Higher Self, which is connected with your soul.
When you focus on that point on your forehead using methods such as meditation whilst entering a state of stillness, then you open the door to your Higher Self, your soul, and thus to universal power and wisdom.

"Sounds exciting! But allow me to ask a silly question: Why would I want to do that?"

Dr Seer looked at me quizzically. He obviously expected me to demonstrate ever more insight.

Let's take a step back, and consider the overall objective of THE GOLDEN VIEW. What would you say it is?

I found it easy to answer his question, because I'd already completely understood what it was all about. What's more, I had also experienced it in more ways than one.

"The objective is to become conscious and to live in a manner that is consistent with my truth, and my vision. To follow the path of my heart, and to find better ways of solving my everyday problems."

The Doc winked at me appreciatively.

Spot on. 'Look out of the spiritual eye!' supports and accelerates your becoming conscious and finding your own truth by allowing you to look into your own consciousness in its purest possible form. This way of seeing IS pure consciousness in and of itself. Meditation allows you to enter a state of pure consciousness.

"Oh, now I understand something that was never clear to me! Most people associate meditation with entering a weird trance-like state, or going on some sort of mind-expanding trip. As far as I know, some people also use meditation purely as a way to relax."

Dr Seer pushed the water carafe to the very middle of the table. He then arranged my glass and the two candles that were also on the table so that all four items were aligned in a straight line.

Without doubt it is about expanding consciousness. Nonetheless, meditation does not mean losing yourself, but rather centring yourself, both in body and in mind. It is total self-focussing. Only then does the gateway open to greater knowledge and greater wisdom. Then you really can go on different journeys, just as you did in eagle form. These journeys, however, never lead you away from yourself – or, as you so neatly put it, send you into some kind of state or on a trip – but they lead you back to your original self, and to who you could or could once again become.
You have realized that you yourself are your own best counsellor. Why? Because you have followed your vision and intuition. And if you now look through your spiritual eye as well, then you are effectively choosing the most direct path to your truth, to that which your soul desires – to the answers and pointers that lead you there. To where your longing calls you.

The penny dropped. How often in life we discover that we have the completely wrong idea about certain concepts or phenomena. There are probably very few people in the Western world who haven't heard of meditation, but most likely many of them believe, as I did until a few minutes ago, that meditation is just a technique originating from foreign cultures that gurus and their followers use to drift off into weird little fantasy worlds of their own imagining. It also occurred to me that only very few know that it is a way of seeing that could help any person from any culture find their own way, or find specific answers to personal questions.

Dr Seer had followed my insights with interest.

A very valuable thought! Meditation would indeed help and benefit everyone, in some way.

My curiosity was suddenly aroused.

"Doc, could you give me some specific tuition in how to meditate? Right now, today?"

Do you really think I would tell you about another perspective of THE GOLDEN VIEW without showing you how to apply it?

My heart began to pound in my chest.

Meditation can also be used purely for relaxation purposes, of course, because it enables you to find a deep sense of inner peace. Undisturbed by any external factors, you can focus on your being. In doing so, you become fully present.
You can meditate on a particular topic and ask your Higher Self questions. You will then receive answers and suggestions from your expanded consciousness. This activates a different mental level to the one you use when you apply reason or every day conscious thought.

I now felt slightly nervous as well as curious. It was as though I was standing in front of yet another closed door to myself that I would soon be allowed to open. Dr Seer seemed to expect a lot from me today. For all his benevolence, he had become a somewhat demanding mentor.

Patience is key for this perspective. You must try to quiet your expectations, because otherwise your mind blocks the opening to your intuitive knowledge. Meditation has nothing to do with the mind. In fact, the mind needs to fade away during the meditation. You have to curb the impulse that says 'I want'.

"But will I really be able to *see* something when I look through my spiritual eye? How can I look through an eye that isn't there in the first place? Does it work every time?"

In answer to your first question... you will see, you will know, you will feel. You may find that different channels of perception are opened to different extents depending on the particular occasion and person involved. The process relies on you activating the very subtlest of your senses. And these all derive from the same source, your higher consciousness.

As to your second question – you see through the invisible eye using your focus. I will show you the method, don't worry! Before I do, allow me to explain some important aspects to you. I would like you to apply this perspective with the utmost respect, and not out of pure curiosity.

And finally, you ask whether it will work – well, with my guidance, you will experience it today. You will then be able to practise it alone. And practise is incredibly important in this case. It's the only way to master the technique.

"OK."

In a bid to calm my impatience, I looked around the room in search of things I might not have noticed before. As my gaze swept over the familiar scene, I once again found my attention drawn to the image of the eye. I eagerly anticipated finally discovering this eye in myself!

Dr Seer straightened up in his chair as he always did when something was very important to him.

Please note that, in theory, a person could meditate every single day without experiencing any kind of growth in terms of the development of their person, spirit and soul. If you don't take action, then you are no more than dreaming. The first step is to focus. And then it's about action. That means living your life in a focused manner and implementing all you have realized.

"Hm, doesn't sound easy, Doc. It sounds like it would require a lot of self-discipline."

Ultimately, though, it's not hard at all – on the contrary. Initially, maintaining awareness is in some way demanding, yes. And it does in fact require a certain degree of discipline to confront your own thoughts and emotions, and to review yourself and your life. It is a process that may feel quite uncomfortable at times. As you yourself discovered when you stood in front of the mirror for the very first time.

By gradually finding the way to yourself and recognizing where your own true path lies one step at a time, you will steadily find that you have much more energy available. What's more, you will find yourself being increasingly steered towards the life that perfectly corresponds to you and your needs. When you lift the veil of fear and self-deprecation, of repressed experiences and unconscious thought patterns, then you live more intensely, more authentically and thus more happily. Or do you currently feel less happy than you did a few months ago, before you set off on this path?

Dr Seer winked at me, signalling that I wasn't expected to answer the question.

It will enrich your life to see the world through your spiritual eye, if you do it in full consciousness and from the depths of your heart. There are many different ways to meditate. But it is definitely not about sitting on a pillow for hours with incense burning in the background as you wait for enlightenment – or, even more extreme, feeling enlightened simply because you've sat down to meditate.

We both laughed. I enjoyed his ironic yet always affectionate sense of humour, as I often found myself, and all of us, reflected in it.

"I've been meaning to ask, actually... what exactly is 'enlightenment', Doc?"

What do you think it is? What is it that lights up?

"Hm. Individuals themselves, I guess."

And what kind of light is it? Where does it come from?

"Oh, that's a good one. You're the expert, you tell me! Perhaps it's meant symbolically?"

Dr Seer paused for a moment, leaving me hanging. Then he reached out his right hand, took one of the candles from the table, held it at eye level and looked straight into the flame.

'Attaining enlightenment' in the spiritual sense is to bring light and love into one's own being.

Light is the energy of a clear consciousness.

Love is the energy of a pure heart.

The enlightened individual is one who knows their full potential and is able to realize it – one who is fully conscious and lives love. Enlightened individuals radiate light and love to others.

Their actions stem from the highest version of themselves, every day, every hour, every minute.

In every situation they see with the heart.

It's about integrating consciousness and love into daily life.

You'll also experience high consciousness and pure love when you meditate with full intention.

Enlightenment is not a goal. Enlightenment is a path. And if you consciously look at yourself, live consciously and apply and implement THE GOLDEN VIEW, then you are on this self-same path.

Meanwhile the room had grown dark. The absence of light emphasized the flames of the many candles, which flickered and gleamed around us as though we were cast adrift on a sea of light. I was so impressed by Dr Seer's words that I found I couldn't speak. My nervous anticipation had subsided.

After a while, the Doc rose from his chair and walked slowly to where the picture with the golden eye hung on the wall. He removed it with an elegant sweep of his hand, and brought it over. As he sat down again, he placed it on the table in front of me, and softly said:

Would you like to look out of your spiritual eye now, my friend?

A deep sigh escaped my lips.

"Yes."

Alright. There's no need to sit cross-legged, by the way. But I will ask you to sit in a way that ensures your spine is straight. You'll notice that the energy will flow better like that. Inhale as deeply and calmly as you can, please.

I sat upright in my chair and began to breathe consciously again.

Concentrate only on your breathing!

In a calm voice, he guided me onwards.

In – out – in – out – in – out – in – out – in – out – in – out.

I will now guide you through the meditation. You'll start by going inwards. And then you will look out of your spiritual eye. It is not important how long you meditate. Enter a mentally timeless state. It could be ten minutes or three hours. You will feel when it's time to come back. Body, mind and soul will understand what happened, and the body remembers at the cellular level how this state of consciousness feels. You will then be able to enter it again and again.

Please close your eyes when you feel ready to go from the outer to the inner world.

Dr Seer matched his breathing to mine. This made me feel as though my breath was becoming deeper and more powerful. I closed my eyes.

Focus and imagine that light is flowing into your body through your breath. Breathe light in through your nose. Exhale slowly through your half-open mouth. As you do this, allow the light to stream down your spine. Imagine your breath filling your body with light.

From this point on he spoke only in a whisper. My perception of the outside world was similar to my perception when I journeyed as an eagle. It all felt very far away.

Keep your spine straight. And allow the light to flow into you.

I noticed that my body became heavier. After a little while, there was stillness in me. I had returned to myself. I heard Dr Seer speak from afar.

Go deep inside and listen to the silence. Feel the silence in yourself.

Several minutes passed. I began to notice strange sensations inside me. I was overcome by sensations of heat. My eyelids seemed so heavy that, for a moment, I thought I would never be able to open them again. Situations from the last few days flashed by in my thoughts before disappearing again – scenes such as when I told my colleagues that I'd be gone for the next year... or thoughts of how quickly everything had happened, and what I still had to do before setting off on the journey.

Dr Seer seemed far, far away, but I still heard his voice speaking loudly and clearly.

Whenever thoughts or emotions rise up inside you, simply watch and observe them. Don't try to push them away. Allow every thought and emotion to pass by like a cloud, and try not to judge them.

To my surprise, I realized that this seemed to come quite naturally to me. All the mental exercises I had learned through THE GOLDEN VIEW seemed to have prepared me well for what the Doc was asking of me now. Thoughts appeared in my mind every now and again, but I found it pretty easy to just let them go.

Continue to breathe the light. There is more and more light.

After a while, I was overcome by a strange sensation that I'd never experienced before. I felt as though I was bigger, and yet lighter at the same time. It was as though my body was expanding.

Judging by the sound of his voice, I guessed that Dr Seer had stood up in the meantime, and was now slowly walking around me in a big circle. I listened to the instructions that followed.

You are now consciously connecting with the higher dimension – your Higher Self. You are now going to enter into the spirit world.

When I heard these words, I felt goose bumps break out all over my body. And, strange as it may sound, the temperature in the room suddenly dropped. Had the Doc opened a window?

Everything is entirely as it should be. Please continue to breathe consciously. Now focus from the inside on the area between your eyebrows.

I swallowed, and felt tears well up in my eyes.

This is where you will find your spiritual eye.

I looked at this point from the inside. My forehead began to tingle. I felt a huge wave of gratitude come over me, causing tears to run down my cheeks. I felt somehow connected to something greater than myself, or more than me, but that belonged to me. Was it my 'Higher Self'?

Allow your spiritual eye to open... NOW! Look through it!

I focused on the point from the inside and tried to hold back my emotions a little – all the while feeling the tears coursing down my cheeks.

Be patient with yourself. Continue to breathe, and don't expect anything.

A period of time passed, although I had absolutely no sense of how long it was. And then it happened: all of a sudden it was bright! Even though my eyes were closed, I could 'see' light as brightly as if Dr Seer had lit up the room or shone a spotlight on me.

What do you see, Mr Allman? Say it out loud, please.

I found it hard to speak, my throat felt so dry. Finally, I heard myself whisper:

"I see... light."

Is your spiritual eye open?

"YES."

Dr Seer gave me some time.

Look! This is where you will receive all the answers you hope to receive. This is where you have access to universal power and wisdom. This is where you dwell in your pure consciousness.
Perhaps a certain message, picture, or word will come to you. Whatever it is, it is definitely intended for YOU, and no one else.

I lingered a while in this state, and felt an ever increasing sense of happiness... a kind of joy unlike anything I had ever known before. I felt connected to everything. And filled with everything.
After several minutes I began to see a series of images, and then a kind of film, play out before my spiritual eye. I saw myself in it. The images were very real, and comparable to the sensation of being in a very vivid dream. I saw myself walking along a sandy road that led through a green meadow. The sun was shining, and it was warm.

"It's your path", I heard something inside me say.

I saw myself walk further down the path and reach a small square, in the middle of which stood a stone about the size of a table.

I approached the stone to take a closer look. There, on the smooth surface, lay a book. A large, stylized eye was drawn on the cover – similar to the eye in the picture that hung in our room.

My inner voice spoke again.

"This is YOUR book."

My heart was pounding, and I desperately wanted to know more. Hoping to open the book straight away, I maintained my focus. But that scene did not appear. I heard the Doc's voice whispering softly.

Ask what kind of book it is.

I continued to focus on the image. And as I did so, the answer slowly rose within me:

"It is THE BOOK OF YOUR LIFE. You will know."

An indescribable emotion washed over me once again. It was something like humility, and it moved me to tears. I felt truly humbled – by my life so far, and by all the help I had received along the way.
I took a deep breath involuntarily, which showed me that the time had come to go back, as Dr Seer put it. I sensed that he too considered this an appropriate point in time to come back.

Focus once again on your breath, and feel your body. Take your time. And come back slowly, very slowly, to the here and now.

It took me several minutes after opening my eyes to see clearly again. The lights of the candles moved around in the surrounding space like a blur. Then I noticed that the picture with the eye was in my lap. Dr Seer was sat opposite me, smiling.

Thank you.

I found it almost impossible to speak.

"Why? For... for what?"

For opening yourself to the spiritual world and for accepting your path.

I looked at my hands, which still held the picture with the eye.

I would like you to have it, as a gift. It will accompany you on your journey.

Once again my eyes filled with tears.

"Thank you. Thank you, Doc."

And for the first and only time, I saw that Dr Seer was also crying.

23 Look at the big picture!

Understanding life spiritually

I felt as effervescent as the bottle of champagne I carried in my right hand. It was New Year's Eve, and I was on my way to say goodbye to Dr Seer. Back at the flat our backpacks were packed and ready to go. I had sublet the place, with the new tenant due to move in at the beginning of next week. Once I'd made the decision to take a year out, everything clicked into place with ease and practically organised itself. As soon as you start to turn your own vision into reality, all the pieces of the puzzle come together as if guided by an invisible hand – as life had shown me, with absolute clarity.

Our big adventure was due to start tomorrow, on New Year's Day. Emily and I had decided to celebrate New Year's Eve at the café where we had first met. Then, at the stroke of midnight, a new era would begin for us, ushered in by our journey, and supported by our new love and the knowledge that an entire year of freedom lay ahead.

I wondered how I would find the right words when saying goodbye to the Doc. How to thank someone to whom you have so much to be grateful for that it can't be expressed in words? Dr Seer had changed my life completely and elevated it to an entirely new level. I could never in my wildest dreams have imagined that such support existed, let alone that it be available to me. How could it be that I, of all people, had received this blessing? And it truly was a blessing, in my eyes.

Today, the way to his house felt very difficult. My joyful anticipation of our journey mingled with the acute pain that comes with imminent leave-taking, and a certain nervousness began to unfold at the thought that I wouldn't be able to visit the Doc and ask his advice for quite some time to come.

I must have been so lost in thought that I walked right past the house. Puzzled, I stopped. No, I had not walked past; I was standing directly in front of it – and to my astonishment, noticed that the signs were no longer there. Wherever had they gone?

'THE GOLDEN VIEW'. They were gone. The house was still there, looking the same as always, but the signs were missing from both the front gate and the door. Slightly perplexed, I wandered through the front garden, returned to the gate, then went back to the front door. Nothing! What's more, the doorbell plate was missing – or at least there was no name on it any more. My heart began to pound, and for a few seconds I couldn't breathe. A troubling thought crept into my mind.

"Oh, no! Doc, no! You haven't just upped and left, have you? It can't be true. Don't leave me here all by myself. Where are you?"

Somewhat at a loss, I stared at the door and rang the bell several times. But the bright ringing sound echoed against an empty background. The door remained closed. I gave myself a little shake, and tried to take deep breaths. Despite these efforts, a slight panic began to rise within me.
I continued breathing deeply in and out. And then the tears came. They flowed in streams down my cheeks, and there was not a thing I could do about it. So I stood in front of the locked door, and began to talk to Dr Seer from this place of sorrow, feeling the deep pain of parting.

"Doc, I can't take this! I know you said that soon I won't need you any-more – but did it have to be so abrupt? Why can't you just open the door and say 'Good day' to me like you always used to? Or is this another test?"

Like a petulant child, I didn't want to believe what was becoming ever more obvious: Dr Seer was clearly gone. After indirectly announcing his intended departure he had then simply gone ahead and left, in his own unique way. Just as extraordinarily as it had all started, and as every single encounter with him had been, so too was the conclusion of our time together.

In my whole life so far I'd never known a person who had touched me so deeply, to the very depths of my soul. And as close as Dr Seer had come to me and all my emotional inadequacies, my human problems and my heart, he also remained a perpetual mystery to me. And he will remain so as long as I live.

I continued to address the emptiness.

"Doc, you could at least have had one last drink with me. Would it have been too much to ask for us to share a small glass of champagne together, after all we've been through?"

My pitiful attempt to tempt him back was obviously pointless. As were my quiet little utterances intended to assuage the terrible feeling of loss spreading through me. The thought of never again being able to ask him for advice, knowing that from now on he was no longer there to guide me, gave me stomach cramps. My knees felt weak, and I desperately needed to sit down. A low wall at the front of the house came to my aid.

"OK, Doc, I'm going to sit on that wall and pour us both a glass of bubbly. I'll wait for you."

It was already dusk, and as the sun sank slowly on the horizon it painted the sky with striking golden hues. It was cold, the kind of dry cold that chills to the bone. Leaning against the ice-cold wall, I found myself remembering a scene from last summer, when I had smoked a cigarette with Dr Seer. The thought of the Doc with a cigarette elicited a little chuckle... there was something almost comical about it. He stopped at nothing to bring me to my truth – he had led me over and over again to face the mirror. To the rooftop of the house, into my past, into my inner sun. And yes, out of my pain and into my self-confidence. Into my dreams and visions. The memories of each of our many meetings brought me temporary relief. I opened the bottle, placed the two glasses side by side on the wall, and poured the champagne. Then I raised both glasses and clinked them lovingly together.

"Cheers, Doc. Wherever you are. Here's to a happy new year."

Cheers, my friend. It will be a wonderful year!

Confused, I looked around. 'That was Dr Seer's voice, I'm sure of it! Or am I going nuts?' shot through my mind. There was no-one to be seen. I felt a bit like I did when he suddenly appeared behind me, seemingly out of nowhere, that time in the corridor. But this was different. There was no-one here. 'I'm probably just overexcited after all that's happened in the last few days.' I tried to regain my composure, and took another sip.

343

I am with you.

I heard his voice again, loud and clear. I wasn't drunk, that much was certain. This time it freaked me out.

I'll always be with you, as I promised. You may not see me with your physical eyes, but see with the heart, look out of the spiritual eye, and there I will be. You will be able to see, hear and feel me.

I froze.

There's no need to be afraid! You weren't frightened before.

I took a deep breath and tried to calmly tell myself that I had just experienced my first ever clearly diagnosable psychological hallucination. Had my mind received so much input that such an effect was possible?

A few months ago I would have fled the place and thrown myself into some kind of activity to help me forget this bizarre experience as quickly as possible. This time, however, something in me specifically demanded that I stay. Maybe it was my intuition. Or the greatly increased sense of trust I had developed – even in things I couldn't explain.
I closed my eyes and tried to feel what was going on inside me. And after a few minutes I finally ventured an attempt to pick up the dialogue. Whispering, I addressed the icy winter air:

"Oh, Doc. I... I'm just an ordinary person."

You are no ordinary person. Every human being is something very special. Most have just forgotten. There are no ordinary people – just as there are no ordinary paths.

His inimitable chuckle echoed in my ear.

You have understood this already.

"Yes."

In a flash, a realization shot through my consciousness: Dr Seer's voice was coming out of me! The time of his physical presence in my life was over. This too was part of my new reality. Perhaps he had only been here in this place just for me. And wherever he was now, he was also in me. And in this way I would be able to communicate with him.

My friend, please pass the following message on to the world, for it will help many people: Everyone follows their own path to mastery. And all that truly matters is each person's individual development.

From this arises a guiding truth: You shouldn't compare yourself to others! Making comparisons with other people is human, and the conclusions drawn can provide some guidance – especially if the person is growing up and developing their personality and abilities. But comparisons will never advance you on your own unique path.

The self-assessment resulting from comparison does not tell you anything. In the end it only costs you energy because your focus is directed away from yourself – even when you appear to be superior to the subject of your comparison and emerge as the stronger of the two. This strengthening takes place in the ego and not in your heart. You don't know the path of the other; you don't know what his or her learning experiences in life consist of, or what they are longing for.

Use each other as mirrors to gain an impetus for your own development. But don't evaluate yourself and others comparatively. Reverse this thinking for yourself, even if society still lives it differently.

Your Highest Self is tailored only to you! Orientate yourself according to the highest possible version of yourself – nothing else.

Dr Seer imparted these messages in spirit. I had goose bumps all over, and despite the freezing cold, I felt warm inside.

"Thank you, Doc. Thank you, for everything you have done for me!"

I sighed deeply, and tears rolled once again down my cheeks.

"When I found you, I felt empty and grey. And now things couldn't be more exciting or beautiful. I've become a happier person. Yes, I can definitely say that from my heart, even though I'm standing here crying like a baby."

345

The cold was getting to me, as were my runny nose and frozen hands. But I found it impossible to go home, probably because I yearned for more certainty that Dr Seer was really with me. And I wanted that certainty firmly anchored in me, right here in this place where it all began.

As I reached into my jacket pocket for a tissue, a lighter came to hand, probably still there from my days as a smoker. At the same time, a small glass lantern standing directly beside the front door caught my eye. I walked over and picked up the lantern. Inside was a thick, white candle. It felt as if the Doc had left it there for me, and I interpreted this as a further sign that he was now indeed accompanying me.

I returned to my spot on the wall and lit the candle. I placed the shining lantern beside me, alongside the two champagne glasses. The sight gave me a pleasant feeling inside, reminding me of all the times Dr Seer had lit candles while explaining to me whatever it was that I needed to understand. Consciousness is light.

"Doc, I'm so happy with how my life has changed in only half a year. And yet I still can't grasp it all. The last few months were often very stressful. All the ups and downs – and you've accompanied me through all of it with your amazing patience and kindness. For every situation I had to face, you taught me an incredible lesson. So many times I stumbled, and over and over again you were there to catch me, and pick me up."

It was a transformation. With THE GOLDEN VIEW, you looked at each experience and grew through it. Every single time, you then continued more consciously on your way. The path is the transformation.

And so our meeting this evening was happening inside me. I conducted a dialog with Dr Seer without him being physically present. It was fascinating, as I could so clearly hear his answers and messages in my heart. For a moment I once again considered whether I was only imagining all this, or if my fantasy played some significant role, but then I heard his unmistakably powerful words again. And it was certainly not coming from my imagination, because I could never imitate his unique style of formulation and explanation.

Dear Mr Allman, please internalize yet another secret. Every person has a spiritual lifeline. This develops mainly in waveform, meaning it is characterised by ups and downs.

From a spiritual perspective, the downward phases are not merely unpleasant experiences such as personal failure, loss or sadness that we have to go through, and from which we somehow emerge again. Rather, these lows have a greater meaning. There is always knowledge concealed within them, knowledge that wants to be discovered. And this knowledge can make one's life richer and more truthful.

Even if such phases are experienced as very difficult or painful, the real task is to use them to gain insight. Without exception, setbacks and crises offer the chance of a fresh start. You can now create something new in your life, or finally allow something to unfold. Remember that it's about becoming conscious, and that depends on how you see and feel.

'Look closely at what you experience and feel!' Those who internalize this principle become more optimistic and capable of action, and are able to get the most out of every situation. You never have to stagnate as a passive victim.

Such learning phases can also provide the decisive impulse that will help you catch the next upward wave. It is important to keep trusting that that wave will come, and that life is on your side.

Every challenge represents an opportunity. To truly understand this principle, look back and find confirmation of it in your own lifeline. Ask yourself 'What have I experienced? What did I learn? Where has it brought me? And what can my current situation in life teach me? What can I take from it that will help me during the next phase in my life?'

I thought for a moment. It occurred to me that his messages no longer seemed tailored just to me personally, but were meant for everyone. He was now addressing all mankind, and spoke as if from a higher viewpoint. I really wanted to continue this unusual conversation.

"It's as if our time together was representative of how an entire life proceeds. In cycles of ups and downs, right?"

Exactly! I'm impressed that you see it this way. All life follows a cyclical or wave-like motion – the seasons, the tides, the moon cycles, sleeping and waking. After the storm comes the calm. After adventures out in the wider world arises the need to return home. Cyclicality is characteristic of life itself.

On an emotional level, life often feels wavy, too – even throughout the 'upward' development of one's consciousness. When you find yourself going through a difficult phase again, it doesn't mean that you have regressed. It is connected with the next important experience that the soul needs in order to grow.

Remember: it's not about always feeling 'on a high', but about anchoring the experience in one's consciousness and thereby becoming more and more awake.

"Yes."

Once again, I got goose bumps. After a minute or so I straightened up, and took a few steps away from the wall. Standing tall, I looked into the golden evening sky.

"Tell me, Doc, what's it all about? The purpose of our existence?"

The spiritual meaning of your existence is to become ever more conscious, to have experiences, to heal fears, and move closer and closer to your own truth and to live it. That is 'self-realization', my friend. The truth is directly connected to your heart.

All of life, the whole journey, serves the process of realization – realization, development, wisdom and truth. From a higher perspective, emotional ups and downs are not the decisive parameters. All experience, be it pleasurable or painful, serves the purpose of becoming conscious. It's only ever about this.

"So that means that, no matter what I experience, whether at work, in love, health-related, with family or with friends – every experience I have is actually about my own self-awareness?"

That's it. There is a higher meaning in everything and every situation can be viewed in terms of a greater context. Pointers showing the way to something bigger can be found in everything. Trust your life. Trust that every situation can bring you further. Even – or maybe even particularly – situations that are painful or difficult.

Once again a shiver came over me and I felt a strange energy that drove me to question further. I had understood a lot, but apparently I was still missing a piece of the puzzle.

"Why is that? Why should we know ourselves? Who or what determines what I want or what I should experience?"

Consider it again in the spiritual context:
Every soul is a part of the bigger picture – part of the great light, the origin, the creative power, of God, however it may be expressed in human language. Every soul wants to develop; it wants to be bigger and brighter, like everything in the universe. This can happen through earthly experience, and in the form of human existence. The more conscious the soul becomes throughout all its lives, the more filled with light it becomes. Consciousness is light!
On the spiritual level, there are no opposites or polarities. There is no good or evil, no judgment about which state is better or worse. There is only unity and the inherent desire for expansion.
On the earthly plane, everything moves between opposites, be this in emotional, intellectual, material or moral terms. Each experience carries its own opposite within it. A man, for example, is rich so not poor, healthy and thus not sick, part of a community and hence not alone.
For a soul to expand in its light, it needs many lifetimes to experience both poles, to allow it to balance these opposites. In this way, it can grow and become greater and brighter in spiritual terms – provided it has gained awareness of its experiences within the course of its human life.
From the soul's perspective, the much-quoted 'karma' is not a moral burden that it brings with it, or something that it must 'atone for' in life, although some may perceive it as such. On the soul level, it is in essence about acquiring specific kinds of experiences and balancing these within itself.

Think of it like this: Before your soul incarnates – that is, before a human life has begun – it has already chosen what it wants to learn and experience. It chooses which options to experience, and it harmonises with your Higher Self, which represents the mind-based part of your full potential.

As you become ever more conscious, and increasingly learn to sense your intuition, you achieve ever greater access to your soul and your Higher Self. The soul expresses itself through your feelings. Thus you find your way onto the path that your soul would like to take. Your Higher Self speaks to you through your mind and your wakeful consciousness, and leads you on your way. The soul can enlighten itself only through its experiences and by becoming conscious. It cannot be enlightened from the outside.

I paused and closed my eyes. I really wanted to understand these higher laws.

"But what about my freedom of choice? My free will? Does it mean that I can't realize all of my dreams for myself after all?"

If they are your heart's desire, which means they are in concordance with the path of your soul, then yes, you can. It's like this: The creative power of the mind is principally unlimited. However, the goal is not to go around wishing for things left, right and centre in a bid to prove your own power of manifestation, nor is it to chase after a so-called fulfilled life. Rather, the aim is to sense and discover what your soul requires to unfold its full power.

Feel what you truly need, and attract that into your life. What really brings you joy? What wish do you harbour deep in your heart, but have perhaps never dared to voice? What have you wanted to do for years, but never found the courage to do?

Yes, I had understood this. I had already taken that step. It had been my decisive step – one that many people still have ahead of them. Dr Seer continued.

The path of the soul is the only path to true happiness. And there is no shortcut.

In fact, you have free will in the sense of freedom of choice in what you do. However, the relationship works as follows: The more you are in harmony with the path of your soul, the more unconditionally you will decide in accordance with it. Your will chooses that which your soul needs to experience. Do you remember?

You express your free will by your actions. If you now decide to choose something that does not correspond with what the soul needs as a next step, it will only work in the short term. Ultimately, it will just be a detour. Because at some point later on you'll have to travel this part of your path again.

You keep getting the chance to undertake the learning experience over and over again, until you finally accept it. To pass over or even dodge what you actually already unconsciously feel will only ever be a temporary step, lasting only until the moment when the opportunity comes around again.

It will be infinitely helpful for you to understand this spiritual principle of human life. If the same thing happens to you again and again when the same problem repeatedly occurs – for example, falling many times into a similar, difficult relationship pattern with partners, making the same 'mistake' time and again, or experiencing similar disappointment many times over – then all this means is that you're being offered the same opportunity for development repeatedly.

If and when you finally accept the opportunity by consciously looking at the experience and feeling what this experience does with you emotionally, then you can grow from it, dissolve the associated pain and gain something from it. The golden key is to always ask: What kind of feeling does this situation trigger in me? Because feelings are the bridge to the learning experience. The soul always communicates through feelings. The nature of what needs to be recognized or learned is always indicated by the feeling that the particular situation produces within you.

You start by understanding it through your feelings. Then comes insight. Then you act. With this, the experience is completed and integrated.

"That all sounds very plausible! But is it really possible to live with such a constant sense of awareness? Some situations are acutely painful. How is one to find the higher perspective in these situations, and trust that it's all good for something?"

That's true, my friend. At first, the immediate situation appears to be the most important. The detachment from the subjective experience, towards an expanded, higher perspective requires both clear sight and a willingness to be open to this perspective. Remember when you looked back from the future. You were in an acute situation with all its attendant thoughts, emotions and choices. Looking back from the future, you could free yourself from the situation in order to clearly see what was right for you.

I was silent for a moment. Today's lesson with Dr Seer was undoubtedly one of the most mentally challenging – not least because it took place outside in freezing temperatures, and without my mentor being physically present.

"I just wonder whether another perspective can be derived from everything you're telling me today. To go the way of the soul, to accept experiences, even those that hurt, and to be aware of what messages are hidden in them. To view your own life spiritually, and starting from this perspective, to then strive to become brighter and more awake... Is there another perspective from THE GOLDEN VIEW underlying it all?"

There was no answer, and I felt that I should try to find this out myself.

"Let me try – I'd say it was *'Look at the big picture'*!"

Fantastic! As I mentioned before, you no longer need me. This is the 23rd perspective. Had you not noticed that one was missing?

I sensed Dr Seer was now unable to resist a smile. I was proud that I had worked out the name of the last perspective of THE GOLDEN VIEW – even though I didn't enjoy the fact that the Doc considered this part of the justification for his physical disappearance.

"I think I understand. And I'm guessing that *your* big picture is far greater than the big picture I can see. You probably have the entire cosmos in view."

Certainly, the process of becoming conscious can always be taken one step higher, one step further. It's a never-ending progression. You have arrived at the next level. This is a huge step.

Now the time has come to stop processing. It's now no longer a matter of observing experiences, of understanding, or of making decisions. Live! Move! Say 'yes' to what is now. And enjoy it! You deserve it. Everyone deserves it. Life itself is your teacher now.

I took a deep breath, and absorbed his words as I did so. At that very moment a strong gust of wind swept through the front garden. From the corner of my eye I could see that my little arrangement on the wall was undisturbed. I remained standing straight and motionless, with my gaze directed at the sky. Dr Seer continued.

By the way, time is also a factor when looking at the big picture. Sometimes it is necessary to act immediately, and sometimes it simply takes some time until what you need or hope for is revealed. It might be that a further process or transformation within ourselves is required for a change to manifest itself on the outside.

When you feel that something is right for you, then stick with it and don't give up! Stay with it by believing in yourself and the cause. And if it takes much longer to achieve your goal than you expected, then ask yourself: 'Have I done my best?' If you can answer 'yes' to this question, then patience is called for. If the honest answer is 'no', then ask yourself why you have not given your all in this particular case. It may be an indication that you should be asking whether it's the right path. Do you really want it? Does it correspond with your inner truth?

"Hm. And what if I need you, Doc? Or even a new golden perspective, whenever there is something new to understand or process?"

THE GOLDEN VIEW, with its 23 individual perspectives, is comprehensive and complete. You have learned everything you need in order to move forward. Always listen to your feelings, because they speak the truth. Feel deep in your heart and you'll know what the next step is. Look closely, and you will know! If you need help, ask and you will receive it.

Tears welled up in my eyes yet again.

"Doc, I see the truth... I see that you are here. Just as you came when I needed you and was ready to receive your wisdom, so you have now left at the point that I attained a higher level of consciousness. Is that right?"

It is! To use another image: Do you remember the mirror that suddenly disappeared? You didn't need it at the time, literally as well as metaphorically. This is how the material world changes when you no longer need a certain mirror for the experiences you have in the outer world. You had the experience, and have integrated the knowledge into your life. Everything old that has been resolved no longer poses a challenge. Emotionally, it has been healed. And you are free to make new experiences.

"And so, as one door closes, a new one opens. The door to your office may be closed, but the door to my new life is wide open!"

Yes, Mr Allman. That's exactly how it is.

I felt an inexpressible gratitude, and at that moment realized what our meeting actually represented. Not only was Dr Seer my advisor, mentor and good friend – he was also my spiritual master.

In spirit he would always be close by me. It was a magical moment marked by great clarity – and I thanked the universe with deep humility for sending me Dr Seer.

Now you know.

"Doc, I feel so strongly connected to you. It feels as if we've known each other for ages. I trust you completely. How could such a close bond develop in such a short time?"

That's how it feels when an encounter takes place at the soul level. I see you. I've always seen you. I perceive you in your true essence and meet you heart to heart. Time is relative. It's a man-made concept that serves as a framework. It depends on the intensity, on the moment.

I leaned gently back against the wall. I wondered if we'd actually spent months together... and if Dr Seer had ever been real.

Sometimes recognition takes years, sometimes just one hour. Sometimes a whole lifetime and sometimes just a moment! I was real, my friend, and I'm still real and will be for all of time.

"Still, I wish our time together could have lasted longer."

YOU're leaving too.

"Yes, but I'll be back!"

Are you so sure about that?

Had Dr Seer been with me in person, he would have looked at me with a mischievous smile at this point. I once again felt touched.

"But that's no consolation right now. I just don't want to let go."

I know. I see it. Thank you for your trust.

"Doc, I'll never forget you!"

For a brief moment I worried that I'd spoken out loud, as a few people went past the house that very second. But at the same time I realized that I didn't care if anyone overheard as I addressed the sky with tears in my eyes.

My love is with you! Always take good care of yourself.

His voice grew louder and more insistent.

The answers to your questions are inside you. Always follow your heart and you'll always receive inner guidance.

There then followed a deep silence.

Something changed within me. I felt as though I had suddenly woken from a kind of daydream. It was pitch dark. A glance at my watch showed that three whole hours had passed. My body was freezing, but I didn't feel cold.

"Doc?"

There was no answer.

Those were the last words that I heard from Dr Seer.

Passers-by were gradually making their way to their New Year's Eve parties. Somewhat dazed, I followed them into the city centre. I found it hard to move, and tears kept filling my eyes. What I had experienced today could not be described in words – even if I've tried to do so here. Step by step I moved towards my new life. And with every step there arose an increasing feeling of happiness within me – the feeling of a new kind of freedom, a feeling that put a spring in my step.

When I opened the door to the café, I felt ready. It was time to celebrate my life.

⁎⁎⁎⁎⁎⁎⁎⁎⁎⁎

The Book of my Life

Just as did the planning of our trip, the start of our journey went as smoothly as if guided by an angel's hand. After an enjoyable flight and connecting bus transfer, Emily and I arrived at the port, and a few days later were sailing the South Seas on a three-master. We had booked three whole weeks on this beautiful sailboat, followed by some time on the island where the boat would be moored.
It was late afternoon and the sun was beating down. I had trouble accepting that the brightness of the air and the blueness of the sky were real. Sitting on the deck of this magnificent sailing boat, the thought kept flashed through my mind that I might actually be sitting in my office chair,

about to wake up from a dream-filled power nap. Thus I was overcome with pure elation every single time I realized that it was all very real – as real as the salty taste on my tongue and the infinite ocean, stretching to the horizon far into the distance before my very eyes. How often had this image appeared in my mind's eye! It had been firmly rooted in me ever since – and now it had become a reality!

A light, pleasant breeze blew, and the cries of the seagulls and the repetitive sound of the waves put me into an almost meditative mood. Time stood still. Emily lay next to me in a brightly coloured bikini, enjoying the sun.
I gazed for a while at the deep, blue sea and felt infinitely happy. I would have plenty of time to think about my future career plans and to try out new things. Above all, I wanted to write. Here too Dr Seer's hints had been accurate. How often had he mentioned that I would write something someday. And just as I had felt at the beginning of our journey together that it was better not to tell anyone about our meetings, I now received a clear, inner message: I should reveal my experiences to the world!
I had become aware that the path I had travelled with the help of Dr Seer was not only *mine*. It is the path *we all* follow. It is everybody's learning process and we may all pass through these stages. I travelled this path as a representative of us all.

The pages of my book were still unwritten. I looked into the sky and down at the glittering surface of the water. And I felt a wonderful force rise up in me. Deliberately, as if in slow motion, I took my pencil in my right hand. And in big letters I wrote on the first page:

THE GOLDEN VIEW

What was to follow these words would prove to be unlike anything I had experienced in my life so far.

My name is *Allman,* and I've told you my story.

The Golden View	Areas of application	Key sentences & mantras
1 Look in the mirror! *How do I actually feel?*	• Inventory of emotional and physical state • Honing self-perception • Describing one's self image • Connecting with yourself • Diagnosing the status quo • Confronting your reflection face-to-face	▪ I see myself. ▪ I perceive myself. ▪ I recognize myself. ▪ I am attentive to myself. ▪ I face myself. ▪ I create and maintain a connection to myself.
2 See yourself from the outside! *Gaining awareness of the impression you make on your surroundings*	• Uncovering and resolving discrepancies between your inner desires/intentions and outward behaviour • Creating authentic interaction • Communicating clearly in line with your goals • Avoiding/correcting misunderstandings	▪ I state my wishes. ▪ I act according to my underlying concerns. ▪ I gain awareness of how I come across. ▪ I dare to let myself be seen. ▪ I remain true to myself.
3 Look at the situation from above! *Being the neutral observer*	• Detaching from experiencing events as burdensome • Gaining clarity by adopting the perspective of neutral observer • Obtaining an overview • Relativizing premature judgments • Constructively resolving tensions within group situations • Understanding complex situations comprehensively	▪ I rise above it all. ▪ I don't waste energy on everyday drama. ▪ I look at things objectively. ▪ I clarify. ▪ I see clearly.

4 See with the eyes of a tiger! *Finding the courage to face upcoming changes*	• Working past doubt and fear of failure • Being ready to face challenges • Taking the initiative and breaking stagnation • Realizing fear-laden objectives with focused intention	▪ I can do it. ▪ I'm courageous. ▪ I'll go for it. ▪ I have the guts to do it. ▪ I face the situation.
5 Look in their eyes! *Truly connecting with those around you*	• Creating direct interaction/relationships • Consolidating interpersonal and emotional ties • Strengthening the connection to strangers and people you know in conversation • Creating trust in conflict situations	▪ I see you. ▪ I'm brave enough to look at you. ▪ I open myself to our connection. ▪ I encounter people at a deeper level.
6 See with the eyes of a role model! *Achieving the seemingly impossible*	• Being able to take action when faced with tasks that seem unachievable • Creating your own blue-print for action by taking your lead from a role model • Recognizing and activating latent potential • Demystifying seemingly unresolvable challenges	▪ I can do it, too. ▪ I believe in myself. ▪ I become conscious of my abilities. ▪ I awaken my potential.
7 See through the other person's eyes! *Classic perspective-taking: the basis of human interrelation*	• Assisting in situations where different positions/opinions collide • Smoothing out disagreements • Resolving conflict situations	▪ I assume your perspective. ▪ I can relate to your point of view. ▪ I understand your way of seeing. ▪ I respect other opinions.

8 Look from within!
 	
Recognizing and living your true needs
	• Dissatisfaction/discomfort as a starting point
	• Identifying true needs
	  ○ physical
	  ○ mental
	  ○ emotional
	• Analysing existing behaviour patterns and rituals
	• Determining optimal behaviours for satisfying needs
		▪ I recognize what I actually need.
		▪ I act according to my needs.
		▪ I have the courage to honour my needs.
		▪ I take the best possible care of myself.

9 Look at the decisive moment! *Making the right decision – intuition will ultimately provide the answer*	• All decision making	▪ My decision process holds valuable insights. ▪ My intuition already knows the answer. ▪ I take the time that's needed. ▪ If I can't decide, then the decision's not ready yet.
10 Stare into space! *When you are stuck...*	• Identifying cognitive/ creative blocks • Unclogging jammed work-flows • Being open to beneficial impulses and new solution approaches • Maintaining flow in result-oriented tasks	▪ I'll start by letting go. ▪ If I stop doing, my creativity will return. ▪ The solution will come to me. ▪ Take a break!
11 See with the eyes of a child! *Invigorating day-to-day life*	• Re-evaluating routines • Discovering something new every day by keeping an open mind • Embedding childlike curiosity as a basic principle in life • Intensifying your sensory perception and giving your intuition more space	▪ I open myself to the situation. ▪ I'll let myself be surprised. ▪ I'm open to discovering new things. ▪ Each day is eventful.

12 Stop right there! *Breaking destructive behaviour patterns*	• Understanding addictions as a behaviour pattern • Becoming conscious of automatic behaviour patterns/habits and recognizing the underlying needs and emotional root causes • Identifying day-to-day triggers, such as stressful situations • Identifying and implementing signals/anchor points for breaking behaviour patterns • Choosing positive ways to act	▪ Stop right there! ▪ I break my negative patterns. ▪ I know myself and my needs. ▪ I consciously choose that which does me good. ▪ I am master of my habits.
13 Look into your past! *In-depth understanding and resolution of emotional burdens*	• Recognizing and changing the causes of counterproductive behaviour and thought patterns • Clarifying and healing the key issues underlying old wounds • Releasing energy by resolving blockages	▪ I am free. ▪ I forgive those who have hurt me. ▪ I lovingly let go of the past.
14 Look into your inner sun! *Drawing new strength*	• Alleviating burdensome circumstances • Mitigating stressful situations • Optimizing your own energy balance	▪ I am calm and relaxed. ▪ I draw strength from my inner source of energy.

15 Look at yourself with kindness!
 	
Revealing and reversing negative self-judgments
	• Changing negative self-judgment:
	  ○ low self-esteem
	  ○ negative self-image
	  ○ self-accusations, guilt, shame
	  ○ lack of self-confidence
	  ○ devaluing oneself
	• Strengthening self-love
		▪ I believe in myself.
		▪ I trust myself.
		▪ I forgive myself.
		▪ I love myself unconditionally.

16 Look into the distance! *Dealing with emotional crises*	• Alleviating acute emotional distress • Letting go of fixation on problematic situations such as separation, loss • Letting go of emotional rigidity/blockages • Freeing yourself from emotional drama • Gaining confidence	▪ It won't always feel how it feels today. ▪ A high always follows a low. ▪ I'll gradually feel better. ▪ There is always hope.
17 Look upon what's to come with joy! *Influencing the future positively*	• Resolving feelings of being powerless, passive and unable to influence situations • Allowing positive experiences to resonate using visualization and positive emotions	▪ I can create my own feelings. ▪ My imagination determines my reality. ▪ I can influence every situation positively. ▪ I recognize my own creative power.
18 SEMO – See more than meets the eye! *Understanding the emotional dynamics of interactions*	• Interaction with others: Understanding what motivates people's actions • Recognizing that each person is responsible for their own feelings • Dealing with personal hurt • Protecting oneself from being influenced by the negative feelings of others	▪ I don't take anything personally. ▪ I am master of my feelings. ▪ My counterpart doesn't want to hurt me. ▪ Other people's behaviour is rooted in themselves.

19 Focus!
 	
Using your own resources productively
	• Defining goals
	  ○ for daily and routine activities
	  ○ for work
	  ○ for life
	• Achieving goals by consciously focusing attention
	• Managing your own energy reserves
		▪ I define what I want.
		▪ I deploy my energies consciously.
		▪ I keep my eye firmly on the goal.
		▪ I focus.

20 Look back from the future! *Discerning what really matters on your life's journey*	• Identifying personal passions • Realizing possibilities as they present themselves • Making life decisions • Seizing opportunities • Eliminating life's 'woulda/shoulda/couldas' • Setting boundaries for the opinions and judgments of others	▪ I recognize what I really want. ▪ I have the courage to live what really matters to me. ▪ I go my own way. ▪ I don't miss out on opportunities.
21 See with the heart! *Love as way of life*	• Initiating positive feelings around you • Achieving peaceful interrelationships • Breaking negative communication spirals • Resolving conflicts	▪ I respect, love and value every living being. ▪ My stance is love. ▪ I am kind. ▪ I am love.
22 Look out of the spiritual eye! *Connecting to higher energy*	• Finding inner peace • Centering yourself • Recognizing and sensing the Higher Self • Gaining access to universal wisdom	▪ I receive the answers I need. ▪ I am one with everything. ▪ I am filled with light.
23 Look at the big picture! *Understanding life spiritually*	• Receiving answers to life's big questions • Picking up metaphysical thought impulses	▪ Everything has a higher meaning. ▪ I trust that every situation helps me to grow. ▪ My feelings are messages from my soul.

Sabine zur Nedden

Sabine zur Nedden holds a degree in psychology and is a qualified integrative coach (ECA). As an expert in a wide range of psychological matters, she frequently features on shows for the German TV channels WDR, RTL, VOX, ProSieben and *n-tv*. As well as appearing in front of the camera, she also works behind the scenes as a psychological counsellor and coach to actors and producers in the television and film industries.

Having established herself as a creative mind, source of ideas and author in the film and media sector, some ten years ago she began combining her knowledge of psychology with her expertise in drama and has since advised on the content of numerous projects and formats and has co-developed scripts. She has also worked as a research associate and lecturer in social and media psychology at the University of Cologne, Germany, and has been a communications trainer and coach for vocational guidance and personality development in the educational sector.

In her own practice for psychological and spiritual counselling, consciousness training and energy work in Cologne, she works with people from all walks of life and of all personality types. Sabine zur Nedden is gifted with pronounced intuitive abilities and expertise with which she is able to give her clients renewed energy and guide them towards realizing their full potential and innermost confidence. She has a unique way of combining psychology and spirituality, and has inspired and supported many people to follow a new path and to live a life of self-realization.

Contact:
www.wissenstor-verlag.com

Simone Alz

Simone Alz holds a degree in psychology and is a qualified coach (CPCC). She has two decades of international experience working with global companies and organisations.
Having begun her career in a renowned consulting company as a human performance and change management consultant, she then worked for the United Nations in both New York and Rome. As an Associate Expert for the UN Department of Economics and Social Affairs, her remit included strategic personnel allocation and staff delegation and development. In her role as staff counsellor for the UN World Food Programme, she not only worked as a psychological advisor but also provided crisis intervention and training for staff at headquarters and on WFP missions. She then went on to develop crisis intervention programmes for the UN Department of Safety and Security.

Within the private sector, she has led international teams and held executive responsibility for the departments People and Organisation Development, Leadership Development, and HR Strategy and Change Management.

From her base in Munich, southern Germany, Simone Alz currently works as an independent consultant to senior executives and coaches team, personality and consciousness development for multinational clients. Alongside mediation and conflict-management expertise, she also provides coaching and facilitation training. Her work is characterised by her strategic way of thinking and her distinctive talent for facilitating transitions with intuition and clarity.

Contact:
www.wissenstor-verlag.com